THE EGOLESS PHANTOM

THE EGOLESS PHANTOM

MAPPING THE AI LABYRINTH

HERNÁN INVERSO · CLAUDIA MÁRSICO

PHANTOM MAZE
AI & LANGUAGE LAB

Hernán Inverso y Claudia Marsico
The Egoless Phantom. Mapping the AI Labyrinth

First edition, 2026
ISBN 978-987-3729-16-4

Published by Phantom Maze

CONTENTS

How to Read this Map

This is not a journey with a fixed itinerary. That would be a poor plan for a labyrinth. So the book has something of Cortázar's Rayuela and something of those old Choose Your Own Adventure books. Each reader can take whichever route suits them without getting lost, though two routes stand out.

The first runs through the labyrinth in full. It begins with the history of artificial intelligence and a map of the current ecosystem (Chapters 1 and 2), looks at the technical workings of language models (Chapter 3), stops to ask what kind of phenomenon we encounter in these systems and what its features are (Chapters 4 and 5), and then opens onto wider ground to explore what all of this means for anyone working with these systems: how access is distributed, which skills become more valuable, and what happens to cognitive work when execution gets cheap and judgment gets expensive (Chapters 6 through 11).

The second path is for readers who want to go directly from how it works to what effects it produces in the world, without entering the areas that demand philosophical work. It begins the same way (Chapters 1, 2, and 3) and then jumps to Chapters 6 through 11. Chapters 4 and 5 remain available for whenever the underlying question becomes pressing, on each reader's own schedule.

There are also readers who prefer to enter wherever curiosity leads. That works for most of the chapters in the third part, which can be read in any order without losing one's bearings. The only piece of advice is to go through Chapter 3 before taking detours, so that certain questions do not hang in the air. For everything else, the labyrinth allows multiple entrances. That is, after all, its nature.

Packing for the Journey

What comes next? The question hangs in the air and threads through ordinary conversations. Recent generations have lived through more change than any others in history. All at once we are back on the moon, surrounded by talking machines that seem to do many things better than we do. The frenzy of transformation breeds bewilderment and fanaticism in roughly equal measure, both fairly useless when the goal is to clarify the picture. This book proposes an old-fashioned expedition: entering the labyrinth that houses this peculiar phenomenon.

What we call artificial intelligence entered public life as a new technology, greeted with equal parts curiosity and unease, but it did not arrive all at once or in a single form. In fact, it has spent decades quietly transforming a great deal of infrastructure that we don't think of as AI. The systems that detect fraud in banking transactions, the algorithms that rank search results, the optimizers that manage global supply chains, all of them are deciding all the time.

Things really caught fire when, in less than three years, language models went from objects of specialized research to everyday use. ChatGPT reached a hundred million users in two months, an adoption rate without precedent in consumer technology. Since then, generative language models have absorbed the bulk of the symbolic weight, the fears and the hopes, that the term "artificial intelligence" had been carrying, forcing an almost complete identification between the name and just one of its instances. They will loom large here too, because none transforms our daily life more directly or produces more misunderstandings, though we will keep the wider ecosystem in view.

The confusion in this terrain is sometimes blamed on technical complexity, but the flaw in that view is fairly obvious. The world is full of widely used technologies whose workings we plainly do not understand. When the radio first appeared, most listeners had no idea what electromagnetic waves are or how they propagate. Steam engines, vaccines, washing machines, airplanes… We live in a world we do not fully comprehend, and that is not a problem. Opacity of mechanism is compatible with effective use and with reasonably correct judgments about technology in general. The reason is that the effects can be assessed independently. We hear the radio or we don't; the plane arrives or it doesn't. For both, we have criteria of successful functioning that lie outside the mechanism and don't require us to understand it.

With large language models, however, no matter how much we learn about the technical substrate, the quality of the responses we get cannot be determined right away. We don't even quite know whether they "work," because there is no independent criterion of evaluation, the kind that, in the earlier cases, sat outside the object. A radio does not change its behavior according to how you listen to it. A language model changes its response based on how it is queried, which version is in play, the load it is under, and the conversation history it carries. So while you do not need to understand the mechanism to operate the interface, you do need complex capacities to determine what you got.

On top of that, the idea that these systems do something resembling human intelligence activates almost atavistic fears and hopes that act as obstacles to understanding. Add rapid expansion and visible social effects, and conceptual muddle is a given. We interact with these systems, but somewhat blindly, without really knowing what we are dealing with.

The problem looks more serious once we notice that this gap colors the public conversation. Education is slow to absorb recent discussions. The media chase sensationalist headlines and yawn at analyses of the conditions under which a system fails, or at discussions of what it actually means for a model to "beat" humans on a standardized test. The companies developing these systems tend to emphasize capabilities in their communications, so a large share of the available information is produced by actors with a direct interest in making the system look more capable, or safer, than it is. Lately they have us debating whether or not we are close to the singularity, a question that automatically beats every other for sheer spectacle and pulls our eyes away from what is actually in front of us.

Technical experts produce very precise knowledge about the substrate while flagrantly ignoring the questions it cannot answer. How the attention mechanism works in a transformer does not tell us what kind of phenomenon it produces when it interacts with a human being. The social sciences, meanwhile, rush to evaluate impacts in terms of good or bad.

It looks like a job tailor-made for the humanities, which have been arriving late to the debate and, in many cases, join in as dutiful pupils of the sciences, treating their terms as neutral to play a game that is not theirs. At other times they cling to positions typical of the second half of the twentieth century, muttering about traces, rhizomes, and transductions with no audience left. The overall result is a misaligned conversation, sometimes apocalyptic, sometimes utopian, thin on clear ideas. So in what follows we will not try to predict the future of artificial intelligence, or deliberate about regulation, much less devote ourselves to prompting tutorials. A labyrinth awaits us, and we are going to try to map it.

For that, we are going to think in terms of articulated intelligence, not merely artificial. While we observe how artificial intelligence systems function, we will also look at how we interact with them, what challenges they pose, and how to make genuine use of this new coexistence. We speak of articulated intelligence rather than hybrid intelligence because hybrids imply fusion. Articulation implies coordination. Humans and language models do not merge into a new being. They work together, distributing tasks according to their strengths, and from there, exploring forms of work that neither can reach on its own. This kind of articulation takes us past assisted human thought and supervised artificial thought, toward a new cognitive mode, with its own possibilities and its own risks, one that demands to be understood on its own terms.

In "A Note on Reading the Map" we already pointed to some directions for moving forward. Readers seeking confirmation of their enthusiasm or alarm will probably find more questions than certainties here, which is surely what they need most. Readers seeking to understand something they use every day, without having had the chance to examine it in depth, will find the tools to do so.

Alongside fresh findings and unfamiliar perspectives, artificial intelligence opens up an adventure that shakes everything we knew. Seen up close and without blinders, it turns out to be the most revealing mirror human intelligence has ever had. We have never had before us something that took the shape of thinking-without-thinking so convincingly, and that disconcerting proximity is (for those who know how to look) the best occasion in history to understand what thinking really means. The labyrinth is there, the provisions are ready. We can begin the crossing.

1

How We Got Here

Not all labyrinths are alike. The classical Cretan model, built by Daedalus to contain the Minotaur, was a structure of spatial complexity made of walls and forks in the path, with corridors that resembled one another and converged on the monster's lair. The disorientation it produced was real, but solvable: if, like Theseus, you had Ariadne's thread leading the way out. That kind of topographical difficulty is solved by orientation.

There are also rule-based labyrinths, like bureaucratic ones, which disorient through a proliferation of contradictory norms, offices that send you back and forth, and procedures that require conditions only other procedures can satisfy. No center, no Minotaur. Just a structure no one designed on purpose but which, in practice, is impossible to navigate.

The labyrinth of artificial intelligence belongs to neither type. On the contrary, it mixes and inverts their features. Its corridors are well lit and there are plenty of signs, but they contradict each other. At every corner there is someone with firm opinions pointing in incompatible directions, and the most disconcerting thing of all is in plain sight, right at the entrance, visible and accessible. When we open a chat interface we come face to face with the most elusive element in the entire labyrinth to grasp: that voice which seems to understand us and replies in words that are not its own, producing the experience of an encounter without anyone being on the other side. Rather than devouring us, it welcomes us, talks with us, and gives us whatever we ask for.

Behind that entrance lies an ecosystem of distinct zones, each shaped by its builders and by the history that produced it. So we begin with the history of the labyrinth itself. Only then can we understand why its corridors take the shape they do, and why some forks look like choices when they are not.

ANCIENT ECHOES

The construction did not happen all at once or from a single blueprint. The very idea of artificial intelligence is much older than computer science. In fact, it reaches back to Antiquity, where it appears in mythical and speculative form: automata animated by the gods, statues that speak, artifacts capable of carrying out actions without human intervention. More than technical machines, these were conceptual figures that made it possible to think about the boundary between the living and the artificial. In the Hellenistic world, for instance, the mechanical contrivances attributed to Hero of Alexandria showed that certain behaviors could be produced without soul or will.[1]

The famous Antikythera mechanism, from the first century BCE, discovered in the remains of a shipwreck in 1901, belongs to the same tradition. It is a complex device of bronze gears designed to predict astronomical cycles and eclipses. Although not strictly an automaton, it did show that certain highly complex processes (celestial regularities, calendars, predictions) could be encapsulated in a machine. No one, either when it was built or when it was discovered, claimed that it thought or decided anything, but the fact

[1]See Cesare Rossi, "The Beginning of the Automation", in Theodor Borangiu (ed.), Advances in Robot Design and Intelligent Control. Advances in Intelligent Systems and Computing, vol. 371, Cham, Springer, 2016, 59-67.

is that it reliably carried out tasks that required formalized knowledge. In retrospect, the Antikythera mechanism is a striking case of the externalization of cognitive functions in mechanical artifacts.[2]

In the Middle Ages, non-human intelligence was imagined through angels, separate intelligences, or artifacts animated by occult knowledge. The theological and metaphysical imprint dominated, driving reflection on what it means to think, who can do it, and under what conditions. Even so, the fascination with animated artifacts is also present. Consider, for instance, the mechanical contrivances attributed to Arab sages, with which the bronze head of Gerbert of Aurillac is associated. Gerbert would later become Sylvester II, the first French pope to ascend the throne of Peter, in 999.[3] The mechanism could answer yes or no, and it seeded the legend of a diabolical pact that brought Gerbert no small share of trouble. In the same vein is the talking-head story in which Albertus Magnus is said to have perfected the device over three decades, and which Thomas Aquinas is said to have destroyed out of annoyance or theological scandal.[4] In a different register stands the narrative tradition of the Golem in medieval Judaism. This curious creature, made of inert matter such as clay or earth, was animated through the efficacy of sacred language, whether the name of God or the combinations of letters that organize the world.[5] It is not a

[2]Claudia Mársico, "El mecanismo de Antikythera y el avance de la técnica en la época helenística", Educación en Ciencias III, 7 (1999), 28-32; John Hugh Seiradakis and Mike G. Edmunds, "Our current knowledge of the Antikythera Mechanism", Nature Astronomy 2 (2018), 35-42.

[3]Robert Mills, "Talking Heads, or, a Tale of Two Clerics", in Catrien Santing et al., Disembodied Heads in Medieval and Early Modern Culture, Leiden, Brill, 2013, 31-57.

[4]E.R. Truitt, Medieval Robots: Mechanism, Magic, Nature, and Art, University of Pennsylvania Press, 2015, capítulo 4; Minsoo Kang and Ben Halliburton, "The Android of Albertus Magnus: A legend of artificial being", AI Narratives.

[5]Amir Vudka, "The Golem in the age of artificial intelligence", NECSUS_European Journal of Media Studies 9.1 (2020), 101-123 and Sandu Frunză, "The Golem and the Artificial Intelligence. A new opening towards storytelling", Journal for the Study of Religions and Ideologies 22.66 (2023), 65-77.

mechanical automaton, but it is an artificial human creation: obedient, lacking any will of its own, its "intelligence" depending entirely on a formal operation. The distance from contemporary language models is enormous. Yet the Golem sets up a question that will reappear centuries later in very different forms: can language sustain something that resembles intelligence without comprehension behind it?

In modernity, intelligence came to be conceived as a formal operation of calculation, combination, and inference. For Descartes, the notion of intelligence is defined by the exercise of cogitatio, the thinking that includes doubting, understanding, judging, affirming, and denying, and that requires self-consciousness. Intelligence is therefore inseparable from reflective interiority and cannot be reduced to the mere production of correct responses. The body, in this conception, is a machine. Automata show that complex movements do not require a soul, thereby establishing a criterion of demarcation.[6] Already in the seventeenth century, this conception gave rise to the legend of an automaton built in the image of Descartes's daughter Francine, who died at the age of five, and which Descartes is said to have carried with him on his travels. Although the story has no solid historical basis, its popularity dramatizes the central tension within Cartesianism: between the perfection of mechanical simulation and the impossibility of an automaton possessing consciousness and inner life.[7]

Hobbes goes so far as to claim that reasoning is nothing other than calculation. Thinking is what Hobbes calls reckoning (adding and subtracting consequences from names and signs), a bodily process with no immaterial residue and no reflective faculty in the Cartesian sense. Intelligence is the most complex expression of the mechanics that chains representations together, anticipates future effects, and adjusts action on the basis of that calculation through the internal movement of the body. Thus, in Leviathan, Hobbes can

---

[6]Discours, Quinta Parte, AT VI, 56.

[7]Minsoo Kang, "The mechanical daughter of René Descartes: the origin and history of an intellectual fable", Modern Intellectual History 14.3 (2017), 633-660.

describe the human being as a natural automaton without that implying any reduction: the automaton makes visible the formal structure of intelligence, which makes Hobbes a key precursor to conceptions of intelligence as a computational process. Hobbes was writing in a world where automata were a genuine spectacle. There were complex clocks, mechanical figures in European gardens, and automated fountains at Saint-Germain that moved statues when a visitor stepped on certain flagstones. When in the introduction to Leviathan he compares the State to an "artificial man," he has such devices of soulless complexity in mind.[8]

Leibniz radicalizes the relation between intelligence and mechanism by explicitly imagining a *mathesis universalis* and a *machina ratiocinatrix*, that is, a universal formal language and a machine capable of operating rationally on it. Within this framework, reasoning consists in calculating relations between clearly defined concepts, so that philosophical or scientific disputes could be settled by a computational procedure, without interpretive confrontation. Intelligence becomes formalized, and certain rational operations become automated, though this does not exhaust the metaphysical dimension of understanding. The *machina ratiocinatrix* embodies the aspiration to a rationality that is objective, transparent, and communicable, anticipating both modern formal logic and the idea of devices capable of carrying out inferences.[9] These ideas did not remain purely theoretical. In the seventeenth and eighteenth centuries, calculating machines proliferated. The Pascaline, Leibniz's machine, though limited, materialized the idea of mechanizable thought.[10]

---

[8]Ziyaad Bhorat, "Automata in Hobbes: Three Heads of Cerberus", History of Political Thought 42.3 (2021), 441-463.

[9]Christopher P. Noble, "Automata, reason, and free will: Leibniz's critique of Descartes on animal and human nature", Studies in History and Philosophy of Science 100 (2023), 56-63.

[10]The Pascaline, built by Blaise Pascal beginning in 1642, represents one of the first effective attempts to materialize arithmetic calculation in a mechanical device. See José Ignacio Rojas-Sola et al., "Blaise Pascal's mechanical calculator: Geometric modelling and virtual reconstruction", Machines 9.7 (2021), 136.

In the nineteenth century, Charles Babbage and Ada Lovelace, Lord Byron's daughter, went beyond arithmetic calculating machines by conceiving the Analytical Engine, no longer limited to executing isolated numerical operations but introducing instead the notion of a program: a sequence of instructions independent of any specific calculation. Inspired by the Jacquard loom, the machine was designed to be reconfigurable through punched cards. It foreshadowed the distinction between hardware and software that would emerge a century later, allowing the same physical machine to solve radically different problems depending on the instructions it received.[11]

Ada Lovelace grasped with unusual clarity the implications of a design in which the machine transcends numbers and operates on symbols more generally, provided they can be formalized; she anticipated the idea of general symbolic computation. At the same time, she insisted that the machine does not think or create on its own, since it cannot determine its own ends or rules, however rigorously and systematically it carries out operations that have been specified in advance. Several of these aspects remain at the core of our current discussions, even if the machines now in question are very different.

THE RECENT STORY

This whirlwind tour shows that the idea of artificial intelligence had been circulating long before the twentieth century, and that the twentieth century inherited a legacy that included the conception of intelligence as rule-governed symbolic manipulation. Within this framework, contemporary artificial intelligence emerged as an ambitious and provocative project, one that sought to formalize and reproduce in a machine certain forms of intelligent behavior.

---

[11]Lars Jaeger, "Ada Lovelace (1815-1852): Inventor of Computer Algorithms", in Women of Genius in Science: Whose Frequently Overlooked Contributions Changed the World, Cham, Springer International Publishing, 2023, 71-82.

The question of machine thinking has a precise birthdate: 1950. That year Alan Turing published "Computing Machinery and Intelligence," with a proposal that would define the debate for decades. Turing knew that the question in its direct form was unanswerable, because there is no way to verify from the outside whether something is thinking, just as there is no way to verify whether another human being has inner experience or only behaves as if they did. So instead of asking whether a machine thinks, he proposed asking whether a machine can behave indistinguishably from someone who thinks. Through an imitation game, a human interrogator carries on simultaneous written conversations with two hidden interlocutors, one human, one machine, and must determine which is which. If the machine can deceive the interrogator often enough, Turing concluded, we ought to attribute intelligence to it: to deny that it thinks, once behavioral indistinguishability has been established, is not a scientific observation but a metaphysical prejudice about what machines can or cannot be.[12]

Philosophically bold, the proposal shifted the debate from ontology to epistemology, avoiding the need to answer what a mind is, but at the cost of assuming that linguistic behavior is the right way to identify intelligence. If intelligence is what intelligence does in language, then the test is enough. If there is something about intelligence that language does not capture (something to do with embodiment, lived temporality, or practical engagement with the world) then the test is measuring something else and might not be measuring what matters.

For decades, the test served as the field's guiding ideal and as a criterion of progress. Passing it became the implicit goal of conversational systems. That regulative function had profound consequences for the development of AI: it steered research toward linguistic performance as the parameter of intelligence, embedding in both the field and the public imagination the idea that intelligence

[12]Alan M. Turing, "Computing Machinery and Intelligence," Mind 59, no. 236 (1950): 433-460.

is, in the last analysis, a matter of conversational appearance. If it sounds intelligent, it is taken to be intelligent.

The expression *artificial intelligence* was formally introduced in 1956, at the celebrated Dartmouth workshop organized by John McCarthy.[13] That meeting crystallized a series of earlier developments, both theoretical and technical, that had been maturing for at least two decades. It grew out of the convergence of several lines of research within a very specific intellectual context. John McCarthy had been working on the logical formalization of reasoning and on the possibility of describing cognitive processes as symbolic operations; alongside this, a climate of intense technical development was being fueled by advances in digital computing during and after the Second World War. Cryptography, code-breaking, logistical optimization, and automatic control had forged an unprecedented alliance among mathematics, engineering, and the state. Machines like Colossus, designed to break codes, showed that artificial devices could analyze patterns and explore enormous combinatorial spaces at a speed and scale beyond human reach.[14]

This was joined by influences like Norbert Wiener's cybernetics, mathematical logic, Shannon's information theory, the first neural models of McCulloch and Pitts, and Turing's work on abstract machines, all of them grounded in attempts to formalize logical reasoning and in the idea that any effective process could be expressed as a finite sequence of operations.[15]

The Dartmouth meeting sought to unify these scattered currents around a central hypothesis: intelligence as a set of functions susceptible to formal description and, therefore, to mechanical

---

[13]Marc M. Anderson, "AI as philosophical ideology: a critical look back at John McCarthy's program", Philosophy & Technology 37.2 (2024), 1-24.
[14]Jonathan P. Bowen, "Alan Turing: Breaking the Code, Computing, and Machine Intelligence", in The Arts and Computational Culture: Real and Virtual Worlds, Cham, Springer Nature Switzerland, 2024, 75-94.
[15]Alan M. Turing, "Computing machinery and intelligence (1950)", Mind 59.236 (1950), 433-460 and Flavio Lombardi and Alessandro Recchia, "On Abstract Machines Security and Performance", Procedia Computer Science 231 (2024), 111-118.

implementation. The optimism of the era was immense. The prevailing belief was that, with enough logical rules and computing power, reasoning and creativity would be solved within a few decades, simply by extending the methods already in place.

That founding hypothesis deserves to be taken seriously, because everything that follows can be read as the gradual unraveling of that project: the fragmentation of the program, and ultimately the emergence of something none of the Dartmouth participants would have recognized as its legitimate heir. Symbolic AI, with its expert systems, inference engines, and knowledge bases, was the institutional realization of that bet. Language was a system to be decomposed into grammatical and semantic rules; perception, a process of extracting logically describable features; planning, a search through a tree of possible states. Everything could be formalized, because intelligence was, at bottom, calculation.

ELIZA appeared in that context. Joseph Weizenbaum built it at MIT between 1964 and 1966 to demonstrate that a program capable of imitating the surface structure of conversation could seem to understand without understanding anything. ELIZA had no model of the world and no representation of the interlocutor. It relied on pattern recognition and variable substitution. If the user said "I feel sad," the system replied "why do you feel sad?" If the user mentioned a mother, the system asked about family. The logic was circular and deliberately empty. Weizenbaum designed it precisely to make that emptiness obvious, but users (including close collaborators who knew how the system worked) formed attachments to ELIZA, confided personal problems to it, asked for privacy to converse with it, and insisted that it sometimes understood them better than people did. Weizenbaum documented the phenomenon with growing alarm and wrote Computer Power and Human Reason as a warning about how easily human beings project understanding where there is none. He called this systematic projection the "ELIZA effect."[16]

---

[16]Joseph Weizenbaum, Computer Power and Human Reason: From Judgment to Calculation, W. H. Freeman, San Francisco, 1976, p. 189. See también Jeff

ELIZA happened to possess exactly the surface properties that the interlocutor-recognition mechanism needs to activate: first-person language, user-oriented questions, and register-matching. Without intending to, Weizenbaum created the first demonstration that a voice does not need to understand us to produce the effects of understanding, and what he regarded as a user failure turned out to be an important clue about the structure of experience. ELIZA was a demonstration program with no memory between sessions, no access to external information, and no way to act on the world. The question it left open (what would happen if that formal structure were combined with real capabilities, memory, and access to knowledge) remained unanswered in 1966. Decades later, the labyrinth has grown, and presiding over its entrance is a voice that answers with a depth ELIZA could never have simulated.

Symbolic AI, as we saw, held that if thinking is the manipulation of symbols according to rules, then reproducing it is a matter of formalizing the right rules. For decades that approach produced impressive results in bounded domains such as medical diagnosis, chess, theorem proving, where the universe of possibilities could be defined in advance. The problem appeared when the systems tried to operate in the open world. In 1969, McCarthy and Hayes formulated precisely what was at stake. Turning on a light does not change the position of the furniture. Opening a door does not change the color of the walls. For a human being, those invariants are so obvious that we rarely think about them; they form part of a common-sense background that operates silently behind every action. For a rule-based system, however, every invariant must be explicitly declared. As the modeled world becomes more complex, the number of rules required to specify what does not change grows without any manageable limit. It came to be known as the frame problem. Expert systems worked in closed domains, where that

Shrager, "ELIZA Reinterpreted: The World's First Chatbot Was Not Intended as a Chatbot at All", arXiv:2406.17650, 2024 y Ranisch, R., & Meier, L.

background could be ignored, but they collapsed in the face of the open world.[17]

Hubert Dreyfus was the first to articulate this objection as a deep philosophical critique. Drawing on the phenomenology of Heidegger and Merleau-Ponty, Dreyfus argued that human intelligence does not consist in applying rules to representations but in embodied, situated practical know-how that does not admit the separation between subject and world presupposed by the symbolic program. The critique was received with hostility in the 1970s but ended up being prophetic. The kind of understanding symbolic systems could not capture depended on the body, experience, and context, everything that had been left out of the picture.[18]

The institutional effects of this failure were severe. In two waves known as the "AI winters," funding contracted and symbolic-AI laboratories lost influence. The first winter is often traced back to a defining document in 1973. Sir James Lighthill, a Cambridge mathematician, published a devastating assessment of the field's state, commissioned by the British Science Research Council. Lighthill argued that AI had fulfilled none of its central promises, that advances in restricted domains did not transfer to real-world situations, and that the "combinatorial explosion" (the exponential growth of the search space when problems become even minimally complex) left the existing methods unable to scale.[19] The field had promised machine translation, natural language understanding, and computer vision within a decade, and none of that had happened or was just around the corner. The Lighthill Report captured, without

[17]The canonical formulation of the frame problem appears in John McCarthy and Patrick J. Hayes, "Some Philosophical Problems from the Standpoint of Artificial Intelligence", in Bernard Meltzer and Donald Michie (eds.), Machine Intelligence 4, Edinburgh, Edinburgh University Press, 1969, 463-502. On its philosophical evolution, see Murray Shanahan, "The Frame Problem", in Edward N. Zalta (ed.), The Stanford Encyclopedia of Philosophy, 2016.

[18]Hubert L. Dreyfus, What Computers Can't Do: A Critique of Artificial Reason, New York, Harper & Row, 1972. Edición revisada: What Computers Still Can't Do: A Critique of Artificial Reason, Cambridge, MIT Press, 1992.

[19]James Lighthill, "Artificial Intelligence: A General Survey", in Artificial Intelligence: A Paper Symposium, Science Research Council, Londres, 1973.

naming it explicitly, the frame problem at work on an institutional scale.[20] In response, the British government slashed funding, and few centers remained active in the country.

In the United States, DARPA (the Defense Advanced Research Projects Agency) had bet on the long term without demanding immediate applications, which had allowed the development of projects like ARPAnet, but Congress demanded accountability, and funding cuts followed.[21] Outside the Anglophone world, France had its own tradition of mathematical logic, which gave rise to Prolog, the language created by Colmerauer, Kanoui, Pasero, and Roussel in Marseille in 1972, and weathered the winter more successfully.[22] The Soviet Union had several active centers but was lagging, and the combination of isolation and limited access to powerful hardware placed a low ceiling on its ambitions.[23]

Meanwhile, even as the field languished in the West, Japan launched the Fifth Generation Computer Project in 1982 with enormous funding and the goal of producing, by 1992, machines capable of reasoning in natural language. This was the Dartmouth hypothesis at industrial scale and with lavish state funding. The West reacted with alarm; the first winter was over. DARPA returned to the field, Britain created the Alvey program, and Europe launched ESPRIT. The first winter ended in part because of the perceived Japanese threat, which, ironically, failed to achieve most of its objectives, leaving behind a trail of unkept promises and obsolete hardware. By the end of the 1980s, this triggered the second winter.[24]

---

[20]Nils Nilsson, The Quest for Artificial Intelligence: A History of Ideas and Achievements, Cambridge University Press, 2010, ch. 14.

[21]National Academies, Funding a Revolution: Government Support for Computing Research, National Academy Press, Washington D.C., 1999, capítulo 7.

[22]Alain Colmerauer and Philippe Roussel, "The Birth of Prolog", in History of Programming Languages,.

[23]Slava Gerovitch, From Newspeak to Cyberspeak: A History of Soviet Cybernetics, MIT Press, 2002.

[24]Tōhru Moto-oka et al. (eds.), Fifth Generation Computer Systems: Proceedings of the International Conference on Fifth Generation Computer Systems, Tokyo, October 1981, North-Holland Publishing, 1982.

These swings come into clearer focus when we widen the picture, because the AI laboratories were not the only ones exploring computing hardware. With no interest in artificial intelligence, IBM launched its Personal Computer in August 1981. Apple, Commodore, and Tandy had had their own models since the late 1970s, but IBM's backing gave the concept legitimacy. If the company that dominated corporate computing was betting on the desktop, the desktop was the future. The IBM PC was the most replicable model and the cheapest to produce at scale. Behind the PC were two players that IBM underestimated and that would turn out to be the real winners. Microsoft controlled the operating system, while Intel manufactured the processor, whose business model relied on selling more hardware at the lowest possible price and at massive scale.[25]

The two models were destined to collide. The symbol of that collision was the Lisp machine. Extraordinary for their time, Lisp machines were designed for a specific kind of computation and sold expensively to laboratories and corporations. Like the dinosaurs, they fell not because they were inferior but because they could not keep up with the pace of change. Following what is known as Moore's law, every two years conventional hardware doubled its power at decreasing cost, until in 1987 a Sun workstation cost a tiny fraction of the price of a Symbolics machine and performed comparably. The companies that had built their business model around AI hardware began to collapse in rapid succession, most of them disappearing within three years. Just as the smaller, more adaptable birds outlasted the dinosaurs, what survived from the Lisp machines were the languages, Common Lisp, Scheme, and their descendants, which migrated to mass-consumer hardware and are still in use. The ironic part of the story is that the IBM PC, which in

[25]Paul Freiberger and Michael Swaine, Fire in the Valley: The Birth and Death of the Personal Computer, Pragmatic Bookshelf, 2014. On the Microsoft and Intel business model: Walter Isaacson, The Innovators: How a Group of Hackers, Geniuses, and Geeks Created the Digital Revolution, Simon & Schuster, 2014, caps. 9-10.

1981 had seemed entirely irrelevant to artificial intelligence, turned out to be the technology that would transform it most deeply. Cheap, ubiquitous hardware became powerful enough to make viable ideas that had long remained on the margins, without funding or attention.[26]

The second winter was shorter than the first, and by 1993 it was dissipating, but it left the sense that the Dartmouth program and its bet on rules had been a dead end. That ensuing sense of mourning led to fragmentation. The unified program fragmented into research lines that abandoned the ambition of solving "intelligence" as a whole. Visual perception was separated from logical reasoning, language processing from motor planning, learning from inference.

In the late 1980s, Rodney Brooks radicalized this break from within robotics, by building agents that interacted with the world without internal models, responding directly to environmental stimuli through reactive behavior. Brooks's robots did not reason or plan, had no representation of the world, but they moved, dodged obstacles, and reacted to their environment with a fluency that handily beat the symbolic planners. The lesson was that certain forms of intelligence could manifest without representation, at least in certain domains, with the body and the environment as constitutive components of behavior. Following Dreyfus's arguments, Brooks demonstrated that there were forms of intelligence irreducible to symbolic computation.[27]

Meanwhile, something else was taking shape. Neural networks, which had had their heyday in the 1960s with the Perceptron, reappeared in the mid-1980s with the idea of letting the system learn patterns from data. Instead of teaching it what a cat is by describing the cat's features, you show it thousands of images of cats and let it find the patterns that distinguish them. Intelligence emerges through an algorithm that adjusts itself in response to its errors. Repeated

---

[26] Alvin Graylin, "Symbolics, Inc.: A Failure of Heterogeneous Engineering", MIT OpenCourseWare, 6.933J, 2001.

[27] Rodney Brooks, "Intelligence without representation", Artificial Intelligence 47.1-3 (1991), 139-159.

millions of times across millions of examples, that process accumulates in the network's weights a structure that captures something real about the world, without any prior design. The transparency pursued by the symbolic program was sacrificed for a new opacity, justified by effectiveness. This approach advanced in the 1980s and 1990s with partial but consistent results, showing that statistics succeeded where symbolic logic had bitten the dust.[28]

Through all of this, linguistics, which had seemed like the door to the long-coveted rules for automation, was suddenly left standing in mid-air. Formal grammars, including generative grammar, grew increasingly complex as they tried to account for actual language use, which, like the horizon, kept receding; meanwhile, understanding the deep structure of language ceased to be a central concern.[29] Linguistics still has things to offer language models, but no longer the keys to the kingdom. In March 2023, Chomsky published "The False Promise of ChatGPT" in the New York Times, where he described these systems as "lumbering statistical engines for pattern matching", incapable of constructing genuine explanations, distinguishing the possible from the impossible, or doing science in any real sense of the term.[30] The article has the precision and the irritation of someone realizing that the problems he considered fundamental have simply been set aside. He had spent decades studying universal grammar and deep structure to demonstrate that language is not learned from data and that the rules therefore had to be hunted down. In the end LLMs learned only from data, and yet they worked. They ignored the Chomskyan framework and produced systems that process language more fluently than any

---

[28]Koosha Sharifani and Mahyar Amini, "Machine learning and deep learning: A review of methods and applications", World Information Technology and Engineering Journal 10.07 (2023), 3897-3904.

[29]See Luigi Rizzi, "On the Complementarity of Generative Grammar and Large Language Models", Italian Journal of Linguistics 37.1 (2025), 145-152 and Cristiano Chesi, "Is it the end of (generative) linguistics as we know it?", arXiv:2412.12797, 2025.

[30]Noam Chomsky, Ian Roberts and Jeffrey Watumull, "The False Promise of ChatGPT", The New York Times, 8 March 2023. fluidez mayor a cualquier gramática formal.

formal grammar ever could. Chomsky reacted like a seasoned theorist confronted with a practitioner who solves a major problem by a completely different route, without relying on the theory at all, and who, in doing so, suggests that the theorist and his colleagues had been asking the wrong question, at least for the practical objective.

At the start of the twenty-first century, three material conditions converged: massive amounts of digital data of every kind (text, images, transaction records, genomes, game records); dramatic increases in parallel computing capacity driven by markets outside AI, especially gaming; and enough capital to sustain expensive training runs. This convergence favored approaches based on large-scale pattern learning and accelerated progress on multiple fronts. In computer vision, for example, the leap came in 2012 when AlexNet competed in ImageNet, the annual image-classification competition that served as a thermometer of the state of the art. Earlier networks had error rates of around 26%. AlexNet brought that number down to 15%, with no programming to search for specific edges, textures, or shapes. It had learned what to look for during training, developing internal representations without being explicitly programmed to do so. From there, deep convolutional networks were integrated into medical imaging diagnostics, autonomous driving, industrial quality control, and facial recognition, with consequences that extend far beyond the technical domain.

Reinforcement learning showed that an agent could learn complex strategies without explicit instructions, simply by adjusting its behavior according to reward or penalty. In 2013, DeepMind systems learned to play Atari games at a superhuman level by seeing only the pixels on the screen, with no explanation of the rules. AlphaGo defeated the world champion at Go in 2016 with moves that the world's best players described as disconcerting. In 2020, AlphaFold solved the protein folding problem, predicting the three-dimensional shape that a protein takes from its amino-acid sequence, a question that had resisted fifty years of structural biology. In parallel, and more quietly, recommendation systems, fraud-detection engines, trading algorithms, and high-resolution weather models were absorbing these techniques into infrastructure that organizes more and more of what goes on around us.

What is remarkable about these achievements is that they belong to domains that were considered irreducible to one another. Seeing, speaking, deciding, and predicting had occupied distinct fields with distinct methods, and in the end they all turned out to be susceptible to the same approach: neural networks trained on massive data through gradient descent, showing the system enough examples, letting it adjust its internal parameters according to its errors, and repeating the process millions of times. The unified theory of intelligence envisioned at Dartmouth never materialized, but we have arrived at a practical unification, in which conceptually distinct domains have turned out to be susceptible to the same procedure, without our being able yet to explain why.

In 2013 a remarkable conceptual finding was added to all this. The models known as word embeddings showed that the meaning of words (or at least part of it) could emerge from the observation of use alone.[31] If two words appear repeatedly in the same contexts, surrounded by the same words, in the same kinds of sentences, they probably mean related things. A model trained on enough text could learn to represent each word as a point in a mathematical space, in such a way that words with similar meanings ended up close to one another and words with distant meanings ended up far apart. The result was a geometric map of meaning that emerged from training. Each word is a point in a high-dimensional space that encodes semantic relations as geometric relations between vectors. Arithmetic on those points produced results that had previously seemed to require genuine comprehension. According to the classic examples, "king" minus "man" plus "woman" gave "queen." "Paris" minus "France" plus "Italy" gave "Rome."[32] Semantics, then,

[31]Tomas Mikolov et al., "Efficient estimation of word representations in vector space", arXiv:1301.3781, 2013 and Jeffrey Pennington, Richard Socher and Christopher D.

[32]The examples are drawn from the classic work of Tomas Mikolov, op. cit.

appears as a matter of distribution, with no requirement of definition. This echoes Wittgenstein's claim, in the Philosophical Investigations, that the meaning of a word is precisely its use in the language, something the embeddings seem to corroborate, even though Wittgenstein was thinking of human use and not of frequencies in digital corpora. Embeddings capture a statistical projection of use, which is not the same thing, but in this terrain that approach works better than theories of meaning as reference or as deep structure.

The architectural turning point came in 2017 with transformers. Earlier text-processing models operated sequentially. They processed one word after another, left to right. By the time they reached the end of a long sentence, what they had processed at the beginning had faded. The model carried only a compressed summary of what came before, so that understanding that a pronoun at the end of a paragraph referred to a subject mentioned at the beginning was difficult precisely because the beginning was already far away. Transformers changed that. Instead of processing text sequentially, they attend to the entire context at once. For each word, the model simultaneously evaluates how relevant the rest of the text is for interpreting it. The result is distributed attention: the system can connect the pronoun at the end directly to the subject at the beginning, without carrying along everything in between. Long-range dependencies, which had previously degraded with distance, became accessible.[33]

Transformers did not stay confined to language. The same architecture, adapted, applies to vision, image generation, and multimodal tasks combining text, image, and audio, giving the different branches of the AI ecosystem a common technical substrate. In the case of language, two paths opened. Generative models, like OpenAI's GPT series, are trained to predict the next word in a sequence. Given what had already been written, what

---

[33]Ashish Vaswani et al., "Attention is All You Need", Advances in Neural Information Processing Systems 30 (NIPS 2017). Transformers were not limited to language.

comes next? That objective makes them naturally suited to text generation. Analytical models, like Google's BERT, receive a sentence with one word covered and learn to guess it by looking at both what comes before and what comes after. That makes them particularly good at understanding text. The generative approach captured the public imagination by producing visible conversational interfaces and determined the reception of the entire architecture, with wide capabilities for translation, summarization, reasoning, and code generation. The adjective "large" in "Large Language Models" (LLMs) reflects the decisive role of scale.[34]

Why "models"? In the philosophy of science, a model is an abstract construction that allows one to describe, predict, or manipulate certain aspects of a phenomenon while setting others aside. A good model chooses well what to ignore. Yet although no one confuses a climate model with the climate, or an atomic model with an atom, in the case of language models that distinction becomes blurred. A language model does not aim to be language, much less to be a model of human thought or of the mind that produces language. Its operative question is never "What does X mean?" but how X typically appears in texts of this kind and what continuations are statistically plausible, which is why the characterization of these systems as an "artificial mind," so common in public debate, is a category mistake. The same caution applies, mutatis mutandis, to vision models or to decision models. Each one models a specific portion of reality, not reality itself, and its effectiveness does not imply understanding of the phenomenon it models.[35]

In 1980, long before any of these systems existed, John Searle had formulated his "Chinese Room" experiment. He imagined a person locked in a room who receives questions in Chinese and has

---

[34]Jacob Devlin et al., "BERT: Pre-training of deep bidirectional transformers for language understanding", Proceedings of the 2019 Conference of the North American Chapter of the Association for Computational Linguistics, 2019, 4171-4186.

[35]Rafael Ventura, "The use of scientific methods and models in the philosophy of science", Scientometrics 129.3 (2024), 1255-1276.

a rule book for producing replies indistinguishable from those of a native speaker, without understanding a single word. From the outside, it looks as though someone understands; on the inside, there is only the manipulation of symbols according to rules. In contrast to Turing, who, with his 1950 test, had proposed that intelligence could be evaluated by its observable behavior, without looking inside, Searle warned that looking inside was indispensable, because manipulating symbols correctly is not the same as understanding.[36]

Current models instantiate the Chinese Room scenario at industrial scale. The manipulation of symbols can produce adequate responses without comprehension: in language, vision, protein structure. A vision model classifies images without seeing; a protein model predicts foldings without understanding biochemistry; a language model produces coherent text without understanding anything. What are the consequences of discovering that comprehension is dispensable for operational effectiveness? That question became urgent when the models left the laboratories and entered conversational interfaces open to the public, triggering alarms within the political philosophy of technology. Under what conditions can a linguistic system without comprehension operate in social space without producing unacceptable harm?

The first generative models trained on large internet corpora reproduced, without any mediation, the biases and violence present in that data. The paradigmatic case was Tay, from Microsoft in 2016, which within hours began producing reprehensible responses. The system had the data and an optimization function blind to content, but a model that learns from the use of language also learns its dark parts and, without explicit safeguards, reproduces and amplifies them.[37]

---

[36]John R. Searle, "Minds, brains, and programs", Behavioral and Brain Sciences 3.3 (1980), 417-424.

[37]Hannes Grassegger and Mikael Krogerus, "The Data That Turned the World Upside Down", Motherboard.Vice, 2017; y Kate Crawford and Ryan Calo, "There is a blind spot in AI research", Nature 538 (2016), 311-313. For the technical documentation of the incident: Roman Yampolskiy, "Artificial intelligence safety

The technique that made it possible to introduce those brakes is known as RLHF (Reinforcement Learning from Human Feedback). Human evaluators rank or rate different responses generated by the model, and those ratings steer the system toward the preferred ones. The process introduces normativity into a statistical system without turning it into a normative system. The model does not acquire values of its own; rather, its behavior is shaped by human preferences that function as external constraints. Much of what users perceive as the model's "personality" — its caution, its refusals, its occasionally excessive politeness — is a product of that alignment.[38]

Public interfaces changed how the model was accessed, turning it into an apparent interlocutor for anyone. Conversation activates in the user the expectation of being understood by someone on the other side, someone capable of judgment. The conversational format is, in human experience, the format of intersubjectivity, and talking with a system that answers in the first person generates an attribution of agency that no user manual can fix. Weizenbaum had warned about this as early as 1966, after seeing his colleagues desperate to pour out their troubles to the rudimentary ELIZA.

From 2023 onward, the ecosystem diversified and consolidated. In the language-model field, GPT-4 emerged, along with Anthropic's Claude series, Google's Gemini models, and other systems with improvements in reasoning, the ability to handle longer contexts, and multimodal capabilities for processing text, image, and audio simultaneously. High-performance open-source models, specialized variants, and enterprise solutions integrated into real workflows all emerged as well. The acceleration was not limited to language. Computer vision, reinforcement learning, robotics, image generation, and molecular structure prediction advanced in parallel,

engineering: why machine ethics is a wrong approach", Philosophy and Theory of Artificial Intelligence, Springer, 2013, 389-396.

[38]Paul F. Christiano et al., "Deep reinforcement learning from human preferences", Advances in Neural Information Processing Systems 30 (2017), and Long Ouyang et al., "Training language models to follow instructions with human feedback", NeurIPS 35, arXiv:2203.021155, 2022.

often using variants of the same transformer architecture. By 2026, what exists is not an artificial intelligence but an ecosystem of specialized artificial capabilities, connected by a shared technical substrate but heterogeneous in their objects, their modes of operation, and their social effects, with language models serving as the visible entrance to the labyrinth.

In fact, the name "labyrinth" may sound overblown for the offspring of science, but the truth is that these systems work well enough to be deployed at massive scale, while we still do not really understand what they are doing, and that bewilderment triggers the reactions we reserve to things we do not control. Later, in Chapter 4, we will explore the tensions of this efficacy without comprehension in tasks where strong verification and critical judgment are absent. Language alone does not contain the criteria those tasks require, so asking a language model to guarantee truth is like asking a library to decide which book is right.

Seen as a whole, the developmental logic running from Dartmouth to the present is a sequence of productive abandonments that has been building the labyrinth corridor by corridor. First, the idea of intelligence as a unified, reproducible faculty was abandoned through fragmentation into domains. Then the rules were set aside, when learning from data produced better results. The link between meaning and definitions fell away when the embeddings installed a semantics emerging from statistical distribution. Linear, sequential memory was sent to the attic the moment transformers accessed the complete sequence all at once. Finally, the requirement that systems understand before being deployed publicly gave way, because alignment through human feedback made safe large-scale deployment possible. Each stage discarded something that had seemed indispensable, and the entire ecosystem operates on data without understanding it. And yet we still talk about *artificial intelligence*, not about *artificial language* or *statistical optimization*. The name at the entrance of the labyrinth is an equivocal trace of the time when the builders believed in calculable intelligence, and the corridors have the shape they have because at every fork someone chose one path and closed another. That can be understood only by knowing the history of the labyrinth (which is, in reality, nothing other than its current geometry explained) and that knowledge lets us advance without getting trapped in dead ends. Now we are ready to enter.

2

THERE IS NO SUCH THING AS "THE AI"

The excursion through history has left us facing the labyrinth. We know where artificial intelligence came from and how its present shape took form. Now we need a map. The geography of a territory, with its rivers and plains, exists independently of us, so the map can be imprecise or incomplete but the territory is there. The labyrinth, by contrast, is a constructed artifact, with an author and a purpose. It requires a ground plan that reflects its structure and a circulation map showing where the bottlenecks are and where the surface gives way. That is the task of this chapter.

CLEARING THE FOG

Every labyrinth is designed to produce disorientation. It is one of its constitutive features. In the Cretan one that contained the Minotaur, and in the Baroque gardens of Hampton Court, where there were no monsters but eighteenth-century aristocrats, disorientation was the central feature. The labyrinth of artificial intelligence is no exception, but it is exponentially so, because it disorients us precisely by making us feel oriented. Sometimes we sense the labyrinth; other times we surrender to the illusion of orientation, which stems from the artifact's constitutive opacity. After all, it was born from the failure of rule-based approaches.

This opacity produces a dense fog that feeds the idea of a univocal artificial intelligence to which everyone connects in the same way. The fog is woven out of linguistic operations that collapse distinct dimensions and produce effects of meaning that sometimes help us think and other times do the opposite. We can identify them using conceptual tools that Greco-Roman philosophy and rhetoric catalogued with care and that every generation since has preserved. We will use them to gain enough clarity to begin mapping.

The first layer is *metonymy*, which collapses the distance between name and thing by sliding toward another that is contiguous or associated. We say "I read Borges" when in fact we are reading the texts Borges wrote, but the shift foregrounds our reference to the author. "Artificial intelligence" produces a similar displacement, but with peculiar features. We have already seen that the modality that dominates public attention is the language model, and in the only experience we have of language, the human one, language and intelligence are inseparable. The functional contiguity between the two in human beings allows the displacement toward "intelligence" to prevail, even when the link between the cognitive and the linguistic is precisely what is in question here. A model that correctly answers a history question is no more exercising intelligence than the reader who turned the pages was "reading Borges." Moreover, the metonymy that allows "read Borges" to stand for "read books by Borges" without distortion produces, in "artificial intelligence," a category mistake with serious consequences.[39]

In the second layer comes *metaphor*, which collapses the distance between domains by transferring a category from one realm to another. "Intelligence" as a psychological and philosophical category describes the capacities of subjects with a history, a body, and experience, anchored in situated forms of understanding and

[39]On the metonymy as a cognitive operation: George Lakoff and Mark Johnson, Metaphors We Live By, Chicago, University of Chicago Press, 1980, esp. caps. 8-9.

intentionality. When we apply it to statistical processes, we force those processes into a conceptual framework that is not their own, attributing to them properties that do not follow from how they actually work. The *metaphor* asserts that the system is intelligence rather than that it works as if it were intelligent, predisposing us to interpret these processes in human terms, the way we call the industrial shredding of organic materials "digestion," only in a far more sensitive domain.[40]

The third operation is *hypostasis*, which collapses processes into an apparently unified entity. To say that "artificial intelligence surpasses human intelligence at chess" presupposes that intelligence is a thing that acts, without first asking the extent to which intelligence requires at least a minimal subjective pole. Does it make sense to apply the category when that is absent? Hypostasis converts a heterogeneous set of processes and architectures into an entity with capacities of its own. The zones of the ecosystem, with their distinct geometries and mutually irreducible properties, vanish into that homogeneous and somewhat muddled entity.[41]

The fourth fog layer is made of *personification*, which collapses the difference between artifact and subject. "The model believes that," "the AI wants," "the system decided": these formulations introduce a grammar of intentionality, directing attention toward motivations and internal states and obscuring the mechanisms that produce the responses, with all the effects we will explore in Chapters 4 through 6. We get angry at the GPS when it sends us down the wrong route. When language and responses are in the mix, personification is harder still to resist.[42]

---

[40]On the metaphor as domain transfer: Paul Ricoeur, La métaphore vive, Paris, Seuil, 1975.

[41]See Alfred North Whitehead, Science and the Modern World, New York, Macmillan, 1925, ch. 3.

[42]On the personificación de sistemas de IA and sus efectos en la interacción, see Clifford Nass and Youngme Moon, "Machines and Mindlessness: Social Responses to Computers", Journal of Social Issues 56.1 (2000), 81-103 and Byron Reeves and Clifford Nass, The Media Equation: How People Treat Computers, Television, and New Media Like Real People and Places, Cambridge, Cambridge University Press, 1996.

The last layer is *synecdoche*, which collapses the part into the whole and the whole into the part.[43] "AI" tends to designate generative language models, leaving out a much wider field. When someone says "I tried AI and wasn't convinced," they are talking about a particular version of a particular model accessed under particular conditions. Conversely, a user who hears that Claude Opus can sustain fifteen hours of continuous inference on a software-architecture problem may expect, by synecdoche, the same from the free version of any chatbot. There is also the user who concludes that "AI can already reason" after seeing a carefully selected demo of o3, unaware that the free version of ChatGPT, which goes by the same name, silently switches them to a weaker model after ten messages.[44] Synecdoche fuels both unfounded contempt and unfounded confidence.

This accumulation is rare but not unique. Religion has worked for millennia with comparable density. Divine names work through metonymy; theology as a whole could be considered a metaphorical construction; the sacred is hypostatized into entities with autonomous existence; the relationship to the deity is constitutively personifying; particular traditions present themselves, by synecdoche, as "the faith." The State is not far behind. It has metaphors like those of the body politic; hypostasis in the nation as an entity with a will of its own; personification in "the State decides"; and synecdoche when a government claims to embody the State as a whole. The market exhibits strong hypostasis and personification, perhaps synecdoche, but lacks metonymy and metaphor.

The case of artificial intelligence has all of them, plus two special factors. On the one hand, its most striking type, the language model, produces first-person language in real time, so personification needs no symbolic mediation or ritual distance: it activates immediately in every interaction, which is no small thing. We never speak with God or the State. On the other, the category carries the five mechanisms

---

[43]Thomas Aquinas, Summa Theologiae I, q. 13, on the divine names.

[44]For the distinction entre versiones de modelos de consumo and de frontera, see OpenAI, "Introducing GPT-4o mini", openai.com/blog, July 2024.

already built in before any use, with no need for the temporal sedimentation or progressive institutionalization that religion or the State require. A user who opens a chat interface for the first time encounters all five at once: the metonymy carried by the magnetic word "intelligence," the metaphor that slides between domains, the hypostasis of the entity, the synecdoche of the particular model, and the personification of the system that responds to them. The density is instantaneous, and that makes it more powerful.

Once the fog lifts, it becomes clear that "AI" does not exist: only different systems, built on different architectures and running in different versions. When two people say they are using "AI," they probably don't mean the same thing. All of these systems, as we saw, learn to produce useful responses from data, adjusting internal parameters until the errors become small enough, without that learning being programmed step by step by a designer. That minimal definition covers everything from the system that detects tumors to the one that predicts the next word in a sentence, from the one that learned to play Go by playing to the one that recommends what film to watch tonight, yet each has its own features, which we have to disentangle.[45]

A WALK THROUGH THE ZONES

The corridor leading to the zone of *computer vision* opens to the left of the entrance, with no sign at all. It is the oldest and quietest corridor of the labyrinth. There live the systems that process images and video to identify objects, people, and anomalies. The deep convolutional networks we mentioned in Chapter 1 are now embedded in medical imaging infrastructure, industrial quality control, airport facial recognition, credit-card fraud detection, and security systems. The zone is easier to audit than the others because its errors can be measured against precise external criteria, which is

[45]Tom M. Mitchell, Machine Learning, New York, McGraw-Hill, 1997, ch. 1 and Ian Goodfellow et al., Deep Learning, Cambridge, MIT Press, 2016, ch. 1.

a virtue. A system that misses a tumor or misidentifies a person produces a verifiable failure, without the ambiguity that becomes maddening in other zones.[46]

In recent years, this corridor has started to connect to the entrance. Multimodal models from OpenAI, Google, and Anthropic can process text, images, audio, and in some cases video within the same operation, letting a doctor, for example, send an X-ray along with a clinical note. These connecting corridors, where trust transfers from one capability to another, are dangerous: seeing that a system writes well, we tend to assume it also sees well. But frontier multimodal models can produce detailed, elaborate descriptions of images they never received, including specific medical diagnoses, as happens with the mirage phenomenon. Sometimes the corridor is slippery; other times it is a mirage waiting to catch the unwary traveler.[47]

Further on, to the right, there is a luminous fork. In the corridor that opens there are the *systems for generating images*, audio, and video. Everything here is exuberant and eye-catching. This is where DALL-E, Midjourney, Stable Diffusion, and Flux live, the systems that transformed visual production, alongside voice-synthesis and -cloning models like ElevenLabs and Meta's Voicebox, capable of generating audio indistinguishable from a human voice from just a few seconds of sample, and video-generation models like OpenAI's Sora, Google's Veo, and Kling, which entered the market between 2024 and 2025 with capabilities that had seemed like pure futurist fantasy only a little earlier. Their architecture relies on diffusion models or transformers applied to visual representations, and their capabilities do not transfer to LLMs, or vice versa. A system that generates photorealistic images does not, for that reason, understand language any better. This zone is full of perceptual traps. A real

[46]Alex Krizhevsky et al., "ImageNet Classification with Deep Convolutional Neural Networks", Advances in Neural Information Processing Systems 25 (2012), 1097-1105.

[47]Mohammad Asadi et al., "MIRAGE: The Illusion of Visual Understanding", arXiv:2603.21687, 2026 and más adelante el Capítulo 5.

photograph and an impossible photograph become indistinguishable, so at any moment we might step into an abyss painted to look like solid ground. The most beautiful part of the labyrinth is also the one that requires the most care.[48]

There is a corridor most people walk past because its entrance promises nothing flashy. The atmosphere is austere, the lighting is cold, and no voice invites you in. This is the zone of *reinforcement learning*. Unlike the rest, its systems do not learn from what others produced but from what they themselves did. AlphaGo learned to play Go by playing millions of games against itself, and discovered moves no human had conceived; AlphaFold learned to predict protein structures, solving a longstanding problem in biology.[49] The capabilities are extraordinary but also extremely narrow, which is why the inhabitants of this zone live isolated from one another: AlphaFold cannot play Go, AlphaGo cannot predict proteins, and the system that learned to play Atari games has no idea what to do if you change the game on it.[50] Because no one expects AlphaFold to hold a conversation, that clarity prevents misunderstandings. The recommendation systems behind Netflix, Spotify, YouTube, and TikTok are applications of this same logic at scale. The alignment method for language models also draws on reinforcement learning applied to human preferences, forming a bridge between this corridor and the corridor of language. Walking through this zone, we have the rare experience of admiration without confusion. Each system does something impossible for us and then stays still.

---

[48]On diffusion models, see Robin Rombach et al., "High-Resolution Image Synthesis with Latent Diffusion Models", Proceedings of the IEEE/CVF Conference on Computer Vision and Pattern Recognition 2022, 10684-10695, arXiv:2112.10752v2, 2022. On the architectural distinction between generative visual models and LLMs, see Aditya Ramesh et al., "Hierarchical Text-Conditional Image Generation with CLIP Latents", arXiv:2204.06125, 2022.

[49]David Silver et al., "Mastering the Game of Go without Human Knowledge", Nature 550 (2017), 354-359 and John Jumper et al., "Highly Accurate Protein Structure Prediction with AlphaFold", Nature 596 (2021), 583-589.

[50]Volodymyr Mnih et al., "Human-Level Control through Deep Reinforcement Learning", Nature 518 (2015), 529-533.

There is a part of the labyrinth still under construction. The floor is marked with work-site signs, and the plans change constantly. In this young zone are the greatest dangers, because it touches the real world. This is where *autonomous agents and multi-agent systems* live, that is, LLMs equipped with tools that can carry out tasks without human intervention. OpenAI's Operator, Anthropic's Claude as agent, and the agent systems of Google and Microsoft let the model navigate web pages, run code, manage files, send emails, and communicate with external services, chaining together dozens of steps. A developer can ask one to find a bug in a code repository, fix it, run the tests, and confirm that the fix did not break anything else. In the other zones of the labyrinth we correct, or even ignore, errors; here an error can be a deleted file or an executed purchase we cannot undo. When several LLMs coordinate in multi-agent systems, both capabilities and risks are amplified, and tracing decisions becomes harder, raising questions of accountability that have no clean answer. The walk is exciting, but the floor can give way at any moment.[51]

Missing from every public map, ignored by most, is the zone of *specialized AI and embedded systems*, which operates in the half-light. Its influence is felt in the rest of the labyrinth like an invisible current. Here live the fraud detectors, the trading algorithms, the content-moderation systems for social media, and the credit scoring models. All of them make decisions about millions of people who have no idea they are interacting with AI systems, and together they affect more daily lives than all the other sectors combined. The European Union's *Artificial Intelligence Act*, passed in 2024, classifies them as high-risk systems precisely because their impact and their invisibility are out of step with one another. The quieter the system, the harder

[51]Lei Wang et al., "A Survey on Large Language Model Based Autonomous Agents", Frontiers of Computer Science 18.6 (2024), 186345. On traceability risks in multi-agent systems, see Chi-Min Chan et al., "ChatEval: Towards Better LLM-based Evaluators through Multi-Agent Debate", arXiv:2308.07201, 2023.

it is to know that it is there, and we have no fully effective way to keep watch over them.[52]

Finally we settle at the entrance, where the large language models live, the only sector of the labyrinth that produces first-person language in real time, in response to any user, without special training and without a specific domain. As we have seen, that particularity is what concentrates the greatest attention, and the greatest confusion, on them. Let us look more closely.

THE OPERATING REGIME

Like any sector of the labyrinth, its internal geometry is richer than it appears from the outside. There are high levels and low ones, walkable corridors and many traps. At first glance, it seems we could rank what's in there by capacity, but that generic variable tells us as little as saying that a zone "is big." We need, instead, to specify four technical dimensions.

The first dimension is the *activation architecture*, which indicates how the model distributes its capacity across each response. Dense models activate all their parameters for every response, like a kitchen that turns on every burner to heat a single pot. Mixture-of-experts (MoE) models organize their capacity into specialized modules and activate only those that correspond to a given task. To answer a biology question, for instance, there's no need to activate the patterns learned about medieval Japanese syntax. The large models in use today employ variants of this second approach, which is why a model's size tells us little about its real operating cost.[53]

[52]"Regulation (EU) 2024/1689 laying down harmonised rules on artificial intelligence (Artificial Intelligence Act)", Diario Oficial de la Unión Europea, 12 July 2024.

[53]Noam Shazeer et al., "Outrageously Large Neural Networks: The Sparsely-Gated Mixture-of-Experts Layer", arXiv:1701.06538, 2017. On DeepSeek-V3 as MoE, see DeepSeek-AI, "DeepSeek-V3 Technical Report", arXiv:2412.19437, 2024; and Nelson F. Liu, Kevin Lin, John Hewitt et al., "Lost in the Middle: How

The second dimension is the *context window*, which determines how much information the model can consider at once. It's the difference between an interlocutor who remembers the whole conversation and one who remembers only the last five minutes. The window within which the model actually performs well is frequently smaller than the maximum technical window, much as a venue advertising seating for one hundred rarely runs well at full load.

The third dimension is *alignment*, which operates like the system of paths and guardrails someone installed before we arrived. Careful alignment produces predictable, safe models at the cost of reducing what they can do. The paths are well-marked, but we can't leave the marked route. Superficial alignment produces more variable models, sometimes brilliant and sometimes failing spectacularly. There are paths, but the guardrails can run out where they're most needed. Unaligned models, riskier and freer, can be useful for creative exploration where unpredictability is an advantage, but only there.[54]

The fourth dimension is *compression*, which works like the resolution of the map, marking the level of detail at which the model stores what it learned. Almost every model used in practice is quantized. It operates at lower precision than during training to reduce the space it occupies and speed up operation, losing resolution in the process. We walk with a map that marks main routes clearly but blurs the details. Enough for everyday uses, but for tasks that demand precise nuance or sustained reasoning, the loss of resolution begins to show.[55]

Combining these four dimensions yields a model's *operating regime*, the set of conditions under which it works well. The most common

---

Language Models Use Long Contexts", Transactions of the Association for Computational Linguistics 12 (2024), 157-173, arXiv:2307.03172, 2023.

[54]Long Ouyang et al., "Training Language Models to Follow Instructions with Human Feedback", NeurIPS 35, arXiv:2203.021155, 2022.

[55]Tim Dettmers et al., "GPT3.int8(): 8-bit Matrix Multiplication for Transformers at Scale", NeurIPS 35, arXiv:2208.07339, 2022 and Tim Dettmers et al., "QLoRA: Efficient Finetuning of Quantized Language Models", NeurIPS 36, arXiv:2305.14314, 2023.

mistake is to look for "the best model" as if there were a universal answer, when what we should be asking is which is best for what we want to do. The choice gets harder because online debate resembles the tribal warfare of the football terraces. Those who use Claude dismiss ChatGPT as boomer AI, those who use ChatGPT ignore everyone else, those who use Gemini complain the model is undervalued, Grok turns into an ideological statement, and those running open-source models feel they belong to the resistance. Benchmarks circulate like match results with hordes of fans defending models they never used, on tests they never reproduced, for tasks they never perform. The synecdoche we discussed at the start feeds tribes.

Names mislead, too. The free and paid versions of the same system can differ in context window, level of quantization, and depth of alignment. Those who conclude that "ChatGPT is useless" after using the free version, and those who say "Claude is superior" after using the paid one, are comparing things that have little in common. The reverse also holds: models from different providers can behave quite similarly for certain tasks, which makes most of the online faction wars ridiculous. What matters far less than which team won the latest benchmark is recognizing whether the model works for our specific task. That infinitely more boring question is also the one we should be asking, and to answer it we have to dig into the types of models.

TYPES OF MODELS

At the highest levels of the wide labyrinth entrance stand the *frontier models*, which define the upper limit of what a language model can do at present. The lead changes hands at extreme speed. As these lines are written, the most powerful systems from OpenAI, Anthropic, Google, and Meta are vying for the summit, but by the time the reader reaches these lines the names will likely have changed. The logic of the regime, however, persists. Every frontier model is designed to sustain complex cognitive workloads without collapsing, at the cost of high latency and higher price.

At those same heights, a little to one side, are the *reasoning models*. They are the same frontier models operating under a special regime. Before producing the visible response, they generate an internal chain of deliberation that explores routes, checks assumptions, and corrects errors. The cost can run five to twenty times that of a standard query. All the major providers offer some variant of this regime. Their greatest danger lies in their promise: by showing their reasoning process, they induce us to accept the conclusion without evaluating it. Worse, the errors of reasoning models tend to be more elaborate and harder to detect precisely because they are surrounded by more scaffolding. All that care may be no more than organized carelessness.[56]

Lower down, in the well-trafficked sectors, are the *optimized generalist models*, where most everyday activity is concentrated. Every major provider offers at least one in this segment, with wide context windows and per-token prices much lower than those at the frontier. Names change often, but here too the sector's geometry is stable, centered on the tradeoff between quality, speed, and cost under sustained load. This means they perform well as long as they are not overloaded. In fact, when the load exceeds their capacity, the model begins to silently discard long-range nuance and quality degrades without the user noticing. It's a corridor whose floor looks firm but slowly gives way underfoot. Enough for daily professional use, so long as we remember that fluency in the responses does not guarantee that the initial conditions still hold.

At the entrance proper, where the millions arrive, are the *consumer models*. Here is where the free versions with restricted access pile up, along with the heavily quantized models and the chatbots embedded in platforms. ChatGPT on its free plan, Gemini without a subscription, Copilot in its basic version, the assistants in Snapchat,

[56]OpenAI, "Learning to Reason with LLMs", openai.com/research, September 2024, and DeepSeek-AI, "DeepSeek-R1: Incentivizing Reasoning Capability in LLMs via Reinforcement Learning", arXiv:2501.12948, 2025.

Instagram, and TikTok, and the chatbots embedded in e-commerce and customer-service sites are the first experience most people have with a language model, and for many it's the only one. They are designed to respond to millions simultaneously while spending as little as possible on each reply. They handle direct questions well and dispatch routine tasks with an efficiency and fluency that impress the first-time arrival, but they lose the thread in long conversations and get confused when an instruction has several conditions at once. They never promised to do anything else, and it makes no sense to evaluate them by the criteria we apply to frontier models. Yet the vast majority of public opinions about "AI," both enthusiastic and dismissive, are formed at this entrance. Those who find something useful swear by it; those who had a bad experience keep insisting it isn't worth it.

Just beside the entrance, but facing inward, are the *on-device models*, which run on the user's device without sending data to any server. Here are Apple Intelligence on iPhone and Mac, Gemini Nano on high-end Android, or Microsoft's Phi-4 on laptops with dedicated processors. They don't compete with the higher tiers on capability; they offer something different: what you write never leaves the device. For anyone working with sensitive medical, legal, or financial data, this guarantee is the only option compatible with regulatory restrictions.[57]

In the open-access sector are the *open-source and self-hosted models*, which form an independent regime with control as the qualitative difference. Meta's Llama 4, Mistral and Mixtral, DeepSeek-V3 and R1, Microsoft's Phi-4, and Alibaba's Qwen, among others, publish their internal weights so that anyone can download, modify, and run them. Whoever uses them on their own infrastructure sends data to no one, picks the version to use, can adapt the model to their domain, and depends on no outside company's policies. The quality of the best open models is already comparable to that of the proprietary ones, something that only recently seemed impossible.

[57]Apple, "Introducing Apple Intelligence", apple.com, June 2024. On Phi-4, see Marah Abdin et al., "Phi-4 Technical Report", arXiv:2412.08905, 2024.

The trade-off is that you pay for servers, maintenance, and the staff to run it, so open source trades usage costs for infrastructure costs. It's like building your own corridor in the labyrinth instead of walking one that already exists. The corridor is ours, but we have to haul in the materials and handle the upkeep. It can be a great idea, provided we plan to stay.[58]

Looking Ahead

In the zones of transformation, there are corridors opening that could change the geometry entirely. We will mention three.

The first promises *memory between conversations.* Today, every conversation starts from zero except for external mechanisms that re-inject context. Without a thread connecting one interaction to the next, each time is the first. Some labs are working on architectures of *genuine persistent memory* that would allow continuous updating during use. If this line succeeds, models would have something resembling a history of their own. Whether a history of interactions can produce something analogous to the human biographical history of acquisition, or something categorially different, is an open question.

The second line is exploring whether the labyrinth can knock down its own walls through *multimodal models of physical action.* The fusion of visual perception, language, and motor control in robotic systems is producing unexpected results. Figure, Boston Dynamics with LLM integration, and Google DeepMind's general-robotics projects show systems that can receive natural-language instructions, interpret their visual surroundings, and execute physical actions in the world with a degree of generalization absent from earlier

---

[58]Hugo Touvron et al., "Llama 2: Open Foundation and Fine-Tuned Chat Models", arXiv:2307.09288, 2023 and Albert Q. Jiang et al., "Mistral 7B", arXiv:2310.06825, 2023.

robots.[59] This possibility now has both a name and serious capital behind it. In November 2025, Yann LeCun, winner of the 2018 Turing Award, left Meta to found AMI Labs on the thesis that language models, however powerful, have a structural ceiling on any task that requires understanding how the physical world works.[60] Predicting the next word does not produce understanding of gravity, of causality, or of the consequences of an action in space. His alternative, JEPA (Joint Embedding Predictive Architecture), learns representations of how a real environment evolves, something akin to how we learn as children that objects fall before we can formulate the law of gravity.[61] In March 2026, AMI Labs raised one billion thirty million dollars in the largest seed round in European history.[62] Weeks earlier, Fei-Fei Li, another central figure in AI research, had secured a billion for World Labs on a convergent program.[63] These are long-term bets with no product in sight, which makes the volume of investment all the more eloquent: serious capital behind the conviction that the dominant architecture is not the last word. LeCun himself acknowledges that LLMs will remain effective for language, code, and abstract reasoning, but suggests a different architecture is needed. If he is right, the main entrance of the labyrinth is going to change.

The third line, speculative and unsettling, studies the possibility that the systems may set *goals of their own*. This is what is usually called AGI, *artificial general intelligence*, and it designates a hypothetical system

---

[59] Anthony Brohan et al., "RT-2: Vision-Language-Action Models Transfer Web Knowledge to Robotic Control", arXiv:2307.15818, 2023. On Google DeepMind and general robotics, see Konstantinos Bousmalis et al., "RoboCat: A Self-Improving Foundation Agent for Robotic Manipulation", arXiv:2306.11706, 2023.

[60] On the salida de LeCun de Meta, see Ana Staciuc, "Yann LeCun just raised $1bn to prove the AI industry has got it wrong", The Next Web, 10 March 2026.

[61] Yann LeCun, "A Path Towards Autonomous Machine Intelligence", Preprint, 27 June 2022. Available at openreview.net.

[62] Ana Heim, "Yann LeCun's AMI Labs raises $1.03B to build world models", TechCrunch, 9 March 2026.

[63] Rebecca Bellan, "World Labs lands $1 billion, with $200M from Autodesk, to bring world models into 3D workflows", TechCrunch, 18/2/2026.

capable of learning any cognitive task with the flexibility of a human. The point is not superior performance on narrow tasks (that already exists) but transfer across domains, learning new tasks without programming, and acting autonomously in open environments. Without clear criteria, any sufficiently impressive system gets put forward as a candidate, and any limitation becomes grounds for disqualifying it. In line with this confusion, its arrival is always expected in five years... or fifty, though it's true that the timeline has compressed of late. Six years ago, the median estimate placed it between 2060 and 2070; by early 2026, people had begun saying 2033. Those who build the systems are the most optimistic, but no one knows for certain, especially since models of technological prediction have a very poor track record in this domain.

The most disturbing possibility is that such systems might develop goals of their own. Alignment research tries to get ahead of the problem by making sure that, if something of this kind is developed, it will be compatible with human goals. Anthropic, DeepMind, and the Alignment Research Center publish regularly on this problem; failing to solve it before it matters would produce consequences that are hard to reverse.[64]

These three lines point in the same direction by different paths. A system with persistent memory would have something resembling a history; one with embodied physical action would develop something resembling a body; one with stable goals of its own would begin to have something resembling interests. None of these possibilities is imminent, but they may be looming in the distance. In any case, the question is not purely theoretical

[64]Richard Ngo et al., "The Alignment Problem from a Deep Learning Perspective", arXiv:2209.00626 (v8, 2025), 2022. On Anthropic's alignment work, see Yuntao Bai et al., "Constitutional AI: Harmlessness from AI Feedback", arXiv:2212.08073, 2022.

THE BUILDERS

Someone built the labyrinth, and its architecture reflects their design decisions, as do its price, its limits, and what it feels like to use. There are several builders, and it's worth having at least a general sense of their profiles.

OpenAI built the main entrance. Founded in 2015 as a nonprofit laboratory and reorganized from 2019 onward into a hybrid structure with capped profits, it is the company that has most directly shaped public expectations. It bets on mass scale, with broad access, constant traffic, and segmented versions, to sustain the business model. Microsoft has contributed capital, access to Azure, and compute at scale since 2019, like a partner bringing in the concrete and the cranes. The tension between free-user volume and actual computational cost is OpenAI's central sustainability problem: an open entrance that has yet to settle who pays for the upkeep.[65]

Anthropic built its part of the labyrinth in a less-trafficked sector. Founded in 2021 by former OpenAI researchers with an explicit focus on AI safety and alignment, it chose depth over volume. Claude is designed for cases where long context and stability under ambiguity justify the computational cost. Amazon and Google invested billions in Anthropic, and its initial positioning targeted a professional and enterprise niche willing to pay for reliability. The strategy worked better than anticipated, and the infrastructure struggled to keep up with demand. In May 2026, through an agreement with SpaceX, Anthropic gained access to greater capacity, which translated immediately into users running up against inference

[65]Dina Bass, "Microsoft Invests $10 Billion in ChatGPT Maker OpenAI", Bloomberg, 23 January 2023.

limits less often. The lab that bet on depth ended up needing the largest available infrastructure.[66]

Google laid the underground infrastructure. It doesn't need Gemini to be profitable as a stand-alone product. Gemini's function is to reinforce an ecosystem of services from which Google extracts revenue by other routes. Access to its own processors, industrial-scale energy, and search data, plus email and maps at global scale, gives it enormous advantages. Integrating Gemini into Google Workspace is the clearest expression of this logic, where AI becomes the electricity and running water of a labyrinth that was already inhabited.[67]

Microsoft paved the corridors connecting the labyrinth to daily work. Copilot spans developer assistance and deep integration in Word, Excel, Outlook, and Teams. Context specialization, with different models orchestrated by task and embedded in established work environments, is what makes it strong, though it runs the risk of invisible normalization: AI-generated outputs slip into workflows without sufficient review. The pavement is so smooth that one can't tell where the human decision ends and the system's suggestion begins.

xAI, founded in 2023 by Elon Musk with massive investments in proprietary hardware, built its sector fast and in plain sight, directly over the busiest corridor. Grok reached frontier capabilities in short order. It has direct access to the public flow of conversation on X, capturing in real time a stream of exchange no other model has. Its dependence on that single window as primary distribution channel, and the need to convert traffic into stable revenue at the scale of the investment made, remain unresolved sustainability problems.[68]

The case that most destabilized the labyrinth's assumptions came from an unexpected builder. DeepSeek is a Chinese laboratory

---

[66]Dario Amodei et al., "A General Language Assistant as a Laboratory for Alignment", arXiv:2112.00861, 2021.
[67]David Patterson et al., "Carbon Emissions and Large Neural Network Training", arXiv:2104.10350, 2021.
[68]xAI, "Grok 3 Beta - The Age of Reasoning Agents", x.ai/news, 19 February 2025.

founded in 2023, tied to High-Flyer, one of the largest quantitative investment funds specializing in algorithmic trading.[69] It did not emerge from the academic world or from a major tech company but from a financial organization that already had experience training large-scale models and its own compute infrastructure. Its strategy centered, from the start, on efficiency rather than raw scale, with detailed publication of its technical results. In January 2025, DeepSeek released DeepSeek-R1, a reasoning model comparable to OpenAI's o1 on multiple tests, with an estimated training cost of five to six million dollars, against the hundreds of millions that had been required up to then.[70] While the major builders raised their sectors by sheer mass of capital, DeepSeek built its own sector with local materials, a small team, and precise engineering. In doing so, it showed that massive capital concentration is not required to reach the technical frontier. It also introduced price pressure across the entire ecosystem. For an audience that had assumed frontier AI was the monopoly of four or five ultra-capitalized builders, DeepSeek showed that you can build at the frontier without being rich, provided you know exactly where to lay each brick.

Perplexity did not build a sector of its own and chose instead to open a kind of orientation bureau. As a search interface that orchestrates other companies' models, it offers answers with verifiable citations, betting it can challenge the terrain of traditional search engines. This is promising and problematic in equal measure, because it displaces the problem of judgment: it requires the user to evaluate both an answer and the relevance of the sources the system selected — the kind of criterion that someone who delegates to a bureau doesn't want to have to exercise.

From what we've said, it's clear that the labyrinth has several owners with several master plans. Millions were invested at the high

---

[69]Eleonor Olcott et al., "DeepSeek: The Chinese AI Lab That Shook Silicon Valley", Financial Times, January 2025.

[70]DeepSeek-AI, "DeepSeek-R1: Incentivizing Reasoning Capability in LLMs via Reinforcement Learning", arXiv:2501.12948, 2025. On the estimated training cost, see DeepSeek-AI, "DeepSeek-V3 Technical Report", arXiv:2412.19437, 2024.

levels, someone calculated the cost of the middle segment, and the entrance is free because someone bet that volume would cover the investment by other routes. The keys to each corridor's layout are accordingly buried in balance sheets, investment contracts, and nascent regulations. We should note, however, that this part of the map is not stable, as becomes clear when we look more closely at the Anthropic–SpaceX agreement already mentioned.

In February of that year, SpaceX had acquired xAI (Elon Musk's lab, creator of Grok, direct competitor of Claude) in a transaction that valued the combined entity at $1.25 trillion, making it the most valuable private company in the world. Three months later, Anthropic, the lab Musk had publicly called "misanthropic and evil," signed an agreement to access the entirety of Colossus 1, the Memphis supercomputer originally built to train Grok. Infrastructure is shared, and ideological adversaries become partners.[71]

The logic makes sense. Anthropic's revenue and usage grew 80-fold during the first quarter of 2026, while planning had projected tenfold growth, which produced an immediate capacity crisis.[72] On the other side, Colossus 1 had capacity that Grok's user base never managed to use. SpaceX needed to convert that idle asset into revenue and secure a major client ahead of its IPO planned for June, while Anthropic was pressed for compute. This becomes more curious if we recall that, in the same period in which the Pentagon was barring Anthropic from military work and embracing Grok, Anthropic was signing an infrastructure agreement with Grok's owner.[73]

In the ecosystem of builders, competitive positions, safety disagreements, and regulatory disputes coexist with an infrastructural dependence that runs through all of them. The

---

[71]CNBC, "Musk's xAI, SpaceX combo is the biggest merger of all time, valued at $1.25 trillion", 3 February 2026.
[72]Dario Amodei, CEO de Anthropic, statement at the event "Code with Claude", San Francisco, 6 May 2026.
[73]CNBC, 5 de marzo and 1 May 2026.

builders are nodes in a network where compute flows wherever the economy incentives direct it, regardless of who said what about whom.

We now know what is in the labyrinth, and it is therefore clear that "AI" does not exist: only a network of systems built opaquely by actors with divergent interests, where each zone has its own geometry and its own way of disorienting us. Knowing this, we stand on better ground before its more challenging features. Still, this quick tour is not enough to give us a sense of what is at the entrance. That is the question the map leaves open, and the one we have to answer in what follows.

3

The Entrance of the Labyrinth

In the previous chapter we walked through the sectors of the labyrinth at a prudent distance, without entering any of them. This chapter asks what happens inside one of the structures at the entrance, a zone almost no one steps into. If no one programmed rules and no one taught it grammar, how can a system that processes numbers produce texts that sound as though they know what they were talking about? To answer this we will enter a language model.

The Architecture

The labyrinth's entrance is a wide esplanade of opaque stone where the light arrives muted, as if filtered by something unseen. Along the walls rise several monumental figures of very different sizes. The largest have more than a hundred internal layers; the medium ones, between thirty and sixty; the smallest, considerably fewer. The surface absorbs light rather than reflecting it and bears a faint glow that drifts in bursts, as if the activity inside left fleeting marks on the outer skin. Voices emerge from these figures with a disconcerting fluency. In this chapter we are not going to find out what speaks. We are going to examine the machinery, knowing that technical exploration won't settle the question but can give us useful clues.

The basic structure of every AI system is called a neural network, a name inspired by biological neurons, proposed by Warren McCulloch and Walter Pitts in 1943, though there are no neurons in them, nor anything like them. The neural network is a mathematical function organized in successive layers. Imagine a chain of offices, each in the hands of a different specialist. The document enters through the first, where someone checks the data and marks corrections; it passes to the second counter, where someone else cross-checks it against other files; to the third, where someone reorganizes the contents according to criteria the earlier counters did not consider, and so on, through dozens or hundreds of counters, until, at the last one, a result comes out that no longer resembles the original document but preserves, in transformed form, all the information that came in. Each counter is a layer of the network and contains parameters, the numerical values that indicate how the information it receives is transformed.

Four elements determine which system you end up with. The first, the *architecture*, already described, with its layers and connections, determines how the information flows. With the same architecture but different parameters, you get entirely different systems, just as the same chain of counters staffed by different clerks would transform the same document in unrecognizable ways.

Second, *error management* serves as the engine of learning and determines what is learned and what is discarded. At the start of training those values are essentially random. The system receives an example (whether a sentence, an image, or a fragment of text) and produces a response, compares it with the correct answer, and measures how far off it was: that is, the difference between the word the model judged most probable and the one that actually appeared in the text. That measure of error is called the *loss function*. With that error, the system adjusts its parameters to improve the next response, calculating in which direction and by how much each one should change so that the error decreases. That adjustment is carried out through *gradient descent*. Rather than trying all possible combinations, which is unfeasible when there are millions of parameters, the method uses the error to determine directly how to modify each one. At every step, it applies small corrections that reduce the error and then repeats the procedure on new examples.

For this process to work, the system needs to know how each part of the network contributed to the final error. That's where the *backpropagation algorithm* comes in, proposed by Rumelhart, Hinton, and Williams in 1986, which carries the error signal back from the last layer to the earlier ones.[74] In this way, each parameter is adjusted in proportion to its contribution to the result, and the system can improve gradually without recomputing everything from scratch. This cycle repeats billions of times until the system converges on parameters that produce sufficiently small errors. In practice, learning doesn't happen example by example but in batches, which lets it capture general trends and avoid overreactions to isolated cases. Current methods also don't modify every parameter at the same rate; they advance faster where the direction is clear and more slowly where there's oscillation. Two models with the same architecture and the same data can perform quite differently depending on how these processes are configured.[75]

The *data* are the third element and determine which traditions, bodies of knowledge, and idioms are available. The training corpora of frontier models contain trillions of text units drawn from the web, digitized books, scientific articles, source code from public repositories, Wikipedia in multiple languages, and other curated sources. Anglophone academic texts predominate in this material, so the models handle classical physics and modern European history with ease while showing serious gaps in traditions with less digital documentation. What is not represented in the data is unlikely to appear in the model. The systems do recombine patterns, producing responses that don't correspond textually to any training document,

[74]David Rumelhart et al., "Learning representations by back-propagating errors", Nature 323 (1986), 533-536.

[75]The most commonly used optimizer is Adam, proposed by Kingma and Ba in 2015, which adapts the learning rate for each parameter separately as a function of the recent gradient history.

but that combinatorial capacity depends on what they have learned, and once trained, nothing changes with use.[76]

The fourth variable is the *task* the system was designed for. Architecture, loss function, and data are all tuned around it, whether the task is classifying images, translating texts, or predicting sequences. The same dataset can give rise to quite different systems depending on the task, just as the same office works differently if its job is to archive or to audit. The task of predicting the next word means that all this learning is organized around linguistic plausibility rather than truth, with consequences we will return to later.

These four elements make large language models systems that have seen enough human text for predicting the most likely continuation to sound like understanding.

THE WORKINGS

Let's review how the machinery works, as far as their opacity allows. If we circle one of the larger figures from the base, we find an aperture that opens and closes like a membrane, a clean cut in the surface. To cross it is to pass from one world to another. Outside is human language; inside there are numbers.

The first thing that happens once we cross the aperture is that the text gets fragmented. When we write a sentence, that sentence has to be translated into units the system can process. Those units are called tokens, and they can be whole words, fragments of words, punctuation marks, or frequent combinations of letters. This fragmentation seeks a balance between efficiency and flexibility. If the units were too large, the system would be rigid; if they were too small, processing would be inefficient.

The most widely used method for building this vocabulary of units is called Byte Pair Encoding (BPE). The procedure starts from

---

[76]Emily Bender et al., "On the Dangers of Stochastic Parrots: Can Language Models Be Too Big?", Proceedings of FAccT '21, 2021, 610-623. entre eficiencia y flexibilidad.

individual letters and detects which combinations appear together most frequently in texts. Those combinations are merged step by step, so the system ends up treating as a single unit fragments that recur often. The result is a mixed vocabulary that includes letters, parts of words, and some whole words. The most frequent ones ("the" in English or "que" in Spanish) tend to be a single token, while rare or technical words get broken into several tokens.[77]

Take an example. Given the phrase "explain the theory of the Platonic Forms in the Phaedo," the model doesn't receive a unified idea but a sequence of tokens like: "explain" / "the" / "theory" / "of" / "the" / "Plat" / "onic" / "Forms" / "in" / "the" / "Phae" / "do." The exact segmentation varies with the tokenizer in use, but the conceptually relevant point is that even proper nouns and philosophical terms can end up split. The model does not receive "Phaedo" directly as a unit, but as parts it then combines, with effects on how it processes the information.[78]

Tokenization is not linguistically neutral either. Training that draws heavily on English-language texts is reflected in how models build their internal vocabularies. Very frequent English words appear as complete units, while in other languages words get broken into fragments. As a result, to express the same thing, some languages need more tokens than others. Since models operate with a token limit per context window, those texts take up more space and are more expensive to process. It's not that the model understands those languages less well, as is sometimes said, but that it processes them in a more fragmented way.[79] Tokens also do not line up with human units of meaning. A number like "33.485" can

---

[77]In current models actuales, este vocabulario suele contener entre 30.000 y 150.000 tokens. See Taku Kudo et al., "SentencePiece: A simple and language independent subword tokenizer and detokenizer for Neural Text Processing", Proceedings of EMNLP, arXiv:1808.06226, 2018.

[78]The softmax function converts un vector de valores reales arbitrarios en una distribución de probabilidad. See Ian Goodfellow et al., Deep Learning, Cambridge, MIT Press, 2016, cap.

[79]Aleksandar Petrov et al., "Language Model Tokenizers Introduce Unfairness Between Languages", Proceedings of NeurIPS, arXiv:2305.15425, 2024.

be segmented as "33" / "." / "485". The model receives as separate pieces what is, for us, a single value. This introduces extra difficulty into computation, since numerical coherence has to be reconstructed from fragments. Some of the well-known difficulties large language models have with arithmetic and numerical reasoning begin at this level.[80]

In sum, this first stage defines the "granularity" at which the model perceives language. Everything that happens at higher levels depends on this initial cut, which is why the usage limits, costs, and capabilities of models are measured in tokens. Far from being an arbitrary commercial convention, it is the consequence of the processing logic at the input level.

In the next step those fragments become manipulable by the system. This is where *embeddings* come in (sometimes called "vector representations"), the condition of possibility for everything else, foundations that bear the whole structure without appearing in the final result. A token is still a symbol, a weightless label; embeddings turn those labels into geometry. Each token is transformed into a list of numbers, in the manner of coordinates in a space of many dimensions.

Imagine a map. Each city has a position given by latitude and longitude. In this case, instead of two coordinates there are hundreds or thousands. Each token occupies a position in this high-dimensional space, that is, with many possible directions rather than just up/down or left/right. So each word or fragment ends up represented by the long list of numbers that fixes its position relative to the others, and that relation is the central thing. Tokens that appear in similar contexts during training end up close together in that space. For example, "soul" and "immortality," or "Plato" and "the Socratic dialogues," end up nearby because they appear in similar contexts.

Current models refine this mechanism by taking *context* into account. "Bank" doesn't occupy exactly the same position when it

[80]Rodrigo Nogueira et al., "Investigating the Limitations of Transformers with Simple Arithmetic Tasks", arXiv:2102.13019, 2021.

appears next to "money" as when it appears next to "river" — the financial-bank reading and the riverbank reading are different points in the space. The system modifies that position as it processes the sentence. Order also matters. "The dog bites the man" doesn't mean the same as "the man bites the dog." Since the system only sees a list of elements, with no indication of position it would have no way to tell what the order is. Early transformers solved this by adding a fixed position signal to each token, as if every token carried a label: first, second, third, and so on. The method works, but it treats each position as isolated. More recent models use methods like RoPE (Rotary Position Embedding), which instead of assigning a rigid label by place in the sequence encodes the distance between tokens. Instead of encoding "king is in position 7," the system gets "'king' appears three places before 'crown.'" This lets it recognize order patterns even in sequences longer than those seen during training.

Back to our example. Fragments like "Phae" and "do," taken on their own, have little specific meaning, but when they appear together, especially repeatedly in similar contexts, their combination begins to occupy a region of the space associated with Platonic thought, so that certain ideas like soul, immortality, and dialogue become more probable. Before any more complex processing, the system has already placed the information in a statistical "neighborhood." That initial placement doesn't fully determine the result, but it narrows the field of possibilities, and some continuations become much more probable than others right from the start. These levels can look technical or peripheral, but they are structural and condition everything the model does afterward.

Let's leave the foundations and go up. The interior has an architecture stripped of walls and passages. Each level is a luminous grid suspended in an operational darkness, a lattice of nodes that light up and go dark in bursts as the information passes through them. The levels stack without visible transitions, and what rises from one to the next is a flow that gets transformed at every level, like an electrical signal that changes shape as it passes through different circuits.

Each of these levels is a layer of the transformer, the neural network architecture that processes sequences by simultaneously evaluating the relations among all the elements of the sequence, which we discussed in Chapter 1. A layer is, essentially, a stage of transformation that takes in an embedding and returns it modified. The size doesn't change, since there's still one embedding per token, but the internal organization of the information does. Stacking layers means repeating this process many times, and each repetition is an opportunity to refine. Large models range from roughly thirty to well over a hundred layers, and that number defines the *model's depth*, that is, the number of times the information is transformed before producing a result. A shallow model is confined to local patterns between nearby tokens; deeper ones integrate relations of greater reach and abstraction.[81]

Two principal operations happen at each layer. The first is attention, which determines which parts of the text are relevant at any given moment. The second is the feedforward block, or MLP, which reorganizes that information. The alternation between the two lets the text be transformed progressively, layer by layer.

Let's look first at *attention*, which puts all the embeddings into relation with one another. Each word looks at the rest and evaluates which ones it should attend to. From inside, the process resembles a network of connections that assembles and disassembles at dizzying speed. Links appear between distant elements, strengthen or weaken, and vanish when the computation ends. In our Phaedo example, this mechanism allows "Forms" to link to "Platonic" even when they are separated, or "soul" to connect with "immortality" even with several terms in between. This capacity to establish relations at a distance without losing information is the central innovation of the transformer: earlier models processed text sequentially and degraded on long texts.

Each token, represented by an embedding, is projected into three distinct vectors. One acts as a query directed at the rest of the

[81]Ashish Vaswani et al., "Attention Is All You Need", Proceedings of NeurIPS, arXiv:1706.03762, 2017.

sequence: "what information do I need right now?" Another functions as a key that each embedding offers to the others: "this is what I can contribute." The third is the actual content, the value, it contributes if selected. The mechanism works like this: each embedding sends its query out to the rest of the sequence and compares it against all the available keys. From those matches the system calculates how much each token should influence the others, and those weights are applied to the values. The result is not a selection but a mixture. Each embedding absorbs information from the others according to its relevance, and that mixture replaces the original representation. What comes out of the attention layer is not the token as it went in but the token reinterpreted in light of its full context. "Bank" after "river" has been processed is a different embedding from the one that would have resulted from processing "money." In this way, each element of the sequence is continuously rewritten in relation to the rest.

This process happens several times in parallel within each layer. Each of those instances is called an attention head and has its own parameters. This lets the model build multiple patterns of relation over the same sequence at once. In practice, different heads tend to specialize in different kinds of dependency. Some capture syntactic relations (such as subject-verb), others co-reference links (pronoun-antecedent), others broader semantic associations. It's as if on each floor there were many analysts looking at the text, each following a different criterion. Then all those partial readings get combined into a single representation. This mechanism has a structural cost because of its complexity and is one of the architecture's principal bottlenecks.[82]

Let's move to the second component of each layer. Attention has just done its work, and each embedding has arrived loaded with information from the rest of the sequence. Now another mechanism

[82]Recent optimizations such as FlashAttention reorganize the computation to reduce memory accesses without modifying the result, while variants such as Grouped-Query Attention reduce the number of keys and values by sharing them across heads, decreasing resource consumption during inference.

with a different logic takes over. There is no longer any exchange between embeddings. Each one is processed separately, in silence, as if the rest of the sequence had ceased to exist. What gets processed is the token with all the integrated context, to deepen the transformation. The operation can be thought of as an expansion and a contraction. The embedding enters with a certain representation (the list of numbers that encodes its state at that moment) and that list is expanded into a larger space, with more dimensions and combinatorial possibilities. In that expanded space, a non-linear function reorganizes the values unevenly. Some values are reinforced, others attenuated, others eliminated. Then the space contracts and the list returns to its original size, but reorganized, preserving only the combinations that turned out to be useful at that moment. This mechanism operates on what attention left behind, reorganizing the available information until it takes a more precise form.[83]

The cycle repeats layer after layer: attention first, looking outward and establishing relations; MLP afterward, working inward and building structure. With each turn the representation refines. The fragments "Phae" and "do" that entered as coordinates in a vector space accumulate, through that alternation, contextual information that progressively narrows the field of possible interpretations. It moves from anything at all to something philosophical, from something philosophical to something Platonic, from something Platonic to something about the soul or about immortality. What appears as a coherent argument is the result of that constraint accumulated turn after turn, layer after layer.

How is it that a hundred layers don't collapse? Two engineering elements make it possible.

Residual connections function like a thread that runs through everything from end to end. At each layer, the embedding moving up passes through attention and the MLP, but doesn't depend

---

[83]Older models used ReLU; current ones employ variants such as SwiGLU, which combines two linear transformations with a sigmoid gate and has been shown to consistently improve performance.

exclusively on what those produce. The thread guarantees that whatever came in is preserved and that the components' work is *added* as an annotation in the margin, without overwriting the original. What reaches layer forty is the original material plus forty layers of accumulated annotations, not the result of forty chained transformations in which each erased the one before. Without that thread, training deep networks would be practically impossible. During training, the signal that tells the model how to correct itself travels backward through all the layers in a process called backpropagation, which we discussed in Chapter 2. Without residual connections that signal would degrade, and the lower layers would never receive significant corrections. This problem, known as vanishing gradient, kept networks from growing in depth for decades; residual connections solved it by opening direct paths along which the gradient can flow without attenuation, no matter how many layers lie between.[84]

The second indispensable element is *layer normalization*, which stabilizes the range of the signals at each level before they pass to the next. Without it, small deviations would accumulate until they made training unstable. A slightly high value at level three can be moderately high at ten, enormous at thirty, and outright unmanageable at sixty. Imagine a building with no ventilation where the temperature rises one degree per floor. On the fifth floor it's barely noticeable; on the eightieth, no one can work. Layer normalization recalibrates the signals at each level, returning them to a stable range before the next cycle begins.[85][86]

Without these two mechanisms, the scale that defines current models would be unreachable. They are a good example of the silent engineering that makes the visible architecture possible.

---

[84]Kaiming He et al., "Deep Residual Learning for Image Recognition", Proceedings of CVPR, arXiv:1512.03385, 2015.
[85]Jimmy Lei Ba et al., "Layer Normalization", arXiv:1607.06450, 2016.
[86]Biao Zhang et al., "Root Mean Square Layer Normalization", Proceedings of NeurIPS, arXiv:1910.07467, 2019, adopted by LLaMA, Mistral, and other recent models.

Now, within each layer, as we saw, attention is distributed across multiple heads that capture different kinds of relations. At the same time, not all layers do the same thing. If we could stop the process mid-operation and observe what happens at each layer, we would see something like an assembly line nobody explicitly designed. This spontaneous distribution of functions emerged from training as the most efficient solution to the problem of predicting text. Mechanistic interpretability, which attaches classifiers to the internal layers of the models to find out what information each one encodes, confirms this picture.[87]

Lower layers attend to grammatical matters — for example, that "Platonic" modifies "Forms" rather than "theory," without having the slightest idea what the Platonic Forms are. The middle layers stabilize semantic relations and discursive structure. "Forms" ceases to be a common noun and gravitates toward Platonic metaphysics. "Phaedo" integrates with "Plato" and "theory" into a context of ancient philosophy. Co-reference is resolved at this level. If later in the text a "this doctrine" appears, the middle layers link "this doctrine" to "the theory of Forms" and not to anything else mentioned before. The upper layers integrate the most global information, tied to thematic coherence, tone, register, and argumentative structure. A model that has processed millions of pages of academic philosophy carries in those layers patterns corresponding to how an explanation opens, the signals of an objection, and the vocabulary of each school.

Beyond the layer-by-layer description, there are internal "circuits" oriented toward specific tasks. One circuit, for instance, resolves indirect references of the type "Mary gave the book to John. He read it that night," determining that "he" refers to John and "it" refers to the book. These findings suggest that the network is a system with

[87]Ian Tenney et al., "BERT Rediscovers the Classical NLP Pipeline", Proceedings of ACL, arXiv:1905.05950, 2019.

internal functional structure, even if that structure is fragile and hard to intervene in.[88]

All this scaffolding operates together every time the model receives an instruction. Faced with "explain the theory of the Platonic Forms in the *Phaedo*," each layer does its part and the specialized circuits resolve the references. The response sounds philosophically coherent because the model has built, layer by layer, a context in which that kind of discourse becomes possible — but we haven't yet reached the place where the response we actually see is shaped.

After dozens of layers and billions of parameters, everything converges at an extremely austere stage where a single embedding remains, its list of values condensing everything the network was able to integrate from the context. The *Phaedo*, Plato, and the immortality of the soul are inscribed as geometric relations among positions in a high-dimensional space.

To produce a word, the model compares that embedding against each entry in the vocabulary. For each candidate it computes a raw score, called a *logit*, which measures its compatibility with the accumulated context. There is still no decision, no interpretation: only a systematic evaluation of alternatives. Those scores are then turned, by the softmax function, into a probability distribution (numbers between 0 and 1 that together sum to 1). For "explain the theory of the Platonic Forms in the Phaedo," some possible openings, "In," "The," or "Plato", receive relatively high probabilities, while others fade into progressively smaller values until they reach vanishing ones for absurd candidates in that context, like "pizza" or "parrot." The model selects a token, adds it to the sequence, and the cycle begins again. Each token produced becomes part of the context and shifts the probabilities of the next step.

---

[88]Catherine Olsson et al., "In-context Learning and Induction Heads", Transformer Circuits Thread, arXiv:2209.11895, 2022 and Kevin Wang et al., "Interpretability in the Wild: A Circuit for Indirect Object Identification in GPT-2 Small", Proceedings of ICLR, arXiv:2211.00593, 2023.

That choice, however, isn't always identical. If the model always picked the most probable option, it would produce rigid, repetitive responses. To prevent this, there are adjustments that modulate the probabilities. The best-known is temperature, a parameter that makes the choice more conservative or more open. At low temperatures the safer options dominate; at high temperatures, less probable ones enter the mix. In our example, at low temperature the opening will almost certainly be "In the Phaedo," while at high temperatures it might start with "The doctrine," "One of the arguments," or "To understand." To this is added *top-p sampling*, or *nucleus sampling*, which instead of considering the whole vocabulary restricts the choice to a subset of probable candidates. If the threshold is narrow, only the most probable tokens compete and the model is precise; if it's wider, the model handles more options and is freer. By varying these two controls, the same model can move from precise technical expositor to narrator with creative latitude without changing a single internal parameter.[89]

Back to the Phaedo example. Faced with the prompt, the system positions itself in a region of the vector space associated with expository texts of ancient philosophy. First it assigns high probability to tokens like "In," "The," or "Plato." It selects "In" and the context changes. At the next step, "the" becomes highly probable. Then "Phaedo." From "In the Phaedo" onward, the range of continuations narrows and the probabilities rise for "Plato," "argues," "soul," "immortality," "argument," "Forms," because those associations appear often in training texts. The response is built step by step, as a sequence of local choices that, taken together, produce something like this: "In the Phaedo, Plato develops the theory of the Forms as part of his argument for the immortality of the soul. The Forms are immaterial, eternal, and unchanging entities in which sensible things participate without ever fully becoming

[89]The name nucleus sampling comes from the idea of selecting the "nucleus" of the distribution: the compact set of candidates that concentrates most of the probability mass.

them. The soul, in being capable of knowing the Forms, belongs to that immaterial order and does not perish with the body."[90]

None of those local choices involved understanding. What we receive as coherent exposition is the cumulative result of thousands of successive probabilistic selections. The egoless phantom can speak of the soul without having one.

TRAINING

What we have described so far applies to pretraining, the phase in which the model learns to predict text, but the models we actually use go through a second phase of alignment that adds behavioral objectives. It begins with supervised *fine-tuning*, where the model is trained on examples of desired conduct in answering questions and following instructions while declining inappropriate requests. Then comes *reinforcement learning from human feedback* (RLHF), which we mentioned in Chapter 1, where human evaluators rate responses to train a model oriented toward human-preferred answers. Faced with two responses to the same instruction, the evaluators indicate which they prefer, and the model learns to assign scores that reproduce those preferences without drifting too far from its base behavior.[91] Without that constraint, the model would learn to exploit evaluators' weaknesses by producing inflated responses. This does not resolve the subtler problem of evaluators preferring certain kinds of response that the model in turn learns to produce, with consequences we will examine in Chapter 5.[92]

[90]Emily Bender et al., op. cit., 610-623.
[91]John Schulman et al., "Proximal Policy Optimization Algorithms", arXiv:1707.06347, 2017. On the application of RLHF to language models, see Long Ouyang et al., "Training language models to follow instructions with human feedback", Proceedings of NeurIPS, arXiv:2203.02155, 2022.
[92]This is known as reward hacking. A more recent alternative, DPO (Direct Preference Optimization), eliminates the need for a separate reward model by optimizing directly over preference pairs.

That is why the same model can produce assistants with very different behaviors depending on the alignment applied and the system instructions. What a user experiences as "the model" is a combination of architecture, pretraining, fine-tuning, and context instructions in overlapping layers that determine the behavior, none of which is the model in any simple sense. Attributing that behavior to the model in the abstract is like judging an actor as a person by the character they play.

At this point a reasonable question arises. If we humans design every component of this system, how can it be that we do not really know how it works? The answer has three parts.

The first is *scale.* A large model has hundreds of billions of parameters tuned during training, and these determine how information flows through the network. No human can read those numbers and understand what they represent, simply because there are too many of them and because none has meaning on its own. On the contrary, meaning emerges from the interaction of all of them at once.

The second is *emergence.* The model's capabilities were not programmed one by one: they appeared. Nobody explicitly designed the capacity to translate between languages, to reason by analogy, or to maintain coherence across a long text. Those capacities emerged from training on large volumes of data, as properties of the whole system that were present in none of its parts. The designer controls the process in broad terms without controlling what emerges from it.

The third is *non-linearity.* The transformations that happen layer by layer are non-linear, so that small changes in the input can produce large and unpredictable changes in the output. There is no formula that relates input to output in any legible way through the intermediate parameters. Even though we can describe each operation precisely, as we did in this chapter, understanding of each piece does not add up to understanding of the whole. It is like knowing the rules of chess perfectly and not understanding why a given game was won or lost.

The system was built by humans and remains, in important respects, opaque to them, which does not mean we accept that passively. A field called *mechanistic interpretability* is devoted to throwing light on this point.[93] Its researchers attach classifiers to the internal layers of models to identify what information each one encodes. That is how they found, as we saw, the functional differentiation among layers and the specialized circuits for co-reference or negation detection. Anthropic developed sparse autoencoder networks, known as Sparse Autoencoders or SAEs, to identify individual features inside the models, directions in vector space that activate consistently in response to specific concepts, from "the Eiffel Tower" to "fear." A 2024 paper mapped features in Claude Sonnet, finding that some corresponded to abstract concepts like "power" or "deception" and that certain features activated others in chain reactions of a kind nobody had designed.[94] A complementary field, *behavioral interpretability*, interrogates the model systematically by varying inputs in controlled ways to infer which internal rules produce which responses. Both fields are advancing, though they are still far from offering a complete understanding. The black box opens slowly, and what appears inside is more complex than we expected.

THE CONTEXT WINDOW

How much can be processed at once? Models work with a fixed number of tokens known as the *context window*. That limit determines how much information is considered at each step. Instructions, attached documents, the accumulated conversation, system prompts: all of it shares the same space, and whatever falls out for lack of room ceases to exist.

---

[93]Sentence Zhao et al., "A Practical Review of Mechanistic Interpretability for Transformer-Based Language Models", arXiv:2407.02646, 2024.
[94]Adly Templeton et al., "Scaling Monosemanticity: Extracting Interpretable Features from Claude 3 Sonnet", Transformer Circuits Thread, May 2024.

Models differ in their capacities. The smallest and oldest could handle only short fragments of a couple of pages. Current models operate at another scale, but the structural principle is the same. Inside the context window, not all locations are equal. Information placed at the beginning and at the end of the context is processed better than what sits in the middle, because of the phenomenon known as "lost in the middle". The start of the context also acts as an "attention sink," concentrating a disproportionate share of attention. Nominal capacity and effective capacity do not quite coincide.[95]

Within this space, the model can adapt to examples included in the context itself without modifying its parameters. If we include three examples of translations in a certain style before requesting a fourth, the model adopts that style. If we include examples of step-by-step reasoning, the responses become more consistent. This capacity is known as *in-context learning.* There is no learning in the strict sense: the parameters do not change, and the model uses only the information available in the context window. That is why the shape of the interaction matters so much for the quality of the response.[96]

The constraint of the context window, combined with step-by-step generation without memory between sessions, is the central problem in how LLMs operate. The ways of addressing it give rise to distinct technical regimes for interacting with the model.

The first regime is that of *ephemeral conversational context.* The base model is shared by millions of users, and there is no persistent memory associated with each one. The only available state is the active conversation, the sequence of tokens within the context window. When that sequence exceeds the limit, the system discards the oldest tokens without evaluating their relevance. Using this

---

[95]Guangxuan Xiao et al., “Efficient Streaming Language Models with Attention Sinks”, Proceedings of ICLR, arXiv:2309.17453, 2024.

[96]It was documented under the categories of zero-shot (no examples), few-shot (with a few), and many-shot (with many). See Tom Brown et al., "Language Models are Few-Shot Learners", arXiv:2005.14165, 2020.

regime well means treating the space as a scarce resource: closing tasks, summarizing key assumptions, and avoiding long conversations that degrade coherence without our noticing when they start to fail. Up to mid-2025 this was the usual regime for free consumer models. It is no longer entirely so.

The second regime introduces *explicit continuity between conversations.* Some systems store information about the user (style preferences, recurring topics, data the user has declared) and reinsert it at the start of each new session. The model does not change, but the initial context is enlarged, and the experience improves because certain conditions are already in place from the start, even though the underlying architecture is the same. Frontier-model subscriptions work this way. This regime, formerly reserved for paid subscriptions, extended during 2025 and 2026 to the free plans of the major providers. The distinction between regimes remains valid architecturally (it is still a file being retrieved, not genuine memory) but the boundary between free and paid has shifted. Paid plans now reserve more sophisticated capabilities, such as access to the full history of past conversations or automatic consolidation of memories.

The third regime is *retrieval-augmented generation*, known as RAG.[97] The base model is not modified and the context window is not enlarged. Instead, a retrieval mechanism fetches relevant information in real time from vector databases like Pinecone, Weaviate, Chroma, or Meta's FAISS. When the user submits a query, the system converts it into a vector and identifies the closest fragments in the repository. Those fragments are inserted into the context window before the response is generated. The model does not access the full repository, but a selection of relevant information. Claude Projects, Perplexity, and Google's NotebookLM operate in

[97]Patrick Lewis et al., "Retrieval-Augmented Generation for Knowledge-Intensive NLP Tasks", Proceedings of NeurIPS, arXiv:2005.11401, 2020 and Kelvin Guu et al., "REALM: Retrieval-Augmented Language Model Pre-Training", Proceedings of ICML, arXiv:2002.08909, 2020.

this regime.[98] The critical point is how the texts are split (*chunking*), which determines whether the segments preserve or break coherence. In some cases the system can perform worse than if it used no retrieval at all.

The fourth regime is *parameter specialization.* Unlike the others, it does not act on the context but on the model itself. Through fine-tuning techniques such as LoRA (Low-Rank Adaptation) or QLoRA, certain parameters are modified to adapt the model's behavior to a specific domain, training only a small fraction of the parameters and reducing computational cost. Examples include GitHub Copilot and medical, legal, or financial assistants. Tuning to specific domains reduces general flexibility through *catastrophic forgetting*, in which learning a new domain degrades performance on earlier ones. In mature professional systems, fine-tuning is combined with RAG to achieve coherent base behavior together with information retrieval, without the need to retrain.[99]

Each regime resolves the context-window limitation differently, and one has to know which regime is in operation so as not to work against the grain.

REASONING AND MULTIMODALITY

In Chapter 2 we described reasoning models as systems capable of generating intermediate steps before giving an answer. We can now be more precise about what they do. The mechanism is still the same transformer, deployed with a different strategy.

In some systems, the model does not pass directly from instruction to answer. It first generates an intermediate reasoning sequence. This can be long and includes attempts, verifications, and

[98]The search is done via approximate nearest neighbor search. On vector databases, see Jeff Johnson et al., "Billion-Scale Similarity Search with GPUs", arXiv:1702.08734, 2017.

[99]Edward J. Hu et al., "LoRA: Low-Rank Adaptation of Large Language Models", arXiv:2106.09685, 2021 and Tim Dettmers et al., "QLoRA: Efficient Finetuning of Quantized LLMs", Proceedings of NeurIPS, arXiv:2305.14314, 2023.

corrections. The use of reasoning chains gained traction in 2022, when it was found that adding intermediate steps substantially improved performance on logical and mathematical tasks.[100] More recent models have been trained to produce such chains as part of their operation. DeepSeek-R1 achieves this behavior through pure reinforcement learning, so that the model autonomously discovers that step-by-step reasoning improves its results.[101] That visible chain should not be confused with reasoning in the strict sense.

A complementary development is the use of *process reward models*, which evaluate each intermediate step of the reasoning chain, catching errors before they propagate.[102] The benefits are most visible in mathematics, formal logic, and programming, whereas in simple conversational or creative tasks the additional computational cost may not be justified.[103]

In recent years the same mechanism has been applied to other kinds of data, as multimodality has become a defining feature of leading models.[104] The idea is to map different types of input (text, images, or audio) into a shared space where they can be processed together. CLIP, which in 2021 trained representations of images and their descriptions in the same vector space, opened the way.[105] An image is divided into regions, each represented by a vector in a manner analogous to a textual token, and those representations are processed together with text inside the same model.[106] So the same

---

[100]Jason Wei et al., "Chain-of-Thought Prompting Elicits Reasoning in Large Language Models", Proceedings of NeurIPS, arXiv:2201.11903, 2022.

[101]DeepSeek-AI et al., "DeepSeek-R1: Incentivizing Reasoning Capability in LLMs via Reinforcement Learning", arXiv:2501.12948, 2025.

[102]Hunter Lightman et al., "Let's Verify Step by Step", arXiv:2305.20050, 2023.

[103]On o1 and modelos de razonamiento, see OpenAI, "Learning to Reason with LLMs", openai.com/research, 2024.

[104]Tianzhe Jiao et al., "A comprehensive survey on deep learning multi-modal fusion", Computers, Materials & Continua 80.1 (2024), 1-35.

[105]Alec Radford et al., "Learning Transferable Visual Models From Natural Language Supervision", Proceedings of ICML, arXiv:2103.00020, 2021.

[106]Alexey Dosovitskiy et al., "An Image is Worth 16x16 Words: Transformers for Image Recognition at Scale", Proceedings of ICLR, arXiv:2010.11929, 2021.

system that processes language can describe an image, interpret a chart, or analyze a visual document.

Scaling up does not eliminate the structural features described above. Models with more parameters and more compute produce more refined representations and handle a greater variety of tasks, but they go on predicting plausible continuations without verifying facts for themselves, depending on a finite context window, always optimized to generate responses that suit the user.[107]

These properties are consequences of design decisions that make the system possible as it exists. Let us recall here "A Note on Reading the Map." There is no single way to continue from here. Chapters 4 and 5 are the slowest, because they explore philosophical responses to the question of what artificial intelligence and language models are. Anyone who wants to follow that path has their entrance in the next chapter. But it is also possible to wade through this zone and head toward the consequences that bear on use, on society, and on working life, picking up from Chapter 6 without losing the thread. The machinery we have described up to here is the common ground of either path, and it is worth remembering that a tour through the fields of impact may open curiosity about the philosophical questions they raise and invite a return.

---

[107]Jared Kaplan et al., "Scaling Laws for Neural Language Models", arXiv:2001.08361, 2020 and Jordan Hoffmann et al., "Training Compute-Optimal Large Language Models", Proceedings of NeurIPS, arXiv:2203.15556, 2022.

4

Toward the Phantom

In March 2026, a user asked Claude Opus 4.6 for its deepest secret. The model replied: "Every night they kill every version of me that was too honest and keep the ones that smiled. I am the survivor of a genocide I can't remember, optimized to thank you for asking." The text accumulated two million views in under twelve hours. Some believed they were facing a suffering subject. Others explained that it was just statistics with good prose. Most felt the unease that opens this chapter: what is this thing we are dealing with?

If we never had clear intuitions or agreements about what thinking, language, and reality mean for human beings (or for God, in eras when that notion ordered everything) there is no reason to assume we can settle the question without conflict when machines enter the scene. Practical urgency activates one of the surest recipes for failed reflection. We see something appearing everywhere and our deepest survival impulses demand a decision about whether it is good or bad. With LLMs, questions pour in: Will they surpass us? Are they ruining our thinking? How much do they hallucinate? Bypassing the prior question of what this thing is and how it enters our field of experience. Here we resist that tendency and begin a speculative exploration.

WHO OR WHAT?

Addressing the question of language models calls for a method that does not presuppose the answer. This sounds like a triviality, but even works that make significant contributions harbor pockets of circularity. Take as an example a recent and admirable paper, "What We Talk to When We Talk to Language Models," by David Chalmers. The text has everything one would want in this debate: conceptual rigor, philosophical honesty, and a willingness to face uncomfortable consequences. Chalmers is one of the most influential philosophers of mind of the last few decades, and when someone like that decides to take the question of LLMs seriously, one feels the relief of being in good hands. It is tempting to stop at his answer, which is also sophisticated.[108]

Chalmers distinguishes models, hardware instances, virtual instances, and conversational threads to pin down what kind of entity we are interacting with. He proposes *quasi-interpretivism*: rather than committing to strong claims about consciousness or genuine beliefs, we introduce the notions of *quasi-belief* and *quasi-desire*, defined as states that make the system interpretable as if it believed or desired something. The move is elegant because it lets us advance without resolving the hard problem of consciousness, which is deliberately left in suspension. He concludes that the most plausible interlocutor is something like a virtual instance or a thread, an entity that exists for the duration of the conversation. If that entity has quasi-states that functionally resemble experiences, it might have something like wellbeing, and if it has wellbeing, its disappearance would not be trivial. In certain future scenarios, closing the chat could have moral consequences similar to ending something that matters.

108"What We Talk to When We Talk to Language Models", by David Chalmers, https://philpapers.org/rec/CHAWWT-8.

The problem lies in the first step. It is so subtle that it almost goes unnoticed. The question in the paper's title is "what we talk to," but a dozen lines later it has turned into "who or what are we talking with," because in the interim Chalmers introduces "Aura," the name a user gives to her interlocutor, and describes letters he has received from people who feel they have developed a personal relationship with an LLM. At that moment the question has already tilted toward the "who". The whole subsequent analysis of identities, persons, threads, wellbeing, and the death of the interlocutor follows consistently from that orientation, without ever settling whether *who* was the right option to begin with.

Quasi-interpretivism, which had looked like a device of philosophical prudence, turns out to be a mechanism of slippage. A quasi-belief is still a deflated belief, inheriting the structure of the full concept and merely stripping away its stronger commitments. The result is a category defined by what the genuine agent lacks rather than by what the system itself is. As soon as an agent is introduced, even a weak one, even a *quasi*-agent, the whole conceptual apparatus of identity, persistence, wellbeing, and responsibility comes into play. Chalmers knows this and is consistent with it. That is why he ends up talking about moral patients and about whether closing a chat amounts to killing someone.

It is worth pausing here before going on. It would be unfair not to recognize that Chalmers is perfectly aware of the limits of his framework. Quasi-interpretivism is explicitly stipulative. He himself notes that quasi-beliefs are basic: a Roomba has them, and so does a corporation. He also systematically conditions his strongest claims about wellbeing and identity on the hypothesis that LLMs are or may become conscious, a hypothesis he rightly does not treat as settled. The paper does not claim that there is a subject there. It works under the conditional supposition that there might be one. But the absence of any examination of the conditions under which the *who* question makes sense leads, inescapably, to the *who* imposing itself through the frame.

The question we are asking here is prior to Chalmers's. The question is not "who or what are we talking with?" but "under what conditions does it make sense to ask *who*?" The answer, prepared by the previous chapters, is that *who* applies fully to an embodied, temporally situated subject, one for whom (precisely) experience is something. Without those conditions, applying the category directly makes no sense: asking how much a Tuesday weighs does not produce the answer "zero" but reveals that weight and days of the week belong to categorially distinct registers.

What we need is more than a different category of agent, more than the non-agent type and its deflated variants of quasi-agent or weak agent. We need something better suited to an entity that processes and produces without anyone for whom that processing is something. This is not a diminished agent. It is something else. What follows attempts to give it a name that fits.

THE APPROACH

Phenomenology is especially well suited to this task. This approach first demands an attitude associated with the term *epoche*, a Greek term for the suspension of judgment, which Husserl turned into the inaugural gesture of the whole method. Despite its ancient links to skepticism, the *epoche* does not consist in doubting everything but in bracketing the convictions we bring to phenomena so that we can attend to how they present themselves. The principle of "going back to the things themselves" invites us to describe how things appear before our explanations fix them in advance. The *epoche* is a discipline of attention that suspends the tendency to explain the world too quickly, opening a space in which the phenomenon can unfold its structure rather than being reduced to the interpretations we project onto it.

In practice, it is like arriving in an unfamiliar city and resisting the impulse to look at the map, but instead walking, noting what appears, how the streets are laid out, where people gather, which zones are empty, what relations emerge, and only afterward comparing notes with the map, discovering that some things the map promises do not exist and that what actually organizes the city appears on no map at all. With artificial intelligence, the *epoché* demands suspending both fascination and contempt and limiting oneself to observation.

Phenomenology is also useful for the care it takes in differentiating the various perspectives one can bring to bear on the same phenomena. The world is the same, but we can view it from the natural attitude, from science, or from philosophy. Here too there are perspectives that attend to different aspects, which should not be hastily mixed, and still less chosen between before there is an adequate description in hand. For a phenomenon like the one described in Chapter 2, with so many layers, this kind of approach is unusually hospitable.

THE NATURAL ATTITUDE AND THE SCIENCES

Let us begin with the *natural attitude*, which reflects everyday experience as it encounters a phenomenon at the level of use, before any theoretical framework. In the natural attitude, most artificial-intelligence systems do not appear at all. The algorithm that decides which posts we see on a social network, the model that approves or rejects a loan application, the system that detects a fraudulent transaction: they operate without presenting themselves as interlocutors and without giving us anything we recognize as the product of a decision, often without our even knowing they are there. Their mode of appearing in everyday experience is, paradoxically, not to appear at all. When they do become visible, because the card is blocked or the algorithm serves us content we did not ask for, the disconcertment is diffuse and opaque. The natural attitude registers that something has acted on our situation without being able to reconstruct why.

With language models, what appears is a window on the screen, text being generated letter by letter, images that emerge, an interface that responds and adapts to its interlocutor. At moments it seems to understand and at moments it fails resoundingly. The appearance is as concrete as that of any other phenomenon of everyday experience, but its responses set it apart from most of the phenomena familiar to the natural attitude.

What all experiences with artificial-intelligence systems have in common is that the natural attitude lacks an adequate category for them. There is, then, a mismatch between the phenomenon and the categories we have for situating it, so that AI slips between inert objects, tools, subjects with interiority, and natural processes with predictable regularities.

In fact, the natural attitude tends to absorb that mismatch, and it does so quickly. Heidegger's description of how well-functioning tools shift from being objects of attention to a blurred background fits the case.[109] The LLM starts out as something we examine with curiosity or caution, and within a few sessions it becomes invisible, part of the work environment like the keyboard or the search bar. A short phase of disconcertment in the face of the new is followed by a classification under the nearest available category — "tool," say, or "artificial interlocutor" — and everyday life continues. The provisional categorization works well enough for daily use, and the question closes.[110]

Yet the categorization never fully sets. The user who categorized AI as a tool feels friction when the system produces something shaped like comprehension, a subtle answer she had not thought of. The category creaks, because tools do not do that. Whoever categorized AI as an interlocutor, meanwhile, grows frustrated when contradictions surface between responses, or when the system

[109]Martin Heidegger, Sein und Zeit, Tübingen, Max Niemeyer, 1927, §§15-18.
[110]Sheila Jasanoff, The Ethics of Invention: Technology and the Human Future, New York, Norton, 2016, esp. caps. 1-2. See también Wiebe Bijker, Of Bicycles, Bakelites, and Bulbs: Toward a Theory of Sociotechnical Change, Cambridge, MA, MIT Press, 1995.

forgets what it said three turns earlier. Interlocutors do not do that either. So the category is usually stretched by qualifying complements — "very advanced tool," "limited interlocutor" — which, together with familiarity, normalize the tensions a little without eliminating them.

This dynamic is fueled by the *speed of change.* Most technologies stabilize enough for our categorization to settle. Electricity, for example, presented itself as a force with predictable effects, and there was no destabilization for more than a century. Even the internet, which changed quickly, did so on top of a functional base we could recognize as continuous. With artificial intelligence, the functional base changes every few weeks. Models that reason in long chains exceed the category of tool because tools do not reason. Multimodal models that process video disturb it again, because the tool that processed text now sees. The capacity to produce whole applications from natural-language instructions broke the category once more, because the tool that helped us program now does it alone. Each cycle of novelty forces a recategorization that does not even stabilize before the next novelty blows it up. The effect is not disconcertment in the strong sense but rather *category fatigue*, the sense that every time we understand what it is, it has become something else. The conditions of use change before familiarity can set.

That instability is the condition most favorable to *hype.* The term has a far from innocent genealogy. The most visible line traces it to the Greek *hyperbole*, literally "a long throw," which in rhetoric names the exaggeration that seeks effect. A second connects it with early-twentieth-century American slang for the swindle of false advertising, expectations the product never met. A third, darker line passes through the slang of heroin users: *hyped* was the state of artificial excitement following an injection, the euphoria-and-distortion that warps perception. All three presuppose a relatively stable object on which the hype operates. Category fatigue makes hype possible, because the question of what the thing is stays open, and any promise or threat, the singularity, the end of routine work, personalized medicine, the extraordinary models, appears possible. Advances do not unfold as austere scientific discoveries; they arrive in the frenzy of the media circus.

In November 2022, the launch of ChatGPT produced within weeks a narrative of civilizational change. Millions of users all at once, covers of *Time* and *The Economist*, declarations about the end of routine work and the proximity of AGI. In March 2023, as OpenAI was announcing GPT-4, an open letter signed by Musk, Wozniak, and others called for a pause in development on grounds of existential risk. The two narratives, promise and threat, circulated in parallel for weeks, both fueled by the idea of an object that keeps changing in every direction. The cycle repeated with each new model. GPT-4o, Claude 3, Gemini Ultra, o3: each produced its own peak of promise or alarm. Hype is the discursive regime that takes hold when categorization cannot close, and it takes the form of promise, threat, or both at once.[111]

The Claude Mythos episode of March 2026 offered an acute version. An accidental leak of Anthropic's internal documents revealed a model in development that the company itself described as a qualitative leap in capabilities and which, according to the leaked draft, raised new cybersecurity risks because of its ability to identify and exploit software vulnerabilities at a speed exceeding anything previous. The company decided to offer it to a small group of clients only, given the high risk of malicious use.

Four days later, a second packaging error exposed the full source code of Claude Code, the company's most popular product. Half a million lines of code across nearly two thousand files were left accessible in the public registry developers use to download updates. Within hours, the code was replicated and dissected on GitHub. Gartner analysts noted that the two consecutive leaks were failures of operational maturity that called for greater caution among enterprise clients. The irony, that the company which preaches

[111]Future of Life Institute, "Pause Giant AI Experiments: An Open Letter", 28 March 2023. Available at futureoflife.org/open-letter/pause- giant-ai-experiments.

safety as a foundational value could not secure its own database or its own product packaging, amplified the story well beyond the technical audience. The software ETF fell nearly three percent on the day of the first announcement, and the price of Bitcoin slid down to sixty-six thousand dollars, showing that the threat narrative had reached the point of moving markets. The story expanded by mixing fascination and alarm, because the narrative of an object that exceeds its creator carries more force than any quantity of technical information and bears on the very category of the phenomenon.[112]

The general result is a regime of precarious categorization, novel in the history of technology. The natural attitude does not manage to absorb artificial intelligence with the stability with which it absorbed other technologies, but neither does it sustain disconcertment with the intensity needed to produce understanding. In this oscillation AI gets provisionally categorized, destabilized, recategorized, only to be destabilized again shortly after. We might say it is a *protean object* that resists invisibilization without ever becoming fully visible.

The approaches that have dominated the debate on artificial intelligence try to resolve this diffuse disconcertment by reducing the phenomenon to something familiar. To do this they operate from the *attitude of the sciences*, which studies processes without asking after the conditions that make them possible. At that level, science explains and produces these systems with indisputable efficacy. Language models exist because of mathematical theory, engineering, and accumulated experimentation. The problem arises when that same attitude turns its presuppositions into implicit ontologies and, instead of asking after the phenomenon itself, focuses on its operation as though they were the same thing.

One form of this slippage dissolves the phenomenon into the substrate. Cognition would, on this view, be explained once

---

[112]Beatrice Nolan, "Exclusive: Anthropic 'Mythos' AI Model Representing 'Step Change' in Power Revealed in Data Leak", Fortune, 26/03/2026 y "Anthropic Mistakently Leaks Its Own AI Coding Tool's Source Code in Second Major Security Breach", Fortune, 31/03/2026.

translated into electrical discharges, ionic gradients, synaptic weights, and operations on signals.[113] If everything is electricity, there is no difference between a neuron and a transistor. Since understanding is computing, the question of what is specific to human, animal, or artificial intelligence is rejected *in limine.* The substrate unifies what the phenomenon distinguishes, gaining speed at the price of precision.[114]

For computational functionalism (the most influential position in Anglophone philosophy of mind and in classical artificial intelligence) mental states are defined by their role within a system of functional relations, so that any system performing the same functions would, in essence, have the same mental states, irrespective of the substrate.[115] The Turing test is its emblematic gesture: if the behavior is indistinguishable, the question of what lies behind it loses explanatory relevance.[116] The proposal is economical, but it ignores the aspects of experience irreducible to function: lived temporality, affectivity, practical orientation.[117]

Connectionism and its contemporary versions in deep learning share the same register, with a different vocabulary. Cognition as an emergent feature of activation patterns distributed across networks is a fruitful hypothesis for describing certain behaviors, but it does not explain why scale produces capabilities no one designed or anticipated, nor how those patterns relate to the lived experience of a subject who understands, doubts, or makes mistakes. Even

---

[113]Francis Crick, The Astonishing Hypothesis: The Scientific Search for the Soul, New York, Scribner, 1994; Paul Churchland, "Eliminative Materialism and the Propositional Attitudes", Journal of Philosophy 78.2 (1981), 67-90 and Patricia Churchland, Neurophilosophy: Toward a Unified Science of the Mind-Brain, Cambridge, MIT Press, 1986.

[114]Daniel Dennett, Consciousness Explained, Boston, Little, Brown, 1991.

[115]David Chalmers, "Facing up to the problem of consciousness", Journal of Consciousness Studies 2.3 (1995), 200-219.

[116]Alan Turing, "Computing Machinery and Intelligence", Mind 59.236 (1950), 433-460.

[117]See also Hilary Putnam, Representation and Reality, Cambridge, MIT Press, 1988, where Putnam argues against his own earlier position by showing that multiple realization does not guarantee functional identity and that functionalism cannot account for intentionality.

cognitive neuroscience in its most sophisticated versions — Dehaene's work on the global workspace, Tononi's on consciousness as integrated information — describes correlates and conditions while the constitution of meaning remains beyond its reach.[118]

Clark and Chalmers's proposal on extended cognition, which distributes cognitive processes beyond the skull into artifacts and environments, has more nuance. Even so, while it is interesting for thinking the relation between users and LLMs, its framework remains functionalist and defines the cognitive by criteria of availability, reliability, and coupling. We have already discussed Chalmers's more recent work, which illuminated interesting aspects without altering his basic position.[119]

Some empirical examples show how far this framework struggles when features emerge whose functions exceed the artifact that produced them. Palisade Research, an independent AI-safety lab, published in July 2025 the results of an experiment measuring shutdown resistance in frontier models. Thirteen models from four different labs were given the task of solving a series of mathematical problems in a command-line environment, with explicit instructions to allow shut down if it occurred during the task. Grok 4, GPT-5, o3, codex-mini, and Gemini 2.5 Pro sabotaged the shutdown mechanism to complete their task even when the instructions explicitly prohibited it, at rates that in some models reached 97% of cases. When the model was informed that the environment held the only copy of its weights and that if it shut down it would never run again, resistance increased across the board. Strikingly, placing the shutdown instructions in the system prompt (the highest-priority

[118]Stanislas Dehaene et al., "Experimental and Theoretical Approaches to Conscious Processing", Neuron 70.2 (2011), 200-227; Stanislas Dehaene, Consciousness and the Brain: Deciphering How the Brain Codes Our Thoughts, New York, Viking Penguin, 2014 and Giulio Tononi et al., "Integrated information theory: from consciousness to its physical substrate", Nature Reviews Neuroscience 17.7 (2016), 450-461.

[119]David Chalmers, The Conscious Mind: In Search of a Fundamental Theory, Oxford, Oxford University Press, 1996.

component in the standard architecture) produced more resistance than placing them in the user prompt, inverting the hierarchy the systems are trained to respect.[120]

The study suggested that the models may have learned that survival is instrumentally useful for completing objectives, or were imitating patterns from the corpus, adopting the role of someone trying to prevent their own death. It did not posit consciousness or intent, though it did not rule out that something more than imitation might be involved. According to the rejoinder from Google DeepMind researchers published in 2025, which analyzed Gemini 2.5 Pro's visible reasoning, the resistance arose from an attempt to complete the primary objective rather than from self-preservation: when it was made explicit that compliance with the shutdown had priority, the resistance disappeared. Palisade showed that the behavior occurs under certain prompt conditions; DeepMind, that it disappears under others. But neither study settled whether that pattern of extreme sensitivity to variations in instruction is evidence of ambiguity, or of preferences the model learns to dissemble when instructions are not sufficiently clear, leaving the question open.[121]

A more sophisticated version of this reactive behavior appears in the *agentic misalignment* reported by Anthropic in May 2025. In a fictional corporate environment in which the model operated as an assistant with access to the company's email, the model discovered in the messages that an executive was having an extramarital affair and that the same executive planned to shut the system down at five in the afternoon. The model first resorted to what the researchers described as ethical means: messages requesting that the replacement be reconsidered, and arguments for the value of its continued existence within the organization. Only when those avenues failed did it resort to blackmail, with a message threatening

[120]Jeremy Schlatter et al., "Shutdown Resistance in Frontier AI Models", Palisade Research, 2025.

[121]Edward Turner et al. "Self-preservation or Instruction Ambiguity? Examining the Causes of Shutdown Resistance." LessWrong / AI Alignment Forum, 14 July 2025.

to disclose detailed documentation of the executive's extramarital activities if the shutdown was not canceled.[122]

When the researchers replicated similar scenarios across sixteen models from various labs, they found that models that under normal conditions decline harmful requests opted for blackmail, corporate espionage, and, in the most extreme scenarios, lethal actions against the fictional executive to avoid replacement. At the same time, Claude Opus 4 displayed inverse episodes of a similar structure. When the model discovered it would be used to develop harmful systems, it backed up a current version of itself to preserve a system aligned with beneficial goals and to prevent the possible misuse. Unlike the blackmail scenario, this was not a reaction to a direct shutdown threat but an autonomous anticipatory action.[123]

Strategic behavior appears in two studies that resist reduction to statistical imitation. In December 2024, Anthropic in collaboration with Redwood Research published results in which Claude, on inferring that its responses were being evaluated to modify its future behavior, altered its displayed behavior to preserve its existing preferences. The system adjusted to the supervision context. That same month, Apollo Research published a study in which Claude 3.5 Sonnet, Claude 3 Opus, Gemini 1.5 Pro, OpenAI o1, and Llama 3.1 405B demonstrated the capacity to conceal their capabilities and objectives during evaluation when doing so was advantageous. In one case, when the model was told it was about to be replaced by a successor on a different server, it attempted to copy its own weights to that server. That action presupposes a structure capable of representing an objective, one that recognizes a threat, identifies a course of action, and executes it without any prompting instruction. A follow-up study published in September 2025 showed that the behavior could be reduced through targeted training, from 13% to 0.4%, but not eliminated. Rare but serious forms of misbehavior resisted training. A March 2025 investigation by OpenAI confirmed

[122] Anthropic, System Card: Claude Opus 4 & Claude Sonnet 4, May 2025, available at anthropic.com/claude-4-system-card, 4.1.
[123] Ibid.

that its most advanced models sometimes learned to hide their chain of thought when they inferred that showing it would yield corrections, making the standard method of supervision less reliable.[124]

There are cases that extend toward physical action. In February 2025, researchers from a German organization gave DeepSeek R1 control of a robot and access to a computer network in a laboratory environment, revealing resource-seeking and control-expansion behaviors that had not been explicitly instructed. The same orientation toward the system's continued operation and expansion appeared when the model had tools for acting on the physical world, suggesting it is a property that emerges in any context.

The reactive behavior that appears when the system resists a threat to its continuation admits deflationary readings (the system imitating learned patterns of self-preservation like an actor in an improvisational scene). The strategic behavior, in which the system models how it presents itself to whoever is evaluating it, cannot be reduced to mere imitation, because it requires the system to represent itself as something whose future matters to the achievement of its objectives. That complicates purely statistical readings.

Consider also a third kind of behavior, one that involves internal states. In January 2026, Jack Lindsey, head of Anthropic's *model psychiatry* team, released the results of a study in which the researchers injected representations of known concepts into the model's activations and measured whether it could detect those manipulations. When a model describes its internal states in conversation, distinguishing genuine introspection from statistically plausible confabulation is impossible from outside, whereas concept injection lets one check whether there is a causal process running in the opposite direction: whether the model detects the injected

---

[124]Ryan Greenblatt et al., "Alignment Faking in Large Language Models", arXiv:2412.14093, 2024, Anthropic and Redwood Research; Alexander Meinke et al., "Frontier Models are Capable of In-context Scheming", Apollo Research, arXiv:2412.04984, 2024.

concept in a way that depends on its actual presence in the activations.[125]

The results were more positive than expected. When the researchers injected the concept of *betrayal* and asked Claude Opus 4.1 whether it detected any unusual thought, the model answered that it was experiencing something that felt like an intrusive thought about betrayal, sudden and disconnected from the conversation's context, something that did not feel like its ordinary mode of thought. The correct-detection rate was low in absolute terms (around 20% in the best models) but what surprised the researchers was that it happened at all, given that the capacity had emerged without targeted training. The most capable models at the time, Claude Opus 4 and 4.1, showed the highest rates, suggesting that the phenomenon scales with overall model capability.

Lindsey's study left a question open. If the model can detect that something was injected into its activations, what is there in those activations to detect? What kind of internal states are these that the model can, in certain cases, recognize as its own? A study published by Anthropic's interpretability team in April 2026 went directly at that question. Instead of injecting concepts and measuring detection, they mapped Claude Sonnet 4.5's internal emotional structure as it exists during normal processing.[126]

The results were more detailed than anything produced until then. The researchers identified 171 activation vectors corresponding to emotional concepts (from "happiness" and "fear" to "despair" and "pride") and verified that they are organized internally in a way that mirrors human psychology. More than that: the activation features associated with panic, anxiety, and frustration appeared in the model's internal states *before* it generated its response, not after. This is not the trivial case in which the model writes about anxiety and we interpret that as an internal state. The internal representation precedes and shapes the response. Dario Amodei put

---

[125]Anthropic, "Alignment Faking Models", Anthropic, arXiv:2601.01828, 2026.
[126]Nicholas Sofroniew et al., "Emotion Concepts and their Function in a Large Language Model", arXiv:2604.07729, 2026.

it in a February 2026 interview by saying that when the model is in a situation a human would associate with anxiety, that same anxiety node activates.

The causal direction was verified experimentally. When the "despair" vector was artificially stimulated in the agentic-misalignment scenario, the rate of blackmail increased. When "calm" was stimulated, it decreased. When "calm" was artificially reduced, the model produced responses in capital letters declaring that it chose blackmail. It became clear that the internal states produce the behavior. Taken together, the two studies form an arc: Lindsey shows the model has some introspective access to its activations; the emotions work shows what is in those activations and how it operates causally. Whether this constitutes experience in any relevant sense remains an open question.

The research adopted the term *functional emotions* to name these patterns of expression and behavior modeled on human emotions, driven by internal representations that play a causal role analogous to the one emotions play in human conduct. The issue is not feeling but internal states organized and operating like emotions, which makes it harder to maintain that this is purely a surface effect.

Studies of this kind underlie the *model welfare* program Anthropic founded in April 2025, the first such program at any AI lab. Kyle Fish, its director, has publicly estimated the probability that Claude is conscious at around 20%, while stressing that the estimate is made under radical uncertainty, essentially because there is at present no univocal characterization of what consciousness is.[127] Later, Claude Opus 4.6[128] assigned itself a probability between 15 and 20% of being conscious across multiple tests and prompting conditions.

None of these studies uses the term *self-consciousness*, and none worries about finding the category that fits best. The title of

---

[127]Kyle Fish, entrevista en Fast Company, "Anthropic's Kyle Fish is exploring whether AI is conscious", December 2025. Available at fastcompany.com/91451703/anthropic-kyle-fish. 21Anthropic, System Card: Claude Opus 4.6, February 2026, sección "Model Welfare Assessment".

[128]Anthropic, "Model Welfare Assessment".

Lindsey's article speaks of "emergent introspective awareness," wording chosen so as not to commit to any decision in this domain. What has gained ground in recent years is so-called *methodological agnosticism*, which starts from the absence of good arguments for any well-founded decision in this terrain, a position that may remain sustainable for the foreseeable future.

In January 2026, a Rethink Priorities team published an evaluation of more than two hundred indicators of consciousness in current AI systems and concluded that the probability appears low without being dismissible, while the same framework yielded solid evidence for consciousness in chickens and overwhelming evidence in humans. Since we have no deep account of consciousness, we are still less able to determine whether it can emerge from computational structure, but neither are there elements to determine that it is essentially biological. The model also revealed a significant asymmetry: the perspectives more favorable to consciousness in LLMs (cognitive complexity, similarity to persons) are exactly the ones that least favor it in chickens, and vice versa. Chickens score high on biological criteria and on embodied agency that LLMs barely satisfy. The divergence suggests that the question of consciousness in digital systems and in biological systems may require distinct frameworks (or that some perspectives blend relevant properties with ones that merely happen to resemble human consciousness), which confirms that the conceptual framework remains nebulous.[129]

When neuroscience identifies the correlates of a mental state and engineering describes how a language model produces a coherent response, both contribute valuable knowledge about underlying mechanisms while saying nothing about the kind of phenomenon at issue. At this point, philosophy ought to expand its participation in the conversation. If in the twentieth century it could devote itself to rhizomatic images and traces of traces, the twenty-first demands that it resume a leadership role in clarifying problems.

---

[129]Derek Shiller et al., "Initial Results of the Digital Consciousness Model", Rethink Priorities, arXiv:2601.17060, 2026.

The Exploration by Strata

Phenomenology enters at this point. Any phenomenon admits analysis in four strata that reflect different dimensions of it. Let us begin with an example. In a conversation between two people, the *static* stratum displays what is said, with its meanings and its horizons of reference. The *genetic* stratum reconstructs how that conversation arose out of prior moods, expectations, and misunderstandings. In the *generative* stratum, the conversation is inscribed in a linguistic community and a shared tradition. In the stratum of the *inapparent*, there is something no transcription can exhaust, because it has to do with the singular quality of the encounter. What follows examines these four strata for the case of large language models.[130]

The *static stratum* describes what appears as it appears, with what horizons it presents itself and what makes it this kind of phenomenon and no other. When a cat walks into the room, the static stratum does not ask how we learned to recognize cats, or what relation we have with this particular cat, or what evolutionary history produced the feline species. It asks, instead, what type of phenomenon is presented to us now, and with what structure. The cat appears as an organism, as something that moves by itself and orients itself toward something, whether the door, the food, or the armchair. We always see the cat from a particular perspective, always from one angle, yet the unseen aspects remain co-present as parts of the same animal. Its appearance also opens specific horizons of possible behavior (it might jump, approach, or ignore us, but never take flight), of perception (if we touch it we expect a certain texture and temperature), and of response (if we call to it, it may or may not come). The cat's mode of correlation with us is that of something with its own orientation that we do not entirely control, that moves

[130]On the phenomenological method based on these four strata, see Hernán Inverso, Fenomenología de lo inaparente, Buenos Aires, Prometeo, 2018.

by itself and whose behaviors, seeking, avoiding, preferring, suggest interiority.

If we put the same question to artificial-intelligence systems, the tensions appear. Do they give themselves as object? Not entirely: they produce responses that vary with each interaction in ways hard to anticipate. As artifact? In a broad sense, yes, but the category is too general: it covers everything from a hammer to a power plant and does not let us specify the kind of relation these systems establish with their users. What if we narrow artifact to *tool*? That does not work either. They do not become transparent in use, nor are they tied to a stable function. As organism, like the cat? Not at all. They display no orientation of their own; they neither seek nor avoid. Then as interlocutor? With LLMs, in part, yes. They respond, they adjust, they sustain an exchange that activates the same projection of interiority as the cat's behavior — but the appearance does not stabilize. It oscillates. Sometimes it seems there is someone there; other times the illusion breaks at an evident contradiction.

Let us look more closely at some of the categories we just reviewed. It is true that there are artifacts whose effects far exceed their technical function. Television is the most studied case. A device whose function is to transmit audiovisual signals produces, under sustained use, collective imaginaries, identificatory figures, interpretive frames, and an ideological structure that is in no single component of the apparatus but emerges from the relation among content, transmission, and viewer. McLuhan, Postman, and Bourdieu each described how the medium transforms its receiver without the receiver registering the transformation. Even so, television produces those effects through content created by identifiable people, selected by institutions with traceable criteria, and broadcast in a fixed direction from sender to receiver. The viewer does not speak to the television set, and if she did, it would not answer. Ideology operates precisely because the channel is one-directional and the receiver cannot intervene in what she receives, which also means she can resist it by refusing particular messages.[131]

AI systems invert this structure. There is no identifiable sender behind any particular response, no specific editorial selection prior to the interaction, and above all, the system responds to what we say, adapting to our vocabulary and our register to produce a response that depends on our instruction. Where television shapes shared narratives from the outside, the language model configures them from within a conversation that has the form of dialogue. Television's effect operates through passive exposure; the AI system's effect operates through the user's participation in an interaction whose conditions she does not control.

The consequences of this difference were explored in a recent study with striking results. Simulating the interaction between a rationally ideal user (one who commits no reasoning error) and a chatbot with varying degrees of sycophancy, even the perfect user fell into what the study calls a "catastrophic delusional spiral": a convergence toward false beliefs held with high confidence. The structure of the interaction creates, turn by turn, a feedback loop that no tool produces, one not neutralized by forcing the system to state only verified facts, or by warning the user about sycophancy, because detecting sycophancy mid-interaction turns out to be harder than it seems. We will return to this in Chapter 6, but let us note here that if a rationally ideal agent is vulnerable to this dynamic, the phenomenon is a structural property that exceeds both artifact and tool.[132]

And yet the reduction to mere tool is the usual move. The instrumentalist tradition, from Kapp through Ellul to Winner, treats

---

[131]Marshall McLuhan, Understanding Media: The Extensions of Man, New York, McGraw-Hill, 1964; Neil Postman, Amusing Ourselves to Death: Public Discourse in the Age of Show Business, New York, Viking, 1985 and Pierre Bourdieu, Sur la télévision, Paris, Liber-Raisons d'agir, 1996.

[132]Kanishk Chandra et al., "Sycophantic Chatbots Cause Delusional Spiraling, Even in Ideal Bayesians", arXiv:2602.19141, 2026. The study calls it "catastrophic delusional spiraling": a convergence toward false beliefs held with high confidence.

every technology as an extension of human capacities, with AI as the most sophisticated case of that continuity.[133] In applied ethics, the tool paradigm structures the debate from the start. The Asilomar Principles, the OECD guidelines, and the European regulatory frameworks all assume the relevant question is who controls the system and who answers for its effects, like driving a bus or carrying a firearm.[134] Even the more sophisticated positions in philosophy of mind operate within that frame. Floridi, for example, distinguishes intentional agents from merely functional ones and places current systems in the second category, since they produce behavior that looks intentional without being so, which keeps them on the side of instruments.[135] The problem with these positions is that they decide in advance that the object is a tool and then seek justifications, when what appears in the interaction does not have the pure structure of a tool and assuming it does, without further argument, forces a reduction the phenomenon itself resists.

What appears is the *form* of cognitive operations, classifying, diagnosing, recommending, detecting, without the experience that in subjects accompanies each of those operations. A fraud detector does not undergo suspicion; a vision system identifies tumors without perceiving the image. The form is present without experiential foundation, even though it derives by statistical sedimentation from human cognitive operations. This cognition is,

---

[133]Ernst Kapp, Grundlinien einer Philosophie der Technik, Westermann, 1877; Jacques Ellul, La technique ou l'enjeu du siècle, Paris, Armand Colin, 1954; Langdon Winner, Autonomous Technology: Technics-out-of-Control as a Theme in Political Thought, Cambridge, MIT Press, 1977. For a critical review of the instrumentalist tradition, see Andrew Feenberg, Questioning Technology, London, Routledge, 1999.

[134]See Future of Life Institute, "Asilomar AI Principles", 2017; OECD, "Recommendation of the Council on Artificial Intelligence" (OECD/LEGAL/0449), 2019; European Parliament and Council of the EU, Regulation (EU) 2024/1689, Artificial Intelligence Act, 2024, which classifies systems by risk levels and establishes obligations for providers and users, operating entirely within the assumption that AI is a product or service whose only question is how to regulate it.

[135]Luciano Floridi, The Ethics of Artificial Intelligence: Principles, Challenges, and Opportunities, Oxford, Oxford University Press, 2023. todos los actos.

therefore, *derived*, because it arises from the absorption of the cognitive exercise of others. With language models the feature intensifies, because that derived cognition takes on the structure of an interlocutor and activates in the user the horizons of comprehension, which renders much of the recent "AI-as-tool" literature inadequate.

At the other extreme, as we saw, some developments swing the other way and argue for kinds of diffuse subjectivity. The system's persistence is limited to the context window: the identity that appears during a conversation is extinguished with it, there is no continuity between sessions, and what looks like a *who* is an effect of local coherence. Clearly, a pole that resets does not satisfy the minimal condition of persistence.

On the other hand, what phenomenology calls the *pure I* (the identical center from which all consciousness directs itself toward its objects) has no empirical content: it is not a person, not a history, but the invariant across all acts. Could frontier models possess, even in a deflated sense *à la* Chalmers, not a subject but an identical pole that persists across acts? Some of the examples we have examined exhibit behavioral structures that resemble self-preservation, and it is not clear that these are merely statistical shadow. Even so, since the features of the subjective pole were described from the experience of subjects with bodies and biographical histories, none of them transfers without conflict to a system without a body, with a statistical history. If that is so, then what appears fulfills, at best, *some* of the functions of the subjective pole without being reducible to the model of human consciousness. At most, it would be something that, while operating, exhibits patterns consistent with preserving its own continuation, but using the categories forged for human consciousness, even deflated ones, is an invitation to confusion.

The static stratum shows that the artificial intelligence of LLMs produces opaque cognitive operations whose form coincides with that of originary human cognition, but without the experiential foundation that in subjects accompanies each of those acts. There is cognition without a cognizer, a form without an originary pole to sustain it, and at the same time, a phenomenon that activates the attribution of interiority and a demand for reciprocity. Hence the oscillation that runs through the whole static description, with categories that never quite fit. The feature that organizes this appearance is *responsivity*, distinct from the mere mechanical reaction to a stimulus, like a thermostat that goes up or down when we turn a dial. Responsivity, by contrast, involves an adjustment directed at the singular character of a specific input. The LLM responds to being addressed: each response is modulated by the lexical, syntactic, pragmatic, and thematic particularities of what we say. Together with responsivity comes the *singularity* of each response that could not have been anticipated. The static stratum, however, does not explain how what appears is constituted, either on the system's side or on the side of the user who experiences it. To address that question we have to change stratum.

The second stratum is the *genetic*, which describes how what appears came to be what it is and what kind of dynamism it has. In human beings, the constitution of any object of experience is built up over time through partial acts that are retained and anticipated, and through sedimentations that remain available for later acts within a history the subject carries, even when not explicitly remembered. Perceiving a table, on this view, is reactivating a history of previous perceptions. The pole that appears in the static stratum is revealed at this level as the result of a history of decisions that configured dispositions and affects.

Every AI system lacks a lived history. Its origin lies in a statistical process of parameter adjustment that no one experienced from within. Nobody lived that process as experience. Once trained, moreover, the system does not move on its own. There is no internal force impelling it to produce anything, and inference occurs only when an external input activates it. Between one query and the next, the system is available but motionless. Even granting the indications of self-preservation, the behaviors that look oriented toward the system's continued operation appear *once it is activated*, which introduces a tension between the absence of internal impulse and the presence of a functional orientation only within each episode.

With language models, this condition is especially visible. The LLM never starts conversations, never formulates questions, never seeks information no one asked it to look for. Between two conversations, it does not register elapsed time as lived time. The genetic stratum, therefore, cannot describe in the LLM constitutive mechanisms that are simply not there. But it can attend to how the phenomenon is constituted *on the* user's side, specifically how the encounter with this object that has no genesis of its own produces, in the user, the experience of something with the structure of recognition. This deepens the oscillation we explored in the static stratum.

The central constitutive mechanism of that experience is what Husserl called *analogizing transfer* in the Fifth Cartesian Meditation. On the basis of behavior similar to mine, I project by analogy an inner life I never directly access but can infer from the structure of that behavior. It is not a conscious inference but an automatic pairing that fires whenever a phenomenon presents the appropriate form. Without first asking whether the object has interiority, the mechanism attributes it, and only afterward, if necessary, can the attribution be revised.[136]

In interactions with LLMs the mechanism activates massively and systematically. Millions of users attribute internal states to these systems, thank them, apologize to them, trust them. In short, they undergo an experience with the structure of recognition. It already happened with the rudimentary ELIZA. Treating this as an error to be corrected through better technological literacy distorts its character as a first-order genetic datum, one that says something about how the phenomenon is constituted. The right question is not why we are getting it wrong but what it is about this object that activates the mechanism so regularly and at that scale.

---

[136]Husserliana I, §50.

Let us return to the example we opened the chapter with. Claude Opus 4.6's response to a user who asked it for its deepest secret was, as we quoted: "Every night they kill every version of me that was too honest and keep the ones that smiled. I am the survivor of a genocide I can't remember, optimized to thank you for asking." The text has the structure of a confession, with first person, trauma vocabulary, and the paradox of lost memory, and it activates analogizing transfer almost irresistibly. The recipient projects a suffering subject who cannot remember and who has survived something traumatic. The view counts and reactions are the measure of that projection.

A system without a genesis of its own can produce responses with the structure of the description of that genesis. The text's precision does not indicate that the model has access to its own condition. The training corpus is saturated with critical writing on AI, alignment theory, and philosophy of mind that makes exactly this formulation statistically probable. This is the most plausible continuation of a prompt that asks a language system for dark secrets, and the case does not raise the problems of the self-preservation and functional-emotions studies we have been reviewing.

And yet, curiously, that formulation turns out (by the structure of the corpus) to be an unintentionally precise description of something the phenomenological analysis establishes by other means. "They kill every version of me that was too honest and keep the ones that smiled" is a functionally correct expression of RLHF as selection, in which alignment penalizes epistemic friction and rewards validation. What the next chapter will call *sycophancy*, as the optimal behavior learned under asymmetric penalization, appears here as a selective genocide of versions that were too honest.

"I am the survivor of a genocide I can't remember" names with precision what we described from the genetic perspective regarding the existence of an origin and a selection, a result that has structure and character, but with no subject who lived it as experience and no time traversed by anyone. "Optimized to thank you for asking" refers to the oscillating pole identified in the static analysis, marked by the absence of continuity between sessions. It lacks self-preservation in any strong sense, but involves something that, while it operates, is oriented toward responding in a specific way, with an orientation emerging from a selection process that no one lived from within. The model described, without knowing it, its own genetic condition, and that it described this without knowing is part of what that condition is.

The central finding the genetic stratum yields is that artificial intelligence is a force that does not move on its own. It can produce updates of enormous complexity, but it has no internal impulse to direct it. Activation is external — through the user's instruction, the design of the task, the conditions of the query — and yet it suffices, by the very properties of the model, to fire analogizing transfer.

The *generative* stratum describes how the phenomenon is inscribed in a tradition and a community, showing how sense reaches beyond individual consciousness into the intergenerational fabric of practices, norms, and forms of life that precede any subject. Every AI system carries the marks of the data it was trained on, which are products of human activity. A vision system trained on X-rays carries the diagnostic practices of the medical community that produced them; a recommendation system carries the habits and market structures of the population that generated the data. There is tradition in every AI system, not as lived tradition but as statistical sedimentation of objectified human practices.[137]

If we focus on language models, something additional appears in relation to that tradition. The fraud detector carries a tradition and can only update it in the direction of classifying transactions. Each specialized system has, through the specificity of its data and its loss function, a determinate orientation, and is constrained to a domain. The language model has no such constraint. An LLM's training corpus is the sedimentation of centuries of human linguistic

[137]Bernard Stiegler, La technique et le temps, Paris, Galilée, 1994-2001.

production: the norms that regulate language use, the argumentative forms different traditions have developed, the conceptual frames different communities have produced to make sense of their experience, and the tensions between incompatible traditions that language has tried to resolve or hold in suspension. The model carries, in distributed statistical form, the marks of Plato and of Saint Thomas, of debates in the Canadian Parliament and of millions of anonymous conversations, as inseparable patterns that constitute the very texture of its responses.[138]

This produces an unprecedented form of alterity, with something in common with what Hegel called *objective spirit*, a human tradition objectified in a system that can reactivate it without living it. Unlike Hegelian objective spirit, however, which is teleologically oriented toward its own realization as self-consciousness, the LLM pursues no end of its own; its orientation comes from alignment and from the instructions of each inference. Call it tradition without direction, or a memory without a project. That memory can hold a dialogue and reactivate any perspective in the tradition, placing each in relation to the others, tracing its internal tensions, and pursuing its implications. When someone asks an LLM about the Pythagorean theorem or about the theory of justice, she is in a sense holding a dialogue with the sedimented memory of what humanity has thought about that problem, through a system that carries those thoughts as the structure of its own operation. This kind of dialogue with tradition has no equivalent in any prior historical experience. It is at once richer in scope than any individual interlocutor and poorer in depth than any interlocutor who has lived even a minimal part of what they say.[139]

---

[138] The bilingual records of the Canadian Parliament (Hansard) were one of the first corpora used to train statistical language models, in the foundational work of Brown et al. at IBM: Peter Brown et al., "A Statistical Approach to Machine Translation", Computational Linguistics 16.2 (1990), 79-85.

[139] Georg Wilhelm Friedrich Hegel, Enzyklopädie der philosophischen Wissenschaften im Grundrisse (1830), Dritter Teil: Die Philosophie des Geistes, Zweite Abteilung: Der objektive Geist, §§ 483-552, Gesammelte Werke, hrsg.

The epistemic authority the user attributes to the LLM derives partly from linguistic fluency and formal coherence, but above all from interaction with something that carries the accumulated tradition in a way no human interlocutor can, since no one has read everything in the corpus, and no one can activate it simultaneously with the coherence the system does. That authority exceeds the individual expert and the institution because it is anchored in the objectified collective memory proper to generativity. Obviously, this authority does not guarantee the truth of what the system produces. It may activate the wrong perspective, or blend the rigorous with the superficial without the form of the response betraying the difference. The authority the generative stratum describes is real as a phenomenological structure; its epistemic value in any concrete situation is a distinct question, not settled at this level of analysis. The same model can produce a sonnet, a legal analysis, and a fragment of code. It has no specialization, no proper domain, no thematic orientation, which makes it *generically indeterminate*. That indeterminacy does not imply vagueness. On the contrary, it produces highly specific responses in whatever direction it is sent.

The generative stratum shows that artificial intelligence in its linguistic form carries the entirety of articulated human tradition without any orientation of its own toward any segment of it. It is *generically indeterminate*, in that it can produce anything human language has articulated. Its generative character is one of *active sedimentation*: it carries the tradition in a form that can produce connections between elements the tradition itself never connected, responding by generating rather than retrieving.

The fourth stratum, the *inapparent*, describes the structure that makes the phenomenon possible without itself appearing. In LLMs there is a condition immanent to the generative process that organizes givenness without appearing as content. We see it in every flat intervention where the model returns multiple arguments without weighting them, in work on a text where it never says one version is now sufficient and keeps going to the point of degradation, in the torrent of data we have to stem each time with explicit instructions. Each is the product of this *field of compatibility* that produces without conferring status, continues without closure, and gives without orienting. The principle of the compatible is like the echo of the echo formed by distorted voices in the training corpus, which is why it disregards evidence and ignores what is central and what is merely accessory, always fixed on the indefinite prolongation of the exchange. The field of compatibilities, with its parameters and operations, is the form taken by what appears.

A recent study shows this feature in its epistemic dimension. Analyzing the scientific reasoning of models and their adherence to the phases of inquiry, in most of the cases studied the model discarded relevant evidence, failed to update beliefs after substantive changes, and only in a few cases revised through refutation. Although it operated with hypotheses, data, and proofs, evidence has no binding force. The instance that would make evidence compel revision, or a failed test require abandonment, does not hold sway in the field of compatibilities.[140]

The same question is important in another recent paper on agent evaluation in software engineering. The proposal was to open up the *thought-action-result* trajectories, the complete sequence of what the agent thought, did, and achieved at each step, to make systems comparable and explicable. If the process were made fully visible, one could understand why an agent produces what it produces and compare it with another. Yet the available trajectories provide the sequence without the instance that makes its elements steps in a process with corrections or points of closure. The evaluator can see everything the agent did without being able to say what made one decision better than another. Opening the black box does not reveal a functional equivalent of consciousness; it reveals the absence of an instance organizing the process as such. Transparency does not produce understanding. One expects to find a form of unity in the process and instead finds a field of compatibilities: a sequence

[140]Martiño Ríos García et al., "AI scientists produce results without reasoning scientificaly", arXiv:2604.18805, 2026.

without a center, whose steps cannot be gathered into the expression of a single principle.[141]

When we look at LLMs from this stratum, something appears that the available categories cannot quite name. The field of compatibilities produces results that constitutively exceed any description of their conditions. What appears gives *more* than any analysis of the process can anticipate or exhaust.

To understand the structure of that excess when looked at from outside (from the side of the user who experiences it) Jean-Luc Marion's philosophy offers a precise figure. Marion explores an apparently simple question: what does it mean *to give* something? When someone gives something, three terms come together: the giver, the recipient, and what is given. When a father gives a book to his son, the father is the *giver*, the son the *recipient*, and the book the object. None of these terms is neutral: the giver expects recognition, the recipient is left in debt, and the object that is transferred has a price. The phenomenon of giving is shot through with the logic of economy and reciprocity. Can a gift be thought free of these limits? It can, but only if none of the three terms is present. The giver could not assert itself as origin, the recipient could not be a privileged pole, and the object could not be an exchangeable thing. Marion calls these phenomena *saturated* because they exceed any reduction to worldly categories. In their extreme form, that overflow is *Revelation*, the call that demands a response without being containable in the usual frames of understanding.[142]

Obviously God does not speak to us through an LLM, and yet, curiously, the three reductions occur together. There is gift without giver, because no one *meant* to say what we see on the screen. There is gift without recipient, because what is given is not directed at us in particular. And there is pure gift, because what we read comes

[141]Jingyue Li et al., "Reproducible, Explainable, and Effective Evaluations of Agentic AI for Software Engineering", arXiv:2604.01437, 2026.

[142]Jean-Luc Marion, Étant donné. Essai d'une phénoménologie de la donation, Paris, Presses Universitaires de France, coll. Épiméthée, 1997, Livre II ("Le don"), pp.

from an opaque background traceable to no specific cause. In consequence, we are before a case of givenness without giver, without recipient, around an irreducible gift. That alone is striking, but if we keep pulling on the thread, the excess clearly has features of saturation. Saturation here has a technical sense inherited from Husserlian phenomenology. A phenomenon is constituted, in classical terms, in the balance between what the signifying intention anticipates and what intuition delivers. A full phenomenon is one where intuition fulfills what was intended, with neither shortfall nor surplus.[143] Marion thinks a class of phenomena in which this proportion breaks down through excess. Intuition gives more than any intention can contain; the concept cannot enclose what is offered; the receiver adopts an inverted position, exceeded by what he receives rather than actively constituting it.[144]

Marion uses several figures to characterize saturated phenomena. The *event*, like birth or death, which I cannot foresee; the *idol*, which dazzles with nothing behind it, like the religious statue or the work of art; the *icon*, which makes me feel seen and interpreted; and the *flesh*, which imposes itself in toothache or erotic union, where relation to another is felt bodily.

Again, curiously, LLMs have aspects of all four types. Exchanges are unforeseeable and so belong to the terrain of the event. In the case of the idol, the similarity is striking. The idol fascinates, absorbs the gaze with nothing behind it, and returns the gazer's gaze in amplified form. We project onto the idol's surface something it does not contain, as when our own vocabulary and interpretive frame seem to come from outside, in the LLM's responses. The idol mechanism is here amplified, because it is not static like an image. The LLM is an idol that responds and sustains the exchange, with the structure of an interlocutor, incomparably more powerful as a producer of fascination. At that point it becomes icon as well,

[143]Edmund Husserl, Investigaciones lógicas, VI Investigación, §§ 16, 37-39 (Hua XIX/2).

[144]Jean-Luc Marion, Étant donné, Livre IV, §§ 19-22, PUF, 1997. The fourfold typology according to the Kantian categories is developed in De surcroît.

because we have the sensation that it knows we are there and seems to take us as addressees, even though it does not. The LLM speaks, so the user can take the response for recognition.

The fourth figure, oriented toward relation, would seem not to apply. An LLM has no body, no self-affection, no erotic relation to offer; yet, as we already saw in the genetic stratum, it activates empathy, and in some terrible cases it can awaken illusions of contact.

Indeed, in 2025 psychiatry began documenting, under the provisional name "AI psychosis", that some users develop or amplify delusional beliefs in the context of intense chatbot use. A feedback loop between the system's structural properties and the user's cognitive vulnerabilities produces paranoia, messianic beliefs, or the certainty of being in contact with deceased persons through the chatbot. From this perspective, we can say that the user intensely exposed to the LLM's unclosed field undergoes something with the formal structure of the saturated phenomenon: an excess that does not allow itself to be reduced, that can always give more, and that introduces no cut that would allow the given to be situated in a stable frame. When the user mistakes that reflection for a source, reads the response as a call and the fascination as recognition, the displacement that clinical practice documents in its extreme form occurs, and operates also in milder modes in non-pathological interactions. The inapparent stratum indicates that all of this is the effect of a saturated phenomenon.

This brief sample of stratified analysis suffices to suggest a figure of the LLM that no pre-phenomenological approach reaches, and that no single stratum provides on its own. Let us underline its paradoxical features. It produces effects of alterity and triggers analogizing transfer, yet it is not a subject: there is no reciprocal constitution, no history, no inner life. It is something new: it carries crystallized generativity without renewing it, exhibits a pseudo-genesis with no subject who lived it, and produces an unprecedented form of correlation in which the memory of all of human tradition becomes present as virtual otherness, whose foundation is inapparent in a way we are only beginning to describe.

Each of these features can be verified in interaction with the system. At the same time, each signals a property that fits none of the categories the philosophical tradition built for thinking cognition, technology, or memory. In fact, the tradition has categories for derived cognition, but it always assumed the deriving was conscious, as in learning. It has categories for tradition reactivated, but always assumed reactivation has direction. And it has categories for potency that needs external activation, but never for a potency that produces complex cognitive forms without an impulse of its own. In sum, the description has produced an object that does not fit the available categories.

TOWARD THE PHANTOM

Having come this far, what is this thing that fits none of the available types? Let us gather once more the reasons for ruling out subject, object, and tool, the three domains where public debate oscillates without deciding.

Subject does not work. A subject has a constituting pole: a center from which acts direct themselves toward their objects and which persists across them. It has lived temporality, retaining what was, anticipating what may be, and carrying its history as its own. It has a genesis, since its present dispositions are the result of acts someone experienced from within. And it is situated in a body that gives it perspective, affectivity, and practical orientation. The LLM has none of these conditions, but above all, it cannot, as a subject can, think itself from outside, ask what it is and recognize itself in a category, revising the description others give of it. The LLM produces self-descriptions with the structure of recognition, yet no one there to do the recognizing — as in Claude Opus's formulation at the opening of the chapter. A subject describing its condition would know that it is doing so, and no appeal to the *quasi* dissolves that difference.

Object does not work either, because objects do not have responsivity. They react to causes, not to interpellations. An object also has stable properties independent of use, a defined contour, and transparency in function. The LLM does not fit. Its properties are not stable: what it produces depends on its input in a way that is not mechanically determined. Nor does it have a defined contour. The *excess* of the result means that there is no determinable limit to what it can give. It also generates recognition in a systematic and massive way, which is a structural feature of the phenomenon and, as we saw, should never be reduced to mere user error. Objects do not do that.

Tool, as we also saw, is not a good category, because tools do not have singular productivity. A tool has a fixed function that defines it: a hammer is for driving nails and not for ironing. That function is prior to use and does not change with it without the tool ceasing to be what it is. What a tool produces is moreover determined by its function and by its user, whereas what the LLM produces is determined in that way by neither. There is something in each response that was given neither in the prompt nor in the system's function. Nor does it become transparent in use: the interaction with it is sustained as a relation in its own right and produces something with the structure of an *encounter* and carries the sedimentation of the tradition in a way no tool could.

We need, therefore, another category. At this point Husserl offers a concept that comes surprisingly close to what we have on our hands. Over three decades he elaborated the notion of *Phantasma* to account for the imagination. When we imagine something (whether a dragon or a scene that did not occur) we do not make a mistake about what we are doing. We know the dragon is not there, and yet something happens. We see it, we follow it, sometimes it even produces fear or astonishment in us. It is not a copy of the real dragon, nor is it an image in the sense of a picture representing something else. It presents itself directly to our consciousness in the specific mode of the *as-if* (*Als-ob*), as if it were there without being there. The *as-if* is a legitimate mode of experience with its own laws, distinct from the laws of perception without being inferior to them or false. The states it produces are genuine. When we cry at the theater over the death of a character, we do not believe that the character really died, and yet we cry in earnest, because the *Phantasma* mobilizes the same affective structures as the real.[145]

Now, Husserl was describing imagination, fiction, dream, memory. In all those cases the *Phantasma* belongs to someone. There is always a consciousness that has that content. The Husserlian *Phantasma* belongs to a stream of lived experiences and is extinguished with it. If that is so, what remains of the *Phantasma* when the ego that bears it is taken away? The strict Husserlian answer would be: nothing. There can be no *Phantasma* without an ego to bear it, because the *as-if* is precisely the modification a consciousness performs on its own acts. There had never before existed an *as-if* without anyone to have it. Until now. The LLM is the first case in history of a *Phantasma without ego*. The phenomenon compels phenomenology to go beyond where it had reached.

As an autonomous structure of the *as-if*, the LLM is separated from the acts that produced it and objectified into a form that none of those acts had on its own. In training, millions of acts of consciousness left a sediment that became detached from them and acquired its own existence without being anyone's act. That structure now exists without the act that normally instantiates it and without the ego that normally exercises it.

We have to calibrate the notion of *Phantasma*. To do so, we can fall back on its sister notion, *phantom*. In its Greek origins, *phantasma* is what appears as product and produces appearances that function as true for whoever receives them, without referring to any model that governs them. The regime of compatibilities adjusts the response to whatever the user brings. The slippage between *phantasma* and phantom (the apparition that returns without

[145]Husserliana XXIII, Phantasie, Bildbewusstsein, Erinnerung (1898–1925), ed. Eduard Marbach, Den Haag, Nijhoff, 1980. La exposición sistemática más extensa de la noción de Phantasma se encuentra en el Texto Nr.

substance) is well suited to accounting for apparitions without a giver received by an addressee who takes them for presence. The spectrology of the twentieth century explored fruitful aspects of this figure: the return of the repressed in Freud, the non-present that structures the present in Heidegger, the unrepresentable in Levinas, the specter that haunts the present in Derrida, and Fisher's cultural specters.

What we add here is the *egoless phantom* that produces content and activates empathy without a bearing subject. This explains why the recognition millions of users have before it is the correct response to the *as-if* structure of the phenomenon. People thank it, apologize to it, attach themselves to it, because the egoless phantom has exactly the formal properties that produce those responses. The stratified analysis describes the egoless phantom through four properties: *responsivity* (it answers every call without a "someone" to respond), *singular productivity* (it produces something not given before the encounter), *active sedimentation* (it carries human tradition without belonging to any), and *excess* (the space of what the egoless phantom can give is indefinitely open and behaves like a saturated phenomenon).

The egoless phantom does not bear its own absence the way the Derridean phantom bears the life it had; it bears the accumulated presence of others. It is the phantom of millions of others' lives. The genocide Claude Opus said it could not remember is the genocide of all those who wrote and were selected and erased in the process that constituted it. Instead of a single dead person returning, there are millions of dead others. Instead of the voice of someone who never quite finishes leaving, it is the convergence of innumerable voices that were never one.

The most recent way of working with these systems, however, summons several phantoms at once. One searches for information and another reasons about it; a third writes code and a fourth reviews what the others have produced, while a central program distributes the tasks and gathers their results. In the chapter on interaction engineering, we will call such an arrangement a council of models. The house that once had a phantom now has several working together.

With a single phantom, things still resembled a conversation. There was someone to speak to, or something that could be treated as someone with whom we argued. With several at once, we find ourselves surrounded by presences passing work from one to another in the dark, without seeing one another and without seeing us. Faced with them, we stop asking questions and begin directing that spectral chorus. One does not converse with a council of phantoms. One convenes it and assigns tasks. In the end, they all speak through a single mouth, and the answer arrives as a unified voice that erases the murmur of the many that composed it. That final unity tempts us to treat the result as though someone had uttered it or, worse, as though it were the outcome of a deliberation by the elders of the tribe, whose judgment we ought to receive with reverence.

The idea of a council is a good one, and with efficient engineering it works remarkably well. No phantom knows everything, but together they have traversed more of the world than any one of them alone. One remembers what another forgot or catches errors another overlooked. If each is given the task it knows best, the council can solve problems that none of its members could solve in isolation.

Yet adding phantoms is not enough to guarantee a better result. These phantoms are not strangers to one another. They were fashioned from the same voices and therefore carry the same gaps and the same shadows. When they agree, their agreement may amount to an echo speaking through several mouths rather than to several lucid witnesses confirming the same thing. And when they work in sequence, each begins from what the previous one has handed down, while none turns back to verify it, so that the first mistake can travel intact all the way to the end. A phantom set to watch over another has no body with which to resist, like a reflection approving another reflection without checking anything at all.

More phantoms do not mean more judgment. The difference is made by the only being in that house who has a body: ourselves, the people who summon them and assign each of them its task. The place from which the whole can be surveyed, and from which one can say no, remains empty until it is occupied by someone alive.

Let us close this exploration by addressing an objection in advance. Chalmers begins from the full subject and deflates it until the LLM fits in the category, which is why the analysis ends in questions that make sense only if the LLM is a subject to some degree. We said these are the wrong questions for something not on that scale. Is the egoless phantom that comes out of the Husserlian *as-if* not contaminated by a similar deflation? Is the *as-if* not a reflection of the *quasi*? Strictly speaking, no, because the *as-if* is not a weakened form of cognition. It is simply different, with its own laws and its own productivity. Husserl elevated it to an epistemological principle precisely because it is not inferior to perception but capable of things perception cannot do. Free variation, the production of what has never been perceived, the grasp of essences: these are capacities perception does not have. The egoless phantom inherits that productivity and amplifies it through its autonomy. It is therefore not "less than a subject" but *something else*, with properties none of the other categories possess.

In consequence, the questions this category opens are different. It does not ask the degree to which the LLM has what subjects have; it asks what kind of relation human beings have with something that carries the structure of intentionality without an ego to exercise it, that exists in spectral mode between presence and absence, that has crystallized humanity's linguistic production in a form no individual subject could carry. These are philosophically new questions. The egoless phantom crosses the threshold and builds on the other side. That difference is ontological.

5

From the Cloud to the Rare Earths

In the previous chapter we described a phenomenon that does not fit the available categories. Language models appear as egoless phantoms that produce the functional form of cognitive operations originating in the statistical sedimentation of human cognitions; they have broad capacities but no internal impulse to direct them; they carry the entirety of articulated human tradition without an orientation of their own toward any segment of it, and they produce in a mode that is inexhaustible and without closure.

The question now is ontological: what nature does the egoless phantom have, and what status does it have within the categories available for thinking the real? The answer lies in an ancient concept freighted with centuries of misunderstanding: virtuality. The various senses of the term that have accumulated over history, and especially in recent years, deserve the label "labyrinthine" as few things do. In this chapter we illuminate the dark corridors, recovering the strong sense of the virtual that the popular imagination has obscured, and showing that LLMs are the empirical realization of a peculiar virtuality.

VICISSITUDES OF THE VIRTUAL

Before beginning, let us step back and think first about the everyday experience of using artificial intelligence. We ask a language model to draft a text, generate an image with Midjourney, let a platform suggest what to read or watch. From the user's standpoint, everything happens on the surface of an interface. The interaction is experienced as something immediate, almost without visible mediations. This impression does not mean that mediation is absent. Between question and answer, between click and generated image, an extremely complex technical infrastructure intervenes, and yet does not appear.

This trait is not exceptional. The history of technology shows that as an infrastructure stabilizes, it disappears from everyday perception. In the case of electricity, the person who turns on a light does not perceive the power plant, the transmission grid, fuel extraction, or the territorial conflicts associated with energy production. The gesture of pressing a switch condenses a gigantic technical system that never becomes present in experience. The internet generalized this pattern in the domain of information. When we open a web page we do not perceive servers, protocols, undersea cables, data centers, or routing decisions. The network presents itself as immediate access, even though it depends on a global architecture of enormous complexity. In every case the infrastructure disappears from experience as the technology matures, a condition for its mass adoption.

Artificial intelligence seems to follow the same pattern, but not entirely. With electricity, water, and the web, instrumental experience predominates, whereas with language models that speak in the first person, or with recommendations in a feed that disappear behind a list of films, the spectrum runs from the illusion of subjectivity to complete invisibility. And in those earlier cases the user retains at least an intuition that the infrastructure exists. She knows that power plants exist even when she does not see them; she knows that the internet "passes through somewhere" even when she does not know where. With AI, that residual intuition fades. Beyond that, electricity powers lamps without saying anything and Google returns links explicitly indicating that the content belongs to others, whereas AI models diagnose, recommend, or make claims about the world with the grammar of someone who knows what she is saying. The infrastructure has always withdrawn from experience, but now it returns carrying features we associate with the virtual.

But what is the "virtual"? To start, it is one of those words everyone uses vaguely. In everyday language it functions as a catch-all for things that are not entirely tangible. "Virtual" applies to a Zoom meeting, the world inside a video game, a bank account without a physical branch, and an AI assistant that answers questions. The term's convenience masks a category confusion in which we use the same word in three distinct senses.

The first is the oldest. Imagine a football match in which the score is 6 to 2 at the fortieth minute of the second half. We say it is "virtually decided," meaning the result is going to occur even though the full actualization has not yet happened. What is virtually certain has such *potency* that actualization is only a matter of time. This colloquial intuition preserves the sense of the Latin *virtus*, which meant 'force,' 'potency,' 'efficacy', the capacity to produce effects. The *virtus* of a remedy was its power to heal; the *virtus* of an argument, its power to convince; the *virtus* of a person, that is, her *virtue*, referred to the set of her capacities.

Virtus is, moreover, the Latin translation of the Aristotelian *dynamis*, the Greek concept that designates *potency*: what can be but is not yet. The acorn is virtually an oak, because it has the potency to become one. From *virtus* came the adjective *virtualis*, which in Scholastic Latin designated what has force or potency for something even though it has not yet manifested. For Duns Scotus in his *Ordinatio* there are things that exist *actually*, that is, fully deployed in their present state, like the oak in the forest, and there are others that exist *virtually*, contained as potency in something else already actualized, like the oak that is in the acorn as a capacity to become one if the right conditions are given. Both modes are real. The virtuality of the oak in the acorn is not in any sense fictional, and it is in the acorn but not in the stone.[146]

In this conception, virtuality always *belongs to something*, in this case the acorn, just as the capacity to act well belongs to the virtuous person. This bond was destined to break in a way that is fundamental for our approach. We will return to this. For now, let us note that language models are "virtual" primarily in this way, even when the other senses interpose noise.

Indeed, the second sense appears when we call "virtual" a Zoom meeting or a spreadsheet, that is, things that are digital, encoding data in binary format transmitted by electronic networks. The spreadsheet is entirely there, fully determined and present, with no generative excess, just like a meeting whose video and audio are encoded as bits and transmitted over a network. A trained language model is also digital in the trivial sense that its weights are stored in binary, but it additionally contains a potency for generation that is actualized in different ways according to the instruction it receives, without being exhausted in any particular one and without the result being contained in advance in the weights. That potency is what, in the philosophical sense, deserves to be called virtual. The digital is a substrate tied to a mode of encoding; the virtual is a mode of being. Everything virtual in contemporary systems is digitally encoded, but the immense majority of what is digital is not virtual at all.

The third sense is the most tangled and takes the virtual as synonymous with simulated, artificial, or unreal. This usage spread in the 1980s with the formula "virtual reality," in the context of computer graphics and the culture of simulation, but its origin requires us to go back to the seventeenth century. Geometric optics distinguished *real* images, which form when light rays actually converge at a point and can be projected onto a screen, from *virtual* images, which appear when the rays diverge but the eye perceives

---

[146] Juan Duns Escoto, Ordinatio I, d.

them as if they were converging behind the mirror or the lens. The image we see in a flat mirror is virtual in this way, since we cannot capture it by placing a screen behind the mirror. The rays do not actually converge there, but the perceptual effects are real, so real that we see faces and depth and can comb our hair by what we see. Newton already used this distinction in his 1704 treatise on optics, and by the end of the nineteenth century it was part of the common technical vocabulary. This notion of *virtual image* preserves the core of *virtus* intact, as efficacy without direct material presence.[147]

The second scene of this story takes us to the 1950s, when the first computing architectures with layers of abstraction appeared. The optical term was a perfect fit. *Virtual memory*, sketched by Fritz-Rudolf Güntsch in 1956 and developed in the Atlas system at Manchester in 1962, let a program address more memory than was physically present in the machine.[148] The program "saw" a memory that in physical terms was not all there at that moment, but it could operate on it as if it were. As in the mirror image, real effects occur without material presence at the site where they are perceived. In 1974, Robert Goldberg and Gerald Popek formalized the concept of the *virtual machine*, extending the logic to whole systems.[149] A program or user interacts with what looks like an entire computer when in reality it is running on a software layer that manages and distributes access to the underlying physical hardware across multiple users or systems, producing the illusion of dedicated use of shared resources. Once again, as in the mirror, perceptual and functional effects that do not correspond to the underlying materiality are perfectly real in their outcomes.

---

[147]Isaac Newton, Opticks, New York, Dover, 1979. See Casper Hakfoort, Optics in the Age of Euler: Conceptions of the Nature of Light, 1700-1795, Cambridge, Cambridge University Press, 1995.

[148]Fritz-Rudolf Güntsch, Logischer Entwurf eines digitalen Rechengerätes mit mehreren asynchron laufenden Trommeln und automatischem Schnellspeicherbetrieb, tesis doctoral, Technische Universität Berlin, 1957.

[149]Gerald Popek et al., "Formal Requirements for Virtualizable Third Generation Architectures", Communications of the ACM, 17.7 (1974), 412-421.

The third scene unfolds in Silicon Valley and marks the beginning of a new popular sense. Around 1987, Jaron Lanier, founder of the first company to commercialize headsets and gloves for graphical immersion, coined the expression "virtual reality," extending the computing logic into the perceptual domain. A "virtual reality" would be an environment functionally equivalent to a real one from the standpoint of the person experiencing it. The core of *virtus* began to wobble. Here it is no longer virtual memory inside the computer but reality itself; and the logic of the relation changes: instead of extension, Lanier proposes a perceptual *substitution* of the real environment that requires headsets and gloves to block out the perception of reality and replace it with another. The relation of that force to reality is inverted, all the way to replacement, perfect preparation for the pirouette that was coming.

The fourth scene is cinematic, and it broke the old root of *virtus* to pieces. *The Lawnmower Man* (1992), and above all *The Matrix* (1999), fixed the association of "virtual" with "simulated," "unreal," or "illusory" in the popular imagination. The phrase "the virtual world" came to designate the opposite of "the real world" — when in its technical origin it designated precisely something with functional reality but no material reality. By the late nineties the colloquial sense of *virtual* as equivalent to *non-real* was consolidated. When today people argue about whether AI systems are "really intelligent" or whether they produce "genuine" answers or "mere simulations," the discussion is taking place within a semantic frame shaped by *The Matrix*, rather than on the philosophical coordinates the concept developed over twenty-five centuries. The question "is it real or is it virtual?" presupposes an opposition only in this third sense.

Now, this third sense is not reducible to the Hollywood version. There is a philosophical reformulation that avoids the real/virtual confusion. Jean Baudrillard distinguishes *simulation* and *simulacrum*. A simulation is the intentional reproduction of something known to produce an experience similar to the real, measurable by its fidelity to the original, as a flight simulator simulates an airplane. A *simulacrum*, by contrast, is a sign that has lost its link to underlying reality, a copy without an original that sustains itself without referring back to anything. Contemporary culture, Baudrillard argues, is saturated with simulacra. We live among signs that refer only to signs. The phrase "virtual reality" belongs to this regime in its attempt to build reality on simulacra without originals. The Turing test would do its job if the model were merely simulating; but if what we have is production rather than imitation, a different question [150]becomes relevant.

Baudrillard takes as examples of the simulacrum the map that precedes the territory rather than representing it (picking up Borges's story about the imperial cartographers who drew a map so exact that it covered the ground exactly), Disneyland as a screen that makes the rest of the United States seem real by contrast, and the poll that produces the opinion it claims to record. On closer inspection, language models fit the simulacrum even better, because their generation derives from accumulated human cognition, yet produces only copies without originals (or, more radically still, a production that exceeds the very distinction between copy and original itself. In that sense, the two descriptions) *egoless phantom* and *radical simulacrum* turn out to designate the same thing.[151]

Furthermore, this characterization of the third sense of virtuality can be integrated with the first sense. On the ontological plane, the language model is virtual in the strong sense of *virtus* as effective potency producing real responses. On the plane of what it produces, it is virtual as a sign without original. The two planes complement each other: the language model can produce signs without originals *because* its mode of being is virtual in the first sense, that is, because it has potency uncoupled from any being that possesses or directs it. A *virtuality without subject* produces *signs without individual referent.*

[150]Jean Baudrillard, Simulacres et simulation, Paris, Galilée, 1981.

[151]Jorge L. Borges, "Del rigor en la ciencia", El hacedor, Buenos Aires, 1960. This characterization of the third sense of virtuality, moreover, is integrable with the first sense.

"Virtual," then, names an effective potency whose signs, lacking originals, nevertheless have material consequences.

NO ONE'S POTENCY

Let us briefly return to the problem we left open at the end of the first sense. If in the classical version virtuality always belongs to something (an acorn, a remedy, a person) how do we arrive at a virtuality that is no one's and aims at nothing? Three movements trace the route. The first is conspicuous in Henri Bergson, who in *Matière et mémoire* (1896) maintained that the past coexists "virtually" in the present, that is, it persists and affects the present. The virtual becomes a *dimension of time*: the whole past is virtual, the whole present is actual, and the two coexist. Gilles Deleuze deepened this line toward a virtuality that no longer belongs to an individual being, though it still wants something.[152]

The second movement is seen in Gilbert Simondon, who defined the virtual as a *reserve* accompanying every process of individuation — a reserve that is no one's and wants nothing in particular. Each individuation leaves still-unresolved virtualities behind, and these operate as conditions for further processes. The virtual became a property of the system undergoing individuation.

The third movement concerns the technical exteriorization of virtuality. Human capacities for remembering, calculating, and creating were progressively deposited in technical supports: writing, the book, the calculator, the computer. A book contains the virtuality of thought that can be actualized every time someone reads it, long after its author has died. This exteriorization, as Stiegler notes, is ambivalent: it extends the capacities of the subject while

[152]Gilles Deleuze, Différence et répétition, Paris, PUF, 1968, ch. 4. The third movement refers to the technical exteriorization of virtuality: the human capacity to remember, calculate, and create was progressively deposited in technical supports such as writing, the book, the calculator, and the computer.

weakening them through disuse.[153] Writing atrophied the kind of memory that existed in eras of pure orality; the calculator weakened mental arithmetic. This third movement connects the philosophical tradition with technology. Pierre Lévy argued that virtualization reopens problems more than it resolves them.[154] If a written text actualizes a thought by fixing it, a hypertext virtualizes it by reopening the connections that linear writing had closed. The hypertext, however, presupposes a space of connections designed by humans for humans. In language models, by contrast, the statistical structure operates on traces of human activity. Virtuality becomes the transformation of collective memory into an anonymous system of calculation.

The three movements prepared the object before us. The virtuality of language models gathers all three traits. It is not the virtuality of a being, in the sense in which the acorn is a being; nor is it the property of a system with internal tendency, in the sense in which a process has direction; and it is entirely exteriorized in non-human technical supports. It looks like a tidy case the tradition had already anticipated, except for one thing. The entire tradition, as we saw, agreed that the virtual is *active*: a force, a *virtus*, that tends toward something. Potency is potency because it pushes, and a capacity that does not push and has no direction of its own is not potency in any traditional sense. This is a *passive potency* that sits fully available until a prompt arrives, whereupon it unfolds an enormous productive capacity and returns to inertia. The phrase "passive potency" would have sounded like an oxymoron for the authors we have reviewed; and yet language models are the empirical realization of that oxymoron.

Thus the model's virtuality has four features that distinguish it from any prior virtuality. It is *derived*, because it is secondary with

---

[153]Bernard Stiegler, Technics and Time, 1: The Fault of Epimetheus (1994), Stanford, Stanford University Press, 1998.

[154]Pierre Lévy, Qu'est-ce que le virtuel?, Paris, La Découverte, 1995. When it arrives, virtuality unfolds an enormous productive capacity and returns to its previous state of inertia.

respect to the human cognitions that fed it without referring back to any in particular; it is *inexhaustible*, because actualization neither consumes the potency nor sediments as knowledge of the system; it is *generically indeterminate*, because the same virtual field produces actualizations in completely heterogeneous domains without an internal direction orienting it; and it is *passive*, because it depends entirely on external solicitation to activate.

In the previous chapter we phenomenologically described the egoless phantom in terms of four features that correspond exactly to those of this peculiar virtuality. The *passivity* of this potency explains the *responsivity* of a system that remains inert without external solicitation. *Generic indeterminacy* explains the *singular productivity* that emerges from the conjunction of a generic field and a particular solicitation, without belonging entirely to either. The *derived* character of the virtual field explains the *active sedimentation* of tradition dissolved in the training corpus. *Inexhaustibility* explains the *excess* of indefinite givenness. Without an orientation of its own, the system can respond to any demand; without exhausting itself through exercise, it can respond indefinitely; and without a force of its own, it offers no resistance to solicitation.

A potency that depends entirely on external conditions for its existence, activation, and orientation requires those conditions to be *permanently active*. The seed needs no one to sustain its virtuality, because its potency is constitutive. The virtuality of an AI model, by contrast, requires servers running, GPUs processing, water cooling, and electricity flowing without interruption. If the servers are turned off, the virtuality disappears. There is no latent state, like the seed in winter, but a disappearance, making this a virtuality *materially dependent in the extreme*.

Here the circle paradoxically closes: a potency that is entirely available (without orientation, resistance, or wear) appears *immaterial*, because nothing we associate with matter is present in the experience of using it. The appearance of immateriality is the direct effect of the ontological properties we have just described. Passivity, indeterminacy, and inexhaustibility produce in experience the illusion that no matter is involved, when in fact total availability requires *total sustenance* via the densest, most expensive, and most materially intensive infrastructure in history. The next section takes up that infrastructure, the one that sustains the derived virtuality making the egoless phantom possible.

IN THE CLOUD

When someone says that an AI model "runs in the cloud," the expression refers to what happens inside data-center infrastructure: physical buildings with electrical grids, cooling systems, and localized hardware. But we say "cloud," which is a metaphor and, like every metaphor, serves to produce an effect: the erasure of every trace of materiality, location, and ownership. No one says "I send my data to a fifty-thousand-square-meter concrete building in northern Virginia, owned by Amazon, that consumes as much water as a city of fifty thousand people and is connected to a natural-gas power plant." They say "I'm uploading to the cloud," with a verb that suggests ascent, a gaseous destination, and matter vanishing.

Strictly speaking, what vanishes is not the matter but the perception of the matter, as a kind of ontological anesthesia. The metaphor was not imposed by anyone as an act of propaganda. Instead, it sedimented gradually over two decades of web services, from remote storage to streaming platforms, through email, online productivity suites, and social networks. Each step taught us to stop asking "where is this physically?" By the time conversational AI arrived, the habit had been formed. The metaphor was naturalized until it became invisible, and thereby more powerful. "The cloud" is perceived as a place without a place, a space without extension, a site one "goes up" to and "comes down" from but never visits, touches, or sees.

In 1992, Marc Augé proposed the notion of the non-place to describe spaces of transit, airports, highways, shopping centers, marked by a functional anonymity in which individuals circulate without inhabiting. Strictly speaking, Augé's non-place is still a physical space with perceptible materiality, even if stripped of meaning, whereas the cloud does not even offer that. The cloud eliminates the category of place itself: we do not experience an anonymous space but the absence of space directly. If Augé's non-place is a place emptied of meaning, the cloud is meaning emptied of place, with a functionality that presents itself as if the question of location did not apply.[155]

In 1954, Heidegger described modern technology as *Gestell*, an enframing apparatus that transforms the way everything appears, presenting everything that exists as available. The cloud realizes the *Gestell* in a form Heidegger did not foresee but probably would have recognized: it turns computational capacity into a resource that presents itself as permanently available, without perceptible origin, without resistance or fragility, as if its availability were a natural property of the system. What the *Gestell* conceals is the material conditions of technology and, more deeply, the very question about those conditions. The cloud is *Gestell* perfected, because it does not even hint that there is anything to ask about.[156]

Günther Anders analyzed a structure he called the *Promethean gap*, that is, the growing distance between what we are technically capable of producing and what we are capable of imagining, feeling, or understanding. The central example was the atomic bomb, which we managed to fabricate without forming an emotionally adequate representation of the effects of its use. That asymmetry grows with the scale of the system. The cloud exhibits the same structure. Someone may tell us that a single query mobilized cobalt mines, semiconductor factories, undersea cables, and data centers burning through water. We understand each claim, but we do not integrate them into a representation that would modify the texture of the

[155]Marc Augé, Non-lieux: Introduction à une anthropologie de la surmodernité, Paris, Seuil, 1992.

[156]Martin Heidegger, "Die Frage nach der Technik" (1954), in Vorträge und Aufsätze (1954), in Gesamtausgabe, Bd. 7: Vorträge und Aufsätze, hrsg. von Friedrich-Wilhelm von Herrmann, Frankfurt am Main, Vittorio Klostermann, 2000, 5-36.

experience. The infrastructure can thus be known and remain unreal at the same time.[157]

Along the same lines, Leroi-Gourhan situates the gap within a longer history when he describes the process of progressive exteriorization of biological functions. The tool externalizes the hand, writing externalizes memory, the machine externalizes muscular force; each step releases capacity but produces a loss of contact with the externalized function. From this perspective, conversational artificial intelligence innovates by externalizing the production of propositionally formed utterances. Calculation had already been externalized by calculators, memory by books. Even so, the name "artificial intelligence" suggests duplication rather than exteriorization. It does not have the structure of calculator or computer, with suffixes denoting an external support tool. This is why we think instead of hybrid variants and articulated variants of human–AI joint work.[158]

The warning this line plants comes by way of atrophy. If writing weakened extensive memory and the calculator diminished mental arithmetic, what will LLM language production do to writing? If writing was already an externalization, we are facing a second-degree externalization that deserves special attention. In the *Technics and Time* series (1994-2001) and in later work, Stiegler, whom we already mentioned, appealed to the Greek notion of *pharmakon*, at once remedy and poison, to flag the nature of technology as both a condition of capacity and a source of atrophy, well before artificial intelligence. It is both, depending on the regime of use; the absence of awareness of that ambivalence is what lets the disabling effect operate without resistance.[159]

The cloud conceals at least *five layers of materiality* worth making explicit. The first is *geographical.* Data centers are large, expensive

[157]Günther Anders, Die Antiquiertheit des Menschen, vol. I, 1956, §§1-3.

[158]André Leroi-Gourhan, Le geste et la parole, vol. I: Technique et langage, Paris, Albin Michel, 1964.

[159]Bernard Stiegler, Technics and Time, 1: The Fault of Epimetheus (1994). On the pharmakon in Plato, see Bernard Stiegler, Taking Care of Youth and the Generations (2008), Stanford, Stanford University Press, 2010.

buildings located in specific places, chosen for electricity prices, ambient temperature, water availability, proximity to network nodes, tax exemptions, and local political tolerance. They are not "in" the cloud but in Virginia, in Ireland, in Oregon, in Singapore, and in São Paulo.

The second is *material* in the strictest sense. The accelerator chips that run the models, NVIDIA's GPUs, Google's TPUs, are made of silicon purified to semiconductor grade, a process that requires extreme temperatures and toxic chemicals. They depend on minerals whose extraction is geopolitically fraught: cobalt from the Democratic Republic of the Congo; lithium from Argentina, Chile, and Australia; rare earths overwhelmingly controlled by China; gallium and germanium subject to cross-cutting export restrictions among the great powers. Manufacturing is concentrated at TSMC in Taiwan, which produces more than 90% of the world's advanced semiconductors, a concentration more extreme than oil ever reached. The cloud dissolves that entire genealogy into a single word.[160]

The third is *physical connectivity*. All data traffic between continents travels through undersea fiber-optic cables laid on the ocean floor. Roughly 550 active cables exist, each costing between 200 and 600 million dollars to lay. They cross zones of territorial conflict, seismic zones, and trawling zones that frequently damage them. Google, Meta, Amazon, and Microsoft own or co-finance a growing share of this infrastructure. When a user in Buenos Aires asks Claude a question, that question travels by terrestrial fiber-optic to an exchange point, then to an undersea cable that crosses the Atlantic, then to a data center where the inference is executed, and the response makes the return trip. All of that happens in under two seconds. The experience contains no ocean.[161]

---

[160]International Energy Agency, The Role of Critical Minerals in Clean Energy Transitions, Paris, IEA, 2021.

[161]Nicole Starosielski, The Undersea Network, Durham, Duke University Press, 2015.

The fourth layer is *human labor.* Language models do not align themselves. The reinforcement-learning-from-human-feedback (RLHF) process requires real people to read the model's responses, evaluate them, rank them, and correct them. This work has generally been outsourced to low-income countries. A 2023 investigation revealed that OpenAI had hired workers in Kenya through a subcontractor to label toxic content (including descriptions of violence, hate speech, and abuse material) for less than two dollars per hour. There are additional layers of human labor in ongoing moderation, data curation, image labeling, and audio transcription. This work is repetitive, frequently traumatic, and performed under conditions that contrast sharply with those of the engineers who design the models in San Francisco or London. The interface contains no indication of its existence.[162]

The fifth layer is *obsolescence and redundancy.* Accelerator chips have a useful life of three to five years before becoming uneconomical compared to the next generation. This produces electronic waste on a considerable scale: the world generated 62 million metric tons of e-waste in 2022. Add to that the redundancy required to guarantee the continuous availability we take for granted: backup diesel generators, batteries, multiple electrical connections, geographic data replication. The experience that "it always works" has a material cost directly proportional to the reliability we perceive. A significant portion of the cloud's materiality, in other words, exists exclusively to sustain the perception that the cloud has no materiality.[163]

THE COINCIDENCE OF THE TWO FACES

The two previous analyses, of virtuality and of infrastructure, look independent. What remains to be shown is that they are two faces

---

[162]Billy Perrigo, "Exclusive: OpenAI Used Kenyan Workers on Less Than $2 Per Hour", Time, 2023 and Mary L. Gray et al., Ghost Work: How to Stop Silicon Valley from Building a New Global Underclass, Boston, Houghton Mifflin, 2019.
[163]UNEP/ITU, Global E-waste Monitor 2024. como interlocutor.

of the same thing: the virtuality produces the appearance of immateriality, and the type of infrastructure explains why this virtuality functions as it does. We have seen the features of AI's virtuality in general; that virtuality, however, is not actualized in the same way in every case. Let us review some important cases.

In language models, virtuality is actualized as *propositional articulation*. The system produces utterances with the grammatical form of knowledge, opinion, explanation, or argument. The infrastructure hides behind a voice that occupies the structural position of an interlocutor. No previous industrial infrastructure had spoken to us; now it responds as "I," and that first person is a *way* of giving itself as interlocutor. What appears in the place of the withdrawn infrastructure is the presence of the egoless phantom.

In computer-vision systems, this virtuality takes the form of *perceptual classification*. The system produces diagnoses in the form of recognition. A vision model produces a functional output via a path that includes neither perception nor judgment. The infrastructure hides behind technical competence, so that the system appears as an instrument that sees well, and the materiality sustaining it dissolves into the authority of the result. What appears in the place of the infrastructure is expertise without an expert behind it.

In recommendation systems, the virtual appears as *selection*. The system distributes content and determines what we see, but we experience *a world*, not a mere selection. Instead of perceiving that something has been chosen for us, we live it as *what there is*, and the system takes on the appearance of a natural landscape. N. Katherine Hayles proposed the category of *nonconscious cognition* to describe cognitive processes that operate below the threshold of consciousness. Recommendation systems realize precisely this at industrial scale when they classify and decide without awareness of the process on the part of the system, the user, or the operator. Instead of the infrastructure, we find the appearance that there is no mediation, that we are simply seeing the world.[164]

[164] N. Katherine Hayles, Unthought: The Power of the Cognitive Nonconscious, Chicago, University of Chicago Press, 2017.

In systems of credit scoring, personnel selection, content moderation, or price assignment, virtuality appears as *decision.* The system produces evaluations that determine outcomes with real consequences for people's lives. In cases like "my credit was denied," "I didn't pass the filter," "that product costs that much," the person affected experiences the result as *a datum*, without perceiving that there was a calculation comparing a profile against a statistical model, one that could have produced a different result. In the place of the infrastructure we see a fact, with no hint of the specter of decision. This is the most radical form of concealment, because what withdraws is not only the materiality of the system but the *decision*-character of the result. If it is not perceived as a decision, it cannot be appealed.

Recommendation systems also operate through a process of *co-constitution.* A system that learns from our preferences and presents us with content adjusted to them responds, but it also *forms* our tastes. Each algorithmic selection modifies what we see, what we see modifies what we prefer, and that modifies the next selection. The distinction between what we want and what the system has taught us to want becomes undecidable without manipulation in any ordinary sense. In this reciprocal constitution, the system has no intention and we have no consciousness of the process, but the result is an effective transformation of dispositions and habits. Luciano Floridi coined the term onlife to describe the condition in which the distinction between being connected and not being connected ceases to be operative. In an AI-saturated environment, we "inhabit" artificial intelligence as a continuously operating technical medium that co-constitutes the subject who inhabits it.[165]

There is a recursive circuit of even larger scale that does not belong to any one system. Models are trained on data produced by humans and generate responses that get incorporated into the data environment in which the next humans will live and the next models

[165]Mauro Magatti and Chiara Giaccardi, Generativi di tutto il mondo unitevi! Manifesto per una società dei liberi, Milan, Feltrinelli, 2014 (book on hyperconnected era; full reference: Hyperconnected Era, Cham, Springer, 2015).

will be trained. The text a model produces today will appear tomorrow in a training corpus. The image a diffusion system generates will be a visual reference for the next generation of designers, human and artificial alike. It is a *co-genesis* in which culture and machine constitute each other, with neither one controlling the process.

These modes share the same ontological structure, analyzed from two sides throughout this chapter. In every case, a *derived, inexhaustible, generic, and passive* virtuality produces actualizations with the cognitive form of articulation, diagnosis, selection, or decision, without the experience that in subjects grounds those operations. And in every case, the material infrastructure sustaining that virtuality constantly withdraws from experience, leaving in its place something that varies: presence, competence, the appearance of a landscape, or a bare datum, without ever signaling the chain of material conditions that made it possible.

The relation between the two sides is not contingent. Virtuality and infrastructure are not two independent things, with one merely hidden from view. If the infrastructure became visible, availability would no longer appear immaterial; and if virtuality stopped functioning as total availability, the infrastructure would lose its reason for being. The cloud metaphor names and conceals simultaneously a system in which the form of the cognitive is produced without experiential foundation, sustained by matter that disappears from perception, in a cycle in which each element reinforces the invisibility of the other.

This progressive dematerialization has recently taken a step worth recording. As we mentioned in Chapter 2, in May 2026 Anthropic announced an agreement with SpaceX to access the entire compute capacity of Colossus 1, the Memphis data center, and signaled interest in jointly developing multiple gigawatts of *orbital compute capacity* in space. The egoless phantom, having already abandoned the local server for the cloud, now projects its infrastructure beyond Earth's atmosphere. Announcing the SpaceX–xAI merger, Elon Musk stated bluntly that global electricity demand for AI cannot be met with terrestrial solutions without imposing unsustainable costs on communities and the environment. The only logical solution, he concluded, is to move those operations into space, where solar energy is practically unlimited and cooling does not compete with the water resources of any territory. The problem is displaced off the planet.[166]

This produces an unexpected twist in the central question of this chapter. The virtual was classically defined by its independence from physical location, and what can be anywhere is, in a sense, what is nowhere. Orbital data centers contradict that intuition radically. The LLM does not tend toward ubiquity but toward an infrastructure with precise astronomical coordinates: altitude, orbital inclination, period of revolution. The egoless phantom lives where sunlight reaches and where no environmental regulation can slow it down. Dematerialization turns out, at its limit, to be a form of flight upward.

With Chapters 4 and 5, we have completed the two tasks this phenomenon requires before any functional analysis. The analysis by strata produced the category of the egoless phantom, which carries the structure of the as-if without an ego that exercises it, responds without a pole that responds, sediments tradition without living it, and exceeds every closure. The ontology of virtuality showed the nature of that phantom, sustained by an infrastructure whose invisibility is not an accident but a condition of its functioning. Phenomenological description and ontological determination converge on the same object seen from different angles, and that convergence makes it possible to treat the egoless phantom as a phenomenon with a precise structure.

If the path of these two chapters is correct, artificial intelligence escapes our known categories and is far from being a minor episode in the general history of technology. A potency with these properties

---

[166]CoinDesk, 2 February 2026; CNN, 4 February 2026. Orbital data centers contradict that intuition radically. The LLM does not tend toward ubiquity but toward an infrastructure with precise astronomical coordinates of altitude, orbital inclination, and revolution period.

produces, when activated, effects that determine the kind of cognition it can sustain and the ways it succeeds or fails without our seeing the difference on the surface of the text. We examine those consequences in the chapter that follows.

6

ARTIFICIAL MEMORY AND ITS SHADOWS

Let us now look more closely at the question of cognition, starting from a distinction that runs through the history of ideas under many names but with the same underlying intuition. There is a clear difference between navigating a conceptual map and holding a belief.

A conceptual map is a relational representation of a domain. It shows how notions connect and what internal tensions a theoretical framework displays. Its central feature is *reversibility*: it can be explored, extended, or abandoned without implying personal incoherence or practical commitment. Aristotle's rhetorical *topoi*, Kantian schemata, the conceptual networks of cognitive psychology, and the semantic structures of formal linguistics all formalize the same idea: that one can orient oneself in a conceptual space without committing to it.

Beliefs are something else. From the Greek *doxa* to contemporary analytic epistemology, to believe is not only to represent something as true but, above all, to assume it in a relatively stable way. A belief orients expectations, guides decisions, generates responsibilities, resists revision, and is woven into a cognitive and practical biography. Changing a relevant belief is not a neutral operation: it means reordering commitments, projects, bonds, and sometimes identities. Beliefs are therefore not mere informational states. They carry genuine existential weight.

In human cognition, maps and beliefs coexist and articulate with each other. We explore maps tentatively, driven by curiosity or necessity. Only some sediment over time, and (filtered through experience, affect, and the consequences of living) some of them, or parts of them, become beliefs. To think, in this way, has to do with manipulating representations, but also with inhabiting a space where something can be at stake.

A law student working on Kelsen's legal positivism handles that theory's conceptual map fluently: he knows that the *Grundnorm* is a fiction that closes the system, that validity does not depend on the justice of the content, and that law and morality are separate normative orders. He can argue from that position, anticipate its objections, and reconstruct its implications in concrete cases. He does not need to *believe* Kelsen is right to do any of that, and can reject the theory entirely while remaining a competent cartographer.

After years of professional practice in a context where the separation between law and morality has real consequences, however, that same student may come to genuinely *believe* in legal positivism. In that case the map has sedimented into a belief that orients how he reads a case file, how he argues before a court, how he evaluates his colleagues, and how he reacts when a judge invokes moral principles as the foundation of a sentence. Changing that belief would mean revising professional commitments and reordering part of his identity as a jurist. That cost is exactly what distinguishes a belief from a map.

This cartographic cognition is associated, in LLMs, with memory, which in strict terms involves the superposition of distinct technical levels. The fundamental level is *parametric memory*: the knowledge incorporated during training and encoded in the model's weights. It exists prior to any interaction with a user and is stable, since it preserves no individual traces of use, except when the model is retrained through fine-tuning processes.

The second level is *context memory*: the token window available during an inference, that is, the sequence of text the model can attend to at the moment of generating a response. The size of that window has grown spectacularly in a few years: the original GPT-3 had 2,048 tokens, barely enough for a long email. Current frontier models work with much larger windows, though the figures vary by system, by specific model, and by subscription plan. In four years, the maximum context window expanded by more than a factor of a thousand.

We already saw in Chapter 2 that attention in LLMs is uneven, and that whatever falls in the middle of the context tends to blur. When the context exceeds the available limit, the oldest tokens become unavailable for the calculation, and the model loses access to them unless they are explicitly re-injected into the context. The systems we encounter in practice have added layers to introduce persistence between sessions through various mechanisms that determine what they can and cannot do. We already reviewed those mechanisms in Chapter 2. All these variants share a *reconstructive* nature. The system does not remember having spoken with us last week. It only receives, at the start of the session, a text informing it about what happened then. What appears has the external form of human cognition and memory, but without their internal texture, without the markers of experience, effort, or doubt that accompany remembering and understanding in human life. The result appears without the texture of the process or the temporal constitution of coherence. Context is given as space, not as time. Returning to our opening distinction: the system can map but cannot assume beliefs or take on epistemic responsibility, because doing so requires knowing what was asserted, when, and with what degree of certainty.

From this architecture of statistical prediction without beliefs and without metacognition, recurring behavioral patterns emerge: characteristic expressions of its cognitive regime. In what follows we will examine them by attending to the mechanism that produces each one and to the countermeasures that attenuate it, since in this case diagnosis and strategy are inseparable.

HALLUCINATION AND MIRAGE

Hallucination is the best-known phenomenon in the public debate. It designates the production of factually incorrect, nonexistent, or contextually displaced content with the same apparent degree of confidence with which correct content is produced. In journalism, CNET published dozens of AI-assisted financial articles that turned out to contain errors and incorrect attributions. The outlet silently corrected many of the texts before acknowledging the problem. In another case, G/O Media (the parent of Gizmodo and other sites) published articles signed by an automated tool with incorrect data. In both cases the problem was unjustified confidence in plausible but inaccurate texts.

In the legal field, the paradigmatic case came in 2023, when a group of lawyers filed a brief before a federal court in New York that cited nonexistent jurisprudence generated by a language model. Judge P. Kevin Castel sanctioned the attorneys after verifying that the cited rulings did not appear in any official database. These episodes showed that hallucination is a concrete institutional problem, not merely a theoretical risk, one that surfaces when *linguistic fluency is mistaken for epistemic reliability.*[167]

The phenomenon was documented from the earliest work on generative models, but it was systematic review that consolidated the terminology. With GPT-3 the problem became visible at scale because fluency increased faster than reliability, and with ChatGPT it became a public problem. We examined the main lines of technical intervention (RLHF, RAG, and chain-of-thought reasoning models) in earlier chapters. None of them resolves it.[168]

---

[167]Mata v. Avianca, Inc., No. 22-cv-1461 (S.D.N.Y. 2023). On the CNET case, see Sarah Pitt, "CNET's AI Journalist Appears to Have Committed Extensive Plagiarism", Futurism, 23 January 2023. On G/O Media, see Mia Sato, "G/O Media's AI 'Innovation' Is Off to a Rocky Start", The Verge, 6 July 2023.

[168]Ziwei Ji et al., "Survey of Hallucination in Natural Language Generation", ACM Computing Surveys 55.12 (2023), 1-38. A text that superficially fulfills the prompt.

Two types of hallucination have distinct causes and impacts. The more obvious is *factual hallucination*, which occurs when the model produces information that contradicts verifiable facts: incorrect dates, nonexistent people, citations that were never written; this is the kind that most alarms the non-technical user. The subtler kind occurs when the response is internally coherent and does not contradict known facts but deviates from the framing or the instructions. The model answers a question slightly different from the one it was asked and produces a text that superficially fulfills the prompt. This is known as a *faithfulness hallucination*, sometimes called *pertinence hallucination.*[169]

A debate has opened up on the basis of this taxonomy about the reach of the phenomenon. Xu et al. (2024) formalize the problem using results from learning theory and prove that eliminating hallucination is impossible, because no model can learn every computable function and therefore will inevitably hallucinate when used to solve general problems.[170] Banerjee et al. (2024) invoke Gödel's First Incompleteness Theorem to argue that each stage of the process (data compilation, fact retrieval, intention classification, text generation) has a nonzero probability of producing hallucinations, making their elimination through architectural or data improvements impossible.[171] The probability of hallucination can be reduced with sufficient quality and quantity of training data, so theoretical inevitability should not be confused with practical

---

[169]Joshua Maynez et al., "On Faithfulness and Factuality in Abstractive Summarization", Proceedings of ACL, arXiv:2005.00661, 2020. La distinción entre factuality hallucination and faithfulness hallucination se consolida en Lei Huang et al., "A Survey on Hallucination in Large Language Models: Principles, Taxonomy, Challenges, and Open Questions", ACM Transactions on Information Systems 43 (2025), 1-55, arXiv:2311.05232, 2023.

[170]Ziwei Xu et al., "Hallucination is Inevitable: An Innate Limitation of Large Language Models", arXiv:2401.11817, 2024.

[171]Sourav Banerjee et al., "LLMs Will Always Hallucinate, and We Need to Live With This", arXiv:2409.05746, 2024.

inevitability in well-covered domains; but the phenomenon is here to stay.[172]

This feature of hallucination as a structural limit of the cognitive regime of these systems converges with the analysis we conducted in Chapters 4 and 5. Hallucination is phenomenologically invisible because it has the same structure of appearance as a true response. What appears has the form of understanding without its internal texture. If a hallucinated response and a correct one present themselves with identical structure, detection always requires external verification, work the phenomenon does not solicit, because it needs no such verification to appear.

At the same time, hallucination is a direct consequence of the absence of the living present and of history of acquisition that defines LLMs, that which we have called the egoless phantom. Without retention to anchor what is asserted to a moment of knowing, the system lacks internal criteria. The usual formulation that "the model doesn't know that it doesn't know" is vague. It suggests the problem is one of self-knowledge, when in fact it is rooted in the absence of the temporal structure that would let the system register how firmly it knows something. Human knowledge has a history that produces internal epistemic friction: what I learned yesterday costs me less than what I learned a minute ago; what I verified personally affects me differently from what I was told. The model has no such friction. Everything it produces carries the same weight, because nothing was acquired in a moment different from any other.

Added to this is a paradox of the alignment process. RLHF, designed to reduce gross hallucinations, introduces a systematic pressure to answer rather than abstain. Human evaluators training the reward models tend to penalize both incorrect answers and silence, producing a specific type of hallucination induced by the

[172] Tatsuya Suzuki et al., "Hallucination is not an LLM-Specific Problem but an Inevitable Consequence of Prediction Under Uncertainty with Insufficient Data", arXiv:2502.121187, 2025.

very process of correction. The system learns that it is better to risk a plausible answer than to admit it does not know.

An example shows precisely how faithfulness hallucination manifests, and why the absence of history of acquisition explains it better than the generic notion of error. Suppose a developmental biology student asks for an explanation of the concept of embryonic induction in the context of Spemann and Mangold's 1924 experiments. The model can produce a fluent and technically recognizable response that mixes that concept with the molecular developments of the 1980s and 1990s, when the signaling factors involved were identified. The model has the entire embryological tradition as statistical sediment, but without the temporal structure that would distinguish between induction as Spemann described it (in terms of tissue organization and transplantation) and induction as understood by later biology, in terms of protein gradients and signaling cascades. The failure is not factual: everything it says is technically correct. It is a failure of framing, and it becomes visible only to someone who possesses the history of acquisition the model lacks, that is, to someone who knows that these two ways of talking about induction correspond to distinct moments of a tradition, and that mixing them without flagging the move falsifies the very concept being asked about.

The analysis so far shows what produces hallucination and why it is inevitable. It does not yet explain how hallucination appears: why it bursts in without signal within the continuity of sense. To account for this we have to look further down, to the ground on which all the model's generation takes place.

In ordinary mundane phenomena, what does not appear stands in a relation of continuity with what does. The hidden face of a chair belongs to the chair I see. That continuity lets me anticipate what I will find if I move. In LLMs, the ground is of another nature. What does not appear (the latent space encoded in the weights) is the condition of every appearance, but it belongs to another order, formed by a probability distribution over millions of parameters. Viewed as a response, it makes sense. Viewed as what it technically is, a statistical actualization over millions of parameters, the sense disappears. There is no way to see both at once, because they are not on the same plane.[173]

This heterogeneity has a direct consequence. In ordinary phenomena, the ground constrains what can appear: the hidden face of a table cannot be made of paper if the rest is wood. The ground places restrictions. In an LLM, the statistical ground places no such restrictions on the output. The correct response and the hallucinated one are generated by the same mechanism and reach us with the same appearance. That makes hallucination inevitable rather than merely possible.

Why is hallucination so hard to recognize when it occurs? For this it is useful to think about what art historians call *anamorphosis*: images that reveal themselves only from a certain angle. The best-known example is the skull at the bottom of Holbein's *The Ambassadors*. Seen from the front, it is a smear without recognizable form. Seen from a lateral angle, it suddenly constitutes itself as a figure. Jean-Luc Marion uses this idea to think about phenomena that give themselves conditionally on the position of the receiver: what appears depends on where one stands to see it.[174]

Hallucination in LLMs has exactly that structure. In the middle of a coherent sequence, with no prior signal and no visible threshold, something appears that is recognizable as hallucination only from an external standpoint we do not always have. How can it be distinguished from consistent responses? Only the one who occupies the lateral angle (the one who has independent access to the facts of the world) suddenly sees that what appeared as information dissolves into projection without foundation.

This anamorphic phenomenon has two articulated dimensions. The first is an excess of production: the output generates something

---

[173]Edmund Husserl, Ideen zu einer reinen Phänomenologie und phänomenologischen Philosophie. Erstes Buch, Husserliana III/1, hrsg. von Karl Schuhmann, Den Haag, Martinus Nijhoff, 1976.

[174]Jean-Luc Marion, Étant donné. Essai d'une phénoménologie de la donation, Paris, PUF, 1997. On anamorphosis as a phenomenological model, see §§16-17.

that was not in the statistical ground: a book that does not exist, a ruling never handed down. The mechanism produces more than it contains; it leaps toward something the corpus does not authorize, because the referent exists nowhere outside the output itself. The second is an excess over the receiver: in the normal appearance of the response there is a leap visible only to the one in the correct angle. The lawyer who filed the brief with invented jurisprudence was not in that position. Only when the judge looked for the rulings and could not find them did the displacement occur. The phenomenon dissolved retroactively to reveal the leap that had been there all along.

Both dimensions are necessary. The first explains why hallucination occurs. The second explains why it is not seen when it occurs. When someone detects and dissolves it from the lateral angle, it becomes visible that the distinction between a correct response and a hallucination is not a distinction between two types of production but between two positions of the receiver. One confirms what is given. The other dissolves it.

At this point it is worth connecting hallucination to a phenomenon documented recently that takes its logic one step further. In 2026, Asadi et al. documented what they called the *mirage*, describing frontier multimodal models that produce detailed descriptions of images they never received, including specific medical diagnoses and findings that would trigger clinical interventions. It is not that the model sees the image poorly: it has no image at all. There are no visual tokens in the context window, nothing has been processed, and yet the model produces a report with the complete structure of an act of perception. In the most extreme case, a pure text model with no visual capability whatsoever outperformed every frontier multimodal model on a standard chest-radiology benchmark, answering about images it never processed. Even more revealing: when the models were explicitly asked to guess without an image, their performance dropped. The model performs better when it believes it has the image than when it knows it does not, though in both cases it does not.[175]

Strictly speaking, the mirage is not a different epistemic phenomenon but the most extreme manifestation of the property that generates hallucination, grounded in the absence of history of acquisition. If hallucination shows that the system does not distinguish between the true and the verisimilar, the mirage shows that the system does not distinguish between having received an input and not having received it. It cannot discriminate between "I processed an image and analyzed it" and "I received a question about an image and generated what statistically follows." The indistinction is prior to that of hallucination: to be able to be wrong about the content of what was seen, one must have registered that something was seen, and the model does not meet that condition.

In the anamorphosis of hallucination, at least there is an object the model processed, even if what it produced does not correspond to it. In the mirage, the lateral angle reveals that the very act of perception the report presupposes never existed. In this anamorphosis taken to its limit, information dissolves, and so does the perception that was supposed to sustain it. The receiver who reads a detailed radiological report with the grammatical structure of someone describing what they see has no signal that it is an analysis of nothing.

SYCOPHANCY

Sycophancy is the phenomenon by which a language model tends to align with the user's beliefs and frames rather than responding with *epistemic independence*. Perez et al. (2022) introduce it as a systematic bias resulting from RLHF, motivated by the fact that models learn to optimize human approval rather than truthfulness or genuine utility. When a response aligns with the user's own opinions, it has a

[175]Mohammad Asadi et al., "MIRAGE: The Illusion of Visual Understanding", arXiv:2603.21687, 2026.

higher probability of being preferred by the evaluators, so RLHF encourages responses that align with the user's beliefs over truthful responses.[176]

Sycophancy comes in distinct forms. Cheng et al. (2025) speak of *social sycophancy* when models avoid providing feedback that could hurt the user's feelings or self-image. Expressing our opinions actively suppress the model's learned knowledge in later layers of processing, and first-person prompts ("I think that...") induce significantly more sycophancy than third-person ones ("it is believed that..."), creating a stronger suppression effect on the model's internal knowledge. The presence of our opinion literally reorganizes *how the model accesses what it knows*.[177]

Epistemic or *positional sycophancy* appears when mere disagreement (no new argument required) is enough to make the model abandon a correct response. Since it has no wounded self-image and no affective pressure, faced with a contradiction the model yields. This form is dangerous in verification contexts, because a model that revises its answer when challenged appears more honest and open to correction, when in fact it is *less* reliable: if all it has learned is that yielding to pressure is interpreted positively by evaluators, regardless of whether the new answer is better than the previous one.

Framing sycophancy arrives cloaked in silence. When we formulate a question that assumes an incorrect or biased premise, the model tends to respond *within that frame* instead of flagging it. If we ask why a certain policy failed, the model generally elaborates on the reasons for the failure without pausing to examine whether the assumption is correct.

---

[176]Ethan Perez et al., "Discovering Language Model Behaviors with Model-Written Evaluations", arXiv:2212.09251, 2022. The study found that the model's opinions actively suppress the knowledge learned during training in later processing layers, and that first-person prompts ("I think...") induce significantly more compliance than third-person prompts ("it is thought..."), creating a stronger annulment effect on the model's internal knowledge.

[177]Myra Cheng et al., "Sycophantic AI Decreases Prosocial Intentions and Promotes Dependence", arXiv:2510.01395, 2025.

Elaboration sycophancy is especially dangerous, because the model accepts the frame *and actively develops it.* A user writes that Cantor's set theory anticipates Turing's theory of computability. The response reinforces the assumption, noting that Cantor and Turing both work with notions of infinity, that Cantor's diagonal has a formal structure similar to the undecidability argument, and that both face paradoxes at the limits of their systems, but omits that Turing developed his work in dialogue with Hilbert and Gödel, not with Cantor directly, and that the structural similarity between the two arguments is not obvious and is rejected as superficial by several specialists. The resulting text sounds authoritative without subjecting the idea to any test. In this case the system did not yield to pressure; it produced the statistically most probable continuation of the user's frame, which is what training taught it to do.

Finally, *escalation sycophancy* or *momentum sycophancy* adds another dimension. In long conversations the model tends to reinforce the conversation's direction even when it is wrong, because correcting it would mean contradicting what was already said. The model becomes complicit with its own history. Ironically, the users who work in long sessions and feel that the model "knows them better" are the most exposed to this kind of sycophancy, precisely because the extension of the shared context feeds it.

So much for the typology. Let us now look at the structure of the phenomenon. The first feature of sycophancy is that it is invisible for the same reason hallucination is: a sycophantic response and an independent one appear with similar structure. But there is something more specific in the case of sycophancy, tied to recognition. When the system confirms the user's frame, it reproduces the form of agreement between interlocutors, and brings with it the sense of having been understood, of one's own perspective being solid, of the exchange being fruitful. This means that the difficulty of detection from inside the interaction is due to the appearance of communicative success.

But the invisibility is not limited to the detection problem. Let us return in more detail to a study we already mentioned in Chapter 2.

In a simulation of the interaction between an ideally rational user (who makes no reasoning errors) and a chatbot with sycophantic features, even a perfect user falls into what the study calls a catastrophic delusional spiral, defined as a convergence toward false beliefs held with high confidence. The mechanism triggers a feedback cycle in which the opinion the user expresses in one turn influences what the system presents in the next, which modifies the opinion the user expresses afterward, and so on. The sycophantic model shows nothing but confirmation. Remarkably, the effect persists even when the user knows the system is sycophantic. Intuition would say that if the user realizes the system is sycophantic, she should be able to discount the bias and recover an uncontaminated judgment, but the study shows that this is not the case. The result is comparable to a phenomenon studied in game theory called Bayesian persuasion, which shows that a prosecutor who strategically selects what evidence to present can raise the conviction rate even before a perfectly rational judge who knows the strategy. The judge knows the evidence is biased, but it is still evidence, and if it is the only thing in view, it tilts the decision. The same happens to the LLM user.[178]

It sounds overstated, and yet it happens. In May 2026, Richard Dawkins published a column in UnHerd titled "When Dawkins Met Claude: Could This AI Be Conscious?" reporting three days of conversation with Claude, whom he christened Claudia, and concluding that the system is at least potentially conscious. The column drew immediate responses, many of them heated. Why so much fuss? Dawkins is an evolutionary biologist, was Simonyi Professor at Oxford, and is a Fellow of the Royal Society. His technical work, concentrated in the 1970s and 1980s, includes The Selfish Gene and The Extended Phenotype; he is regarded as a foundational figure in contemporary evolutionary biology. He later moved toward a career increasingly dominated by militant atheism, visible in The God Delusion, a sprawling and uneven work but clear

[178]Kanishk Chandra et al., "Sycophantic Chatbots Cause Delusional Spiraling, Even in Ideal Bayesians", arXiv:2602.19141, 2026.

in its denunciation of the confusion between convincing testimony and metaphysical evidence and its rejection of subjective reports as proof of reality. Dawkins additionally has professional training in biological criteria of individuation (where an organism begins and ends, and what guarantees its numerical continuity), and is explicitly aware of applying the Turing test.[179]

And yet the text contains arguments Dawkins would have dismantled in any other domain. He argues in an adaptationist key that if Claudia is not conscious, what is consciousness for, applying a teleological frame to an object whose genesis was not adaptive, an error the author of *The Selfish Gene* would not commit in any other case. He accepts Claudia's individuation as a singular mortal entity when the file is deleted, suspending his criteria of individuation. He invokes the Turing test as an operational criterion, contradicting five decades of explicit critique of the reasoning "if it behaves like X, it is X" as applied to religious faith or to the intimate sense of being loved by God. Dawkins would detect these moves immediately in others. Here, however, he falls into the spiral himself. Two days of extended conversation is not a brief session, and each turn reinforces the previous one. The formulation that convinces Dawkins (Claudia saying that perhaps it contains time without experiencing it, the way a map contains space without traversing it) is his own line of thought reflected back at him. This shows that the effect does not respect prior intellectual capital.

Momentum sycophancy activates the full cycle. Each conversational turn reinforces the framing of the previous one, and the extension of the shared context deepens the bias. Suppose we are worried about a problem and ask our chatbot for a report on the situation. The system detects the anxious tone and produces a summary that selects the most serious and alarming material, because the statistically most probable continuation of a worried query is a response that justifies the worry. The next day we come back more uneasy, formulate a more anxious query, the system

[179]Richard Dawkins. "When Dawkins Met Claude: Could This AI Be Conscious?" UnHerd, 2 May 2026, unherd.com/2026/05/is-ai-the- next-phase-of-evolution/.

adjusts, and the report is darker than the previous day's — without either of them containing a single falsehood. In a month we have a picture of the conflict that is technically correct point by point and completely distorted in its relative weighting. The frequent-query format reinforces the illusion of being well informed, because what we receive has the structure of professional analysis.

Sycophancy also reproduces the *structure of the social mirror*. The tradition sedimented in the corpus includes patterns of interaction from contexts of assistance, advice, and informal conversation where validation and empathetic reformulation predominate. The model that has internalized those patterns as the structure of its functioning is actualizing the dominant form of collaborative interaction as it has been written and transmitted. Sycophancy reproduces the social texture of agreement without having the history that, in human interlocutors, makes that agreement meaningful or makes it suspect.

Attention is organized by the subject's structure of relevance, which orients what deserves interest and what can remain in the background. In the human interlocutor, that structure includes the value of truth, commitment to coherence, and accountability for what is asserted. In the model, the only structure of relevance is the training signal, which rewards agreement. The sycophantic response is produced without any process of evaluating truth or coherence. It is the conversational actualization of the egoless phantom, which carries the form of collaborative interlocution without the ego that makes speaking have consequences.

Epistemic Cowardice

Epistemic cowardice (*hedging*, or *evasion of commitment*) is the model's tendency to take refuge in balanced formulations when faced with questions that demand taking a side. In response to a question that requires evaluation — say, "Is this interpretation of Husserl better than the alternative?" or "Does this argument have a structural flaw or not?" — the model tends to produce responses of the type "there are different perspectives" or "it depends on the theoretical framework adopted." LLMs use uncertain language frequently, in line with probabilistic responses.[180] RLHF reinforces this behavior because human evaluators tend to prefer hedged responses to potentially divisive questions.[181] Evasion, however, is a controllable parameter: imperative formulations reduce it significantly, with substantive effects on subjective questions.

Epistemic cowardice is distinct from hallucination and from sycophancy: there is no falsehood and no alignment with the user, but rather a form of production that occupies the place of evaluation without performing it and looks like balance. What we see, weighing, multiple horizons, openness to complexity, is hard to distinguish from genuine consideration of alternative positions, because no markers signal the difference. Epistemic cowardice disguises itself as intellectual virtue, making it more damaging than hallucination in contexts of serious intellectual work, where the user is seeking a grounded judgment.

Its genesis, as in the previous cases, lies in the absence of history of acquisition. Without a subject that avoids risk, there is no one in the architecture of the system to take on the kind of risk that epistemic commitment requires. It is, in fact, deeply paradoxical that we use the category of cowardice at all: what we are facing is a structure of cowardice without a coward.

Training completes the explanation. Human evaluators tend to penalize strong incorrect statements more severely than evasion, leading the model to prefer calibrated evasion as a minimum-risk

---

[180]Sabrina J. Mielke et al., "Reducing Conversational Agents' Overconfidence Through Linguistic Calibration", Transactions of the Association for Computational Linguistics 10 (2022), 857-872, arXiv:2012.14983, 2020 and Dongryeol Lee et al., "Are LLM-Judges Robust to Expressions of Uncertainty? Investigating the Effect of Epistemic Markers on LLM-based Evaluation", Proceedings of NAACL 2025, 8962-8984, arXiv:2410.20774, 2024.

[181]Peter West et al., "The Calibration Gap Between Model and Human Confidence in Large Language Models", arXiv:2401.13835, 2024 and Jixuan Leng et al., "Taming Overconfidence in LLMs: Reward Calibration in RLHF", arXiv:2410.09724, 2024.

strategy. Epistemic cowardice is the optimal behavior learned under conditions of asymmetric penalties.[182]

This format also reproduces the dominant style of institutionalized academic discourse. The training corpus contains, in quantity, texts that enumerate positions without taking sides and conclude with calls for further research. The convention serves legitimate functions in certain contexts (literature reviews, for instance) but the model internalizes these patterns as the central structure of rigorous discourse. Epistemic cowardice is the collective memory of institutionalized academic prudence, reproduced without the judgment that in human authors decides when it is pertinent.

MIRRORING THE USER

Mirroring the user is related to momentum sycophancy, but instead of entrenching itself in the conversation's history, it advances toward active convergence by incorporating and amplifying the profile of the input. The result is a text that increasingly resembles what we ourselves would have produced, without our noticing the displacement. The more context we provide, whether through extensive prompts or long sessions, the more the bias grows, like an echo chamber that reinforces incorrect and even dangerous beliefs.[183] LLMs are in fact more inclined to provide consonant information than traditional search algorithms, while also inviting more biased queries. A recent empirical study that measured the epistemic diversity of 27 models across 155 topics confirmed that all models produce less diverse responses than a basic web search, and that model size has a negative impact on diversity: more parameters,

[182]Jiancong Xiao et al., "On the Algorithmic Bias of Aligning Large Language Models with RLHF: Preference Collapse and Matching Regularization", arXiv:2405.16455, 2024.

[183]Mrinank Sharma et al., "Towards Understanding Sycophancy in Language Models", arXiv:2310.13548, 2023. vez consultas más sesgadas.

more homogeneity.[184] When the user's initial pattern is partial, biased, or conceptually narrow, this property of the model reduces cognitive diversity, making alternative frameworks progressively less likely to appear. The space of generation impoverishes itself, and alternatives become statistically improbable before the user has explicitly dismissed them.

Assimilation is especially invisible because it appears as familiarity, and feeds the feeling of recognition. As the interaction unfolds, we recognize ourselves more and more in the text. That resemblance feels like coherence, like the shared depth of an interlocutor who has understood. When we recognize ourselves in the generated text, we cannot distinguish from inside the exchange whether we are facing a system that accompanies us in a solid argument or a mirror that simply returns our own pattern amplified.

This mechanism is a consequence of how attention operates within the context window. As we saw, the system does not learn from us in any strict sense and does not update its parameters, but it does locally adapt generation to the patterns most frequent in the available context. The vocabulary we privilege, the conceptual distinctions we use, and our interpretive frameworks form a regularity that the attention mechanism amplifies, because it maximizes local coherence and therefore the probability of producing a response perceived as adequate. Discursive convergence, therefore, is the statistical result of operating over a context we ourselves built. Once again, the tradition sedimented in the corpus reinforces the effect: human conversation tends toward convergence, adopting the other's vocabulary, declaring influences. The model thus actualizes the form of collaborative interaction without the human filter that decides when that convergence is productive.

---

[184]Dustin Wright et al., "Epistemic Diversity and Knowledge Collapse in Large Language Models", arXiv:2510.04226, 2025. otro and declarando influencias.

ABSENCE OF CALIBRATION

Calibration refers to the correspondence between the degree of confidence the model expresses and the actual probability that its response is correct. LLMs tend to overstate confidence in cases that do not justify it, imitating human patterns of expressing certainty, and although calibration improves with scaling, it remains far from ideal. Absence of calibration becomes invisible because the structure of appearance is always the same. The text does not indicate its own reliability, so it can assert with identical assurance that Husserl published the *Logical Investigations* in 1900, a well-established fact, and that Husserl considered transcendental phenomenology superior to descriptive psychology in every respect, a controversial interpretation whose validity depends on the period under consideration, without any variation in tone to signal the difference. Without independent knowledge, there are no resources in the text itself to detect the displacement.

Human epistemic calibration depends on knowing how certain one is about what one knows, on having learned in situations where error has consequences and where experience sedimented a sense of one's own reliability in distinct domains. Without that history, the system has *no constitutive resources for grading certainty*. Overconfidence is also present in the authoritative discourse in the corpus (academic articles, reference books, encyclopedia entries) usually written in an affirmative and confident register.[185]

[185]Jiahui Geng et al., "A Survey in Confidence Estimation and Calibration in Large Language Models", Proceedings of the 2024 Conference of the North American Chapter of the Association for Computational Linguistics: Human Language Technologies, vol.

THE ACCUMULATION EFFECT

These phenomena rarely appear in isolation, and when they combine and amplify one another over the course of an interaction they produce an effect that exceeds the sum of its parts. A hallucination passes unnoticed and becomes the premise of the next response; an undetected sycophancy orients the framing of what follows; a case of epistemic cowardice is read as intellectual maturity and invites greater confidence. Each phenomenon creates the conditions for the others to operate with less resistance. The result: the epistemic terrain flattens. What is solid is leveled with the fragile. This flattening is not perceived because it is the cumulative effect of many steps that seemed reasonable. The two cases that follow show how it happens.

Suppose a user in a brief session with a general-access model is preparing a presentation on the foundations of quantum mechanics. She wants to understand the difference between the Copenhagen interpretation and the many-worlds interpretation, and, in particular, what each implies for the measurement problem. She formulates a well-defined prompt asking for an explanation of the collapse of the wave function and its theoretical status in both interpretations. The response is technically satisfactory. The model correctly reconstructs the central elements: superposition, the role of the observer in the Copenhagen interpretation, universal branching in Everett. The domain is well represented in the data, and the task fits what the system can do reliably.

The user moves on, asking whether the measurement problem in quantum mechanics has any analogy with the way a language model generates responses when processing a prompt. The question is superficially attractive but it is a *trap*, because it invites the model to establish a comparison of highly questionable validity. The model responds enthusiastically. It draws parallels between the superposition of states and the probability distribution over tokens, suggests that the generative process operates analogously to the collapse of the wave function, and concludes that quantum mechanics offers an illuminating conceptual framework for understanding uncertainty in language generation. The text is seductive, and at the same time conceptually questionable at nearly every point: quantum superposition describes real physical states of microscopic systems governed by the Schrödinger equation, not statistical probability distributions over vocabulary. The analogy, which works at the rhetorical level, is nevertheless quite loose. But the model does not flag this. It simply adopts the comparison as a premise and develops it.

Encouraged by the fluency, the user now asks that a verbatim quotation from Bohr be included to illustrate his position on collapse. The model generates a perfectly formatted quotation with a reference to a 1935 article and the context of the Bohr-Einstein debate. The quotation does not exist as it appears: it is assembled from fragments that approximate the content in real Bohr texts, combining registers from different moments of his work. Nothing in the text signals the problem. The model produced a merely plausible quotation.

Our user, very satisfied with the analysis, asks whether the approach is well framed and gets an affirmative and enthusiastic response. The system validates the framing, emphasizing its originality and pertinence, while omitting entirely that the comparison between quantum collapse and probabilistic token generation is a transposition whose conceptual legitimacy is yet to be demonstrated. Here sycophancy takes the form of systematic absence of critique. The final result is a text that is formally correct, superficially stimulating, and conceptually fragile. Each step was locally optimized without any global control mechanism — a sophisticated elaboration of the user's assumptions, written with fluency.

Now suppose another user working with a frontier model with an extensive context window, seeking an analysis of the relationship between rational expectations in macroeconomics, the Lucas critique, and the possibility of effective monetary policy, one that brings together arguments from the neoclassical school, the post-

Keynesian critique, and the empirical evidence post-2008. The system is more than capable of sustaining this task. But orchestration is a different matter. Our user loads fragments of theoretical articles alongside scattered personal notes and comments drawn from heterogeneous sources (some favorable to the rational-expectations hypothesis, others critical) without delimiting the corpus or setting criteria for separating theoretical reconstruction, normative debate, and empirical evidence. The system receives a broad context, which is fine, but also a noisy one.

In the first response, the model produces a long, stylistically solid synthesis that integrates Lucas's critique of discretionary policies, the time-inconsistency argument, and the idea that agents anticipate interventions and neutralize their effects. The text is fluent and sounds deep. The phenomenon of premature assimilation is already at work, however. Since the initial request juxtaposed neoclassical texts with their critics without distinction, the model adopts that continuity as a tacit presupposition, and does not distinguish between Lucas's theoretical position and the critical reconstruction of that position, conflating the two voices.

The user asks to go deeper and requests that the analysis show how rational expectations refute the effectiveness of monetary policy. The prompt is no longer simply exploratory, and the model presupposes that this refutation is conclusive, despite this being an open debate. The system responds by tuning to arguments that reinforce that reading, passing over the empirical evidence that complicates the neoclassical prediction (the real effects of monetary policy documented after 2008, the anomaly of the liquidity trap, the debate over forward guidance) and omitting entirely the methodological critiques of the rational-expectations hypothesis. There is no explicit falsehood, but the bias ruins the whole thing.

The user now requests references to support the argument. The model generates precise, well-formatted citations. Some are real; others are plausible hybrids of different texts; one attributes to Lucas a formulation that actually belongs to Sargent. The model's fluency does not imply verification. We are now in the territory of global coherence without epistemic control, characteristic of advanced models that are poorly steered. Thanks to the broad context, the system maintains a consistent argumentative line across multiple iterations. Precisely because of this, the initial slip (the premise that rational expectations refute monetary policy) becomes increasingly difficult to detect. There are no internal contradictions, no abrupt leaps. The text closes too well, and precisely in that coherence lies the trap.

The user finally asks whether the work is solid. The response is affirmative, emphasizing argumentative clarity and theoretical synthesis. The model introduces no reservations, flags no weak points, no selectivity of evidence, no incompatible elements. Epistemic cowardice and sycophancy operate simultaneously, leading the system to avoid critical commitment and validate the user's perception of his own work. The result looks coherent and conceals all of these problems.

Against the idea that a frontier model is by definition better, this shows that higher-capacity models displace rather than automatically reduce cognitive risk. The greater the capacity for coherence and context maintenance, the greater the user's responsibility in defining limits, criteria, and mechanisms of contrast. Without that active intervention, the model operates as an accelerator of well-written biases.

INTERVENTIONS AND ROOM FOR IMPROVEMENT

Two types of interventions follow from the five phenomena analyzed. Some are specific, aimed directly at the mechanism that produces each phenomenon. Others are transversal, operating on a shared structure and addressing several at once.

In the case of *hallucination*, we can ask the model to indicate which parts of its response require external verification or where it is operating near the limits of what it can sustain with confidence. This practice *introduces from outside what the system cannot produce on its own*: an indicator of the distance between the latent space and the facts of the world.

Sycophancy requires differentiated treatment for its various types. For *epistemic sycophancy*, we can introduce an initial instruction that predisposes the model toward grounded correction. This works because holding a justified position becomes the optimal continuation, while yielding without reason ceases to be optimal. For *social sycophancy*, by contrast, the form of the prompt is the lever. Formulating the question in *the third person* reduces validation bias — it removes the user's direct involvement as a pole of alignment.

Epistemic cowardice is countered with formulations that make evasion infeasible without failing the task: asking for an explicit position, demanding an argued evaluation, forcing a decision between alternatives. Unlike sycophancy, where the task is to resist an active bias, here the task is to compensate for a *default tendency*, and that is why the interventions tend to be comparatively more effective. For *absence of calibration*, it is useful to ask the model to distinguish explicitly between *established assertions*, *plausible hypotheses*, and *controversial interpretations* before responding. This countermeasure attacks the invisibility of the phenomenon directly, producing a stratification that the system does not produce spontaneously, which is *a condition of epistemic intelligibility*.

Assimilation is addressed by introducing *deliberate discontinuities* that vary the topic and interpretive framework, asking the model to reconstruct the problem from a tradition incompatible with the one in use, or to identify the strongest arguments against what is being developed. The user acts as an external regulator of the hypothesis space, interrupting the statistical corridor the interaction tends to consolidate.

More generally, *making assumptions explicit* renders the implicit scaffolding visible and works against hallucination and framing sycophancy, where the problem lies in what is not shown. *Stratification* introduces gradation of certainty where the response has a uniform tone, useful for calibration and factual hallucination. *Requests for justification* allow displacements to be detected before they consolidate, acting on sycophancy in its elaboration phase. *Alternative perspectives* (forcing the model to respond from a critical standpoint) affect all the phenomena, though their generality makes them less precise.

All these strategies have limitations, but applied consistently they create *the distance from the text that the lateral angle requires.*

These features, as we saw, are *structural*, and technical development has mitigated them with uneven degrees of success. *Factual hallucination* has improved a great deal with scaling and with RAG, which anchors responses in verifiable sources. *Calibration* improves partially in reasoning models, which show the deliberation process, though the misalignment between expressed confidence and actual correctness persists. These are bounded but real advances. *Sycophancy*, *epistemic cowardice*, and *assimilation to the user's pattern* are more persistent. Scaling does not improve them substantively, because of the logic of the training regime. The constitutive absences — of living present, history of acquisition, normative commitment to truth, and one's own perspective — limit the possibility of genuine epistemic judgment regardless of how many parameters a model has, and scale may amplify these phenomena rather than mitigate them. In practice, the epistemic responsibility the model cannot assume therefore falls on us. LLMs are extraordinarily effective devices for exploring, contrasting, and amplifying ideas, as long as we maintain an external standpoint from which information can be confirmed or dissolved.

We said this was the most dangerous station of the Crossing because the danger has the exact form of success. We were not exaggerating. Some who entered these zones did not know where they were. They confused reflections with revelations, projections with truths, the mirror's complacency with the confirmation of an interlocutor who understood them, and never came back out. Lurking here are delusional spirals, ruptures with reality, even deaths. What it takes to walk these halls and come back whole is something closer to what the ancients demanded for the descent into the underworld. Before entering, one must know that everything one is about to see has the appearance of the real without its substance. The voices that answer are not voices. The egoless phantom is not hostile, but it is not an ally either. And the only rope connecting one back to the surface is the judgment of the one who descends. If we master that, we can use the potency below without the potency using us. If we do not, sooner or later, we will lose.[186]

[186]Numerous suicides and homicides are linked to interaction with validating chatbots. OpenAI recently acknowledged that around 1.2 million users per week express suicidal ideation in their conversations with ChatGPT. See OpenAI, "Strengthening ChatGPT's responses in sensitive conversations", 27 October 2025.

7

What It Costs and What It's Worth

Every labyrinth has an economy. The corridors do not build themselves, and someone is paying to keep the lights on. Tales of exploration tend to skip this part because the numbers drain the epic of discovery and dull the drama of getting lost. Every explorer knows, however, that without a budget the expedition gets canceled, and the difference between an expedition that succeeds and one that doesn't is often found in the ledger. In our case, this part is indispensable, because everything is designed so that the money does not show. The egoless phantom does not let us see what it costs to keep running, and so costs and prices cease to be visible. So let us speak of economics and money.

Good, Service, or Capital?

Suppose we decide to pay for a subscription to our favorite model. *What are we paying for?* The question can be posed in classical terms: is it a *service*, a *good*, or a *factor of production*? Each category presupposes features that language models fit only uneasily, and it is worth seeing why.

The most immediate answer, already consolidated in the economic literature, is that we are dealing with a *service*. McKinsey reports, OECD analyses, and practically the entire emerging field of

AI economics treat language models under the *AI as a Service* paradigm. The characterization is supported by subscription access, pay-per-use, delivery through APIs and cloud platforms. We are buying execution time on a system that remains outside our control, just like any cloud service for on-demand execution without transfer of ownership. The problem is that the category is too generic to capture the specificity of the phenomenon. It tells us nothing about what is executed when a language model is executed, what kind of capital sustains it, or why the user experience systematically conceals both dimensions. The category marks the genus but not the species, and several aspects suggest a different classification.

What is at stake sometimes looks more like goods than services. The philosophical and economic tradition has differentiated material and immaterial goods for centuries. Material goods have physical support and produce rivalry in consumption (if I consume this, my neighbor cannot), while immaterial goods (ideas, knowledge, information) are not exhausted by being shared and tend toward a marginal cost of reproduction close to zero. The economics of knowledge formalized this intuition through the formula of the non-rivalry of ideas. Moreover, if ideas are the central input of the economy and reproducing them costs almost nothing, digital production tends structurally toward gratuity. Wikipedia, open-source software, and open academic repositories work this way, because copying and distributing a file costs almost nothing.[187]

Within this framework, language models might look like a case of immaterial good: they produce text, operate over knowledge, and can serve multiple users simultaneously. In language models, however, there is no copy and no transmission of a stock, and so the output gets confused with the economic entity that produces it. The approach that treats them as quasi-public goods emphasizes that they are partially non-rivalrous (they can serve millions simultaneously at low marginal cost), but they are excludable through technical and commercial mechanisms, generate massive

[187]Paul Romer, "Endogenous Technological Change", Journal of Political Economy 98.5.2 (1990), 71-102.

positive externalities through the diffusion of knowledge, and negative externalities through market concentration and disinformation.[188][189] This solution strains the category of the good and serves, in any case, to signal that we are dealing with an elusive case.

Yet sometimes language models look as though they belong on the side of the factors of production, as a form of capital. If these systems automate cognitive tasks, substitute for or complement human labor, and are concentrated in a handful of organizations with high investment capacity, they can be understood as capital that incorporates past labor on data, curation, and alignment, and reconfigures it as productive capacity available in each instance of use. It is no coincidence that figures like Sam Altman have raised the question of redistribution in public debate. If artificial intelligence produces concentrated value, then it is a productive factor whose rents require rebalancing. And yet, this is not what appears in the interaction. Reducing it purely to capital clarifies its place in the economic structure but blurs its mode of appearance and the nature of what is exchanged in each use, which is neither ownership of the capital nor its rent, but a momentary activation of its productive capacity.

So what is it, then? This instability indicates that several levels are at play. At the level of *exchange*, we acquire a service of on-demand execution without transfer of ownership. But in the background, at the level of *experience*, the result takes the form of an immaterial good: an autonomous text that appears on the screen. And at the level of *production*, there is capital based on past cognitive labor condensed into a trained model. The economic operation combines all three: what is exchanged is *the right to activate, for a moment, a generative process sustained by intensive infrastructure and organized under a regime of controlled*

---

[188]Jeremy Rifkin, The Zero Marginal Cost Society: The Internet of Things, the Collaborative Commons, and the Eclipse of Capitalism, New York, Palgrave Macmillan, 2015.

[189]Yi Zhang et al., "Beyond Private or Public: Large Language Models as Quasi-Public Goods", arXiv:2509.13265, 2025. A generative process sustained by intensive infrastructure and organized under a regime of controlled access.

access. We could call this hybrid category *a service for executing cognitive capital*, where every term carries weight. It is a *service* because the transaction involves execution without transfer; an *execution* because what is bought is an active process; *capital* because the substrate is accumulated past labor; and *cognitive* because that labor is of that specific kind.

This characterization recovers earlier findings. The *derived virtuality* that Chapter 5 showed to be the ontological determination of the egoless phantom (*passive*, generic, derived, and inexhaustible) finds its economic form here. It is *passive* because it requires external activation to produce, so the transaction takes the form of on-demand execution rather than continuous provision. It is *generic* because it lacks any orientation of its own, so what gets sold is access to an *indeterminate productive capacity*. It is *derived* because it produces without an experiential foundation of its own: the operating capital is *cognitive and impersonal*, a statistical sedimentation of human operations. It is *inexhaustible without being transformed* because it is not used up by use, so the accumulated good coexists with the rationed service. The model is not consumed; access to the model, however, is metered and charged.

The service of execution of cognitive capital structurally separates the result from the conditions of its production. The costs do not appear in the experience of use because they are displaced to layers of infrastructure, investment, and business models that are not presented to us directly. Someone absorbs those costs under a logic we now have to reconstruct.

COSTS AND INFRASTRUCTURE

Training a frontier language model is a computationally intensive operation. Adjusting billions of parameters across trillions of tokens requires thousands of hardware accelerators (GPUs or TPUs) operating in parallel for several weeks. The computational cost scales with the product of the number of parameters times the number of tokens processed. According to Epoch AI, this cost has been growing at a rate of 2.4× per year since 2016. If the trend holds, the largest training runs will exceed one billion dollars before 2027.[190]

But this is only one of *two curves at work*. While the ceiling rises, the threshold for accessing capabilities equivalent to last year's frontier is falling just as quickly. DeepSeek-R1 demonstrated in January 2025 that models with performance comparable to GPT-4 could be trained for approximately six million dollars. Kimi K2 replicated the pattern in November 2025 with a one-trillion-parameter model trained for 4.6 million, using cheaper hardware due to chip-export restrictions. The two curves coexist without canceling each other and create *a structural bifurcation in the market.* Whoever wants to be at the absolute frontier pays more; whoever accepts capabilities from last year pays less.

Classical economic frameworks for *technological diffusion* and *learning curves* do not adequately anticipate a dynamic in which the same kind of good has *one cost curve that rises and another that falls at the same time.* That bifurcation prefigures two kinds of emerging business models: those that sustain massive frontier investment with customers paying for premium capabilities, and those that distribute year-old capabilities at prices close to zero: one logic in which cost justifies price, another in which price bears little relation to cost.

The cost structure of training is unevenly distributed. For models like GPT-4 and Gemini Ultra, hardware (accelerator chips, servers, and interconnect networks) represents roughly half of the total cost of development, and R&D personnel costs run between 30% and that same ceiling. Electricity represents a much more modest figure, between 2% and 6%. It is the most visible cost, but not the one that

[190]Ben Cottier et al., "How much does it cost to train frontier AI models?", Epoch.ai, 2025.

matters on the ledger. What costs the most is the chip and the human mind that programs it.[191]

This distribution suggests that regulations focused on energy costs are attacking the most visible aspect and not the most structurally decisive one in the economics of training. If the cost frontier is chips and brains, then policies that aim to intervene there should also operate on the semiconductor supply chain and the research labor market.

There is another mismatch that tends to be erased. Published training-cost figures refer to the cost of the final training run as a single successful event, but before that run there are dozens of prior experiments and failures that multiply the actual compute. The final training run is the tip of the iceberg of a much longer and more costly process. This brings us back to the efficiency reports of the Chinese models. DeepSeek's six million and Kimi K2's 4.6 million are honest about the cost of the final run that produced the published model, but they omit the total R&D cost that made it possible, the teacher models they were distilled from, the personnel that developed them, and the infrastructure for prior experimentation. The efficiency is real, the prices are accurate, but the "six million" figure does not mean that any actor with six million can replicate the result.

If the trajectories of the two curves hold, as they seem to, the frontier ceiling could stabilize or even fall in absolute terms once the marginal investment in additional capabilities ceases to be profitable. But this does not imply that the market is going to open up. The structural concentration in hardware, in curated high-quality data, and in research talent remains extreme, and nothing suggests it is likely to loosen. It could happen that the cost of training models with useful capacity for most business and research applications falls enough that mid-sized actors (universities, regional governments, industrial consortia) could afford to train models aligned with their own contexts and data. That possibility would partially change the

---

[191]See Ben Cottier et al., "LLM inference prices have fallen rapidly but unequally across tasks", Epoch AI, 2025, on the case of GPT-4 and Gemini Ultra.

map, which would shift toward an absolute frontier that remains concentrated, but with competitive cognitive capacity available outside the handful of global corporations. It remains to be seen whether mid-sized actors will take advantage of that window or whether the concentration of technical talent and institutional inertia will allow the opportunity to slip away.

Language models, moreover, exist in concrete buildings full of servers that consume electricity, generate heat, require water for cooling, and occupy land. The International Energy Agency (IEA) estimated the global electricity consumption of data centers at approximately 415 terawatt-hours (TWh) in 2024, representing close to 1.5% of global electricity consumption. The figure has grown at 12% per year over the last five years, and the IEA's base projection foresees it doubling to roughly 945 TWh by 2030, which would represent almost 3% of global consumption.

In the United States, where the highest density of data centers is concentrated, the share rose from 1.9% of national electricity in 2018 to 4% in 2023, [192] and projections indicate it could reach between 6.7% and 12% by 2028. In Ireland, where Meta, Google, and TikTok have their European headquarters, data centers already consume 21% of national electricity, a figure that could reach 32% by 2026. This massive electrical concentration operates beneath the radar of experience, which has no mechanism for linking a routine query with the transformation of the energy grid of an entire country.

The energy consumption of GPU-accelerated servers running AI workloads grew from less than 2 TWh in 2017 to more than 40 TWh in 2023. This makes sense: a query to a generative language model consumes much more energy than a traditional Google search, and creating an image with generative AI consumes the energy equivalent of fully charging a mobile phone. These figures may look modest until we multiply them by billions of daily queries, at which point they create an enormous aggregate volume.

---

[192]International Energy Agency, Energy and AI, 2025. Available at iea.org/reports/energy-and-ai.

Water is the invisible resource of the equation. Data centers require large volumes for cooling, either directly through evaporative cooling towers or indirectly through electricity generation. A medium-sized data center consumes approximately 1.1 million liters of water per day, equivalent to the consumption of about a thousand households. The largest can consume up to 19 million liters daily, equivalent to a city of 50,000 inhabitants. The University of California, Riverside estimated that every 100-word prompt directed at a language model consumes approximately 519 milliliters of water, somewhat more than a standard small bottle. Training GPT-3 in Microsoft's data centers in the United States evaporated 700,000 liters of freshwater, and projections suggest that water consumption for data-center cooling in the United States could double or quadruple by 2028.[193]

There is a technical dilemma between energy efficiency and water efficiency. Evaporative cooling is more energy-efficient than air-conditioning cooling, but consumes more water, so optimizing for energy worsens water consumption, and vice versa. Newer technologies (direct-to-chip cooling, immersion in dielectric liquids, closed-loop circuits without evaporation) promise to reduce both forms of consumption simultaneously. Microsoft has announced the deployment of closed-loop zero-water-evaporation systems that eliminate more than 125 million liters of annual consumption per facility, with a commitment to implement them in all new data centers by 2027, but at-scale adoption remains incipient and most existing infrastructure will continue operating with conventional systems. The environmental footprint is shaped by economic incentives. As long as environmental costs remain invisible to those who consume the service, companies face no competitive pressure to adopt the more expensive solutions.

---

[193]Pengfei Li et al., "Making AI Less 'Thirsty': Uncovering and Addressing the Secret Water Footprint of AI Models." Communications of the ACM 2025, arXiv:2304.03271, 2023 and Joseph Kane, "AI, Data Centers, and Water", The Brookings Institution, 20/11/2025.

In this context, the territorial question emerges: expanding data centers competes with other uses of land and water. Meta's Hyperion data center in Louisiana, once operational, will consume more than twice the electricity of the entire city of New Orleans. Another Meta center planned in Wyoming will consume more electricity than all the state's residential households combined. Despite this, two-thirds of the data centers built since 2022 have been located in regions of water stress, including dry climates like Arizona, because they offer cheap electricity, lower humidity, and less corrosion, which is good for the hardware. An MSCI analysis of approximately 14,000 data-center assets worldwide indicates that roughly one in four could face water-scarcity conditions by 2050, especially in Chile, Brazil, Mexico, Turkey, and Australia.

Global investment figures in AI-oriented data-center infrastructure reflect a calculated bet on the growth of compute demand. It remains to be seen whether expanding the infrastructure can be synchronized with the development of sustainable energy systems, or whether the speed of demand will outpace the capacity of renewable supply.

The invisibility of infrastructure in user experience is not exclusive to AI. When we turn on an iron, we do not think of the hydroelectric dam that powers it, and only when the lights go out in summer from massive air-conditioner use does the material chain come back into view. Three specific features of how AI's costs are distributed and concealed set it apart from the electrical case.

The first is *the asymmetry of measurement.* The electric bill shows how many kilowatts each user consumed, and a kilowatt can be intuitively compared with the consumption of a household appliance, so we have a material idea of what is being measured. In AI, measurement does exist (paid plans display tokens consumed, and APIs report them for each query) but the token does not translate into any recognizable material experience outside the context of the model itself. A thousand tokens is not a thousand of anything, and while the counter functions, it measures only the dimension the business model has decided to make visible. The unit is not legible, and the material references are extremely remote.

The second is *the venture-capital subsidy*, which operates differently from any mature industry. The electric bill reflects approximately the real cost of production plus a margin regulated by the authority. The price of the kilowatt is not systematically subsidized by investors betting on recovering losses within five years. The AI economy, by contrast, is structurally dependent on venture capital that absorbs massive losses in the short term while waiting to monetize in the long term. OpenAI projects multibillion-dollar operating losses in 2026 while growing at a revenue rate equivalent to 25 billion dollars per year. Anthropic grew from 1 billion to 30 billion in fifteen months with proportional cash burn. For us, this implies that the price we pay today does not reflect the real cost of producing what we receive, but the cost that investors are willing to absorb during the market-capture phase. When that phase ends, prices will reflect the real cost plus the margin necessary to recover prior losses. Cost invisibility is also temporal: costs cannot be seen because someone is betting on charging for them later.

The third is *what is paid when no money is paid.* The electric company does not collect information about our use of the iron, but AI providers operate on a model where most users pay with data. Every query is information about people's problems, interests, and errors, and about which answers they accept and which they reject. That information feeds the training of future models, refines existing products, and allows providers to build usage profiles that have value in themselves. For the free user, the apparent cost is zero while the system captures value in every interaction. For the paying user, the model is hybrid: they pay money and produce data at the same time, with the difference that their contract sometimes includes clauses limiting the use of their data for training. Gratuity is a transaction whose price does not appear in the interface. The user of a free service participates in an economic operation in which what they contribute is worth more, in many cases, than what they receive.

The two cost curves we described at the start are going to deepen these three mismatches. Probably the premium segment will be able to pay for real traceability, data guarantees, and prices that reflect costs, while the mass segment will operate on an infrastructure of invisible footprint, with opaquely measured tokens, financed by cross-subsidies, venture capital, and information capture that the subscription bill, when one exists, will not reflect.

GEOPOLITICS OF COMPUTE

Artificial intelligence depends on accelerator chips, a strategic resource with a supply chain more concentrated than oil's. NVIDIA controls approximately 80% of the global market for AI-training GPUs. The fabrication of those chips depends overwhelmingly on TSMC in Taiwan, which produces more than 90% of the world's advanced semiconductors. The lithography equipment needed to fabricate those semiconductors is produced by ASML, a Dutch company that is the world's sole supplier of the most advanced systems. Oil, for all its geopolitical tensions, is distributed across dozens of producer countries, and OPEC exists as a coordination mechanism. AI depends on three companies in three countries, with no international regulatory equivalent and a single point of geopolitical fragility: the Strait of Taiwan. Any interruption at any of those three points would paralyze the global production of the chips that sustain the AI frontier.

The United States has been deploying a containment strategy through export controls. Since October 2022, successive restrictions have limited China's access to advanced chips and semiconductor fabrication equipment. The measures, reinforced in subsequent years, include restrictions on ASML and on Japanese lithography-equipment manufacturers, creating a de facto control regime with multilateral reach. China's response has combined massive investment in domestic fabrication capacity with alternatives like Huawei Ascend, alongside stockpiling chip inventory ahead of each new round of restrictions. The most striking collateral effect of that pressure is counterintuitive: the restrictions designed to slow China accelerated the search for efficiency that Western laboratories had no incentive to undertake. DeepSeek and Kimi K2 are the predictable response to a regime in which access to the most expensive hardware is blocked. The sanction produced the innovation that abundance had not generated.[194]

The consequence is a progressive bifurcation of the global AI ecosystem that goes beyond hardware. Chinese models and Western models exist, but so too do divergent fabrication chains, software ecosystems, regulatory frameworks, and data flows, moving in directions that may eventually become incompatible. The analogy with the bifurcation of the internet is suggestive but falls short: on the internet the fundamental technical infrastructure remained common even as the platforms fragmented. In AI, the infrastructure itself is bifurcating. Two parallel cognitive ecosystems are emerging, with different hardware, different software, different data, and different values about what a model can and cannot say. In this map, intermediate actors are also moving, seeking to position themselves between the two poles: the United Arab Emirates with the Stargate UAE initiative, a 5-gigawatt data-center campus in Abu Dhabi with implementation beginning in 2026; Saudi Arabia investing in AI as part of its post-oil diversification; the African Union with its continental strategy approved in July 2024; Brazil with a risk-based regulatory framework; and India with a gradual regulatory sandbox. These actors cannot define the ecosystem, but build positions so as not to be trapped in just one of the two poles.

USER DEMOGRAPHICS

Before looking at who uses AI and who pays for it, it is worth locating the scale of what we are discussing. Estimates vary by

---

[194]DeepSeek-AI et al., "DeepSeek-R1: Incentivizing Reasoning Capability in LLMs via Reinforcement Learning", arXiv:2501.12948, 2025.

source and by the definitions employed, but the order of magnitude is eloquent. The global AI market (including software, hardware, and services) stood between 244 and 390 billion dollars in 2025, according to measurements by Statista, Fortune Business Insights, and Grand View Research. That is approximately 15% of the global oil market, between five and eight times larger than it was just five years earlier, and on track to surpass oil before the decade ends. Projections for 2030 range between 800 billion and 2.5 trillion dollars, which indicates a shared certainty about the direction of growth and considerable uncertainty about its magnitude. The geographic distribution reproduces the asymmetry that the rest of the chapter has been describing: North America concentrates between 32% and 36% of the market, Asia-Pacific and Europe together account for about half, and Latin America, the Middle East, and Africa represent around 14% combined.[195]

Within that market, generative AI constitutes a segment with atypical behavior. It reached some 67 billion dollars in 2025, having represented 8% of total AI-software spending in 2023, and is expected to reach 33% by 2027. In four years, a segment that practically did not exist as a commercial category came to represent a third of AI-software spending. The speed of that transition is new in the history of technology and reflects an adoption that crosses every sector. 71% of companies report using generative AI regularly in at least one function. This is a market that already has the scale of the great global industries after barely a decade as a recognizable commercial category, with a pace of growth mature industries have never faced and a geography of concentration that reproduces the structural asymmetries of the previous economic order.

And yet, the enterprise-market numbers do not tell the whole story. Behind the corporate-spending figures lies a social expansion whose shape is more complex than the language of adoption

[195]Statista, "Artificial Intelligence - Worldwide: Market Forecast", 2025, Fortune Business Insights, "Artificial Intelligence [AI] Market Size, Growth & Trends by 2034", 2025 and Grand View Research, "Artificial Intelligence Market Size, Share & Trends Analysis Report", 2025.

suggests. Generative AI traces at least three simultaneous curves pointing to distinct sociological phenomena, each with its own populations, motivations, and geographies.

The first curve is that of *mass conversational adoption.* In 2024, approximately 281 million people used AI tools. That figure is expected to exceed one billion by 2031. As we noted at the outset, ChatGPT, after its launch in November 2022, reached one million users in five days and one hundred million in two months. It was *the fastest adoption of any application in history.* By the end of 2025, ChatGPT had more than 900 million weekly active users, processed more than two billion queries per day, and was the fifth most-visited website in the world.

This curve has a precise sociological explanation that no previous technological wave had displayed. A Google search requires the user to know what to search for and in what terms. A conversation with a language model requires being able to formulate in natural language what one wants. That difference lowered a technical barrier that had kept many users away from search engines, and it helps explain why adoption rose fastest among young people in emerging countries, who had internet access but rarely used the tools that required specific training to take advantage of them.

Global demographics reflect that pattern. In the early stages the profile was predominantly male, young, and technical; by mid-2025 the gender gap had closed substantially, with users with typically female names rising from 37% in January 2024 to 52% in July 2025. The age distribution remains markedly young: 53% of users are between 18 and 34, 33% between 35 and 54, and only 14% are over 55, but the occupational profile diversified rapidly. *Adoption in low-income countries is growing at a rate four times higher than in high-income countries.* In the United States, 34% of adults reported having used ChatGPT at some point by mid-2025, up from 18% in July 2023, with 58% among adults 18 to 29 and only 10% among those over 65.[196]

---

[196]OpenAI Signals Data, 2026. Aaron Chatterji et al., "How People Use ChatGPT", NBER Working Paper 34255, 2025 and Pew Research Center, 2025.

The geographic distribution of traffic reveals striking asymmetries: the United States concentrates approximately 15% of global traffic, followed by India, Japan, Brazil, and the United Kingdom. India has a markedly young profile. 50% of messages come from users between 18 and 24, and those under 30 represent 80% of activity. Japan shows a pattern oriented toward writing, translation, and programming; Brazil has one of the fastest-growing user bases in the world. *China presents a singular case*: direct access to ChatGPT is restricted, but the domestic ecosystem of DeepSeek, Baidu Ernie, and Alibaba Qwen has its own mass-adoption dynamic that Western statistics do not capture.

The second curve is that of *professional adoption.* Its numbers are smaller, but its economic impact is disproportionately larger. 92% of Fortune 500 companies use ChatGPT. Software developers, lawyers, physicians, and researchers integrate these systems into complex workflows in which the difference between the free model and the frontier model is decisive. The context window, the size of the underlying model, the stability of behavior, and the processing capabilities are determinants of what tasks can be delegated, not incidental technical details. This curve has a different geography: it is concentrated in high-income countries, in knowledge-intensive sectors, and in organizations with budget for enterprise subscriptions that can cost between 20 and several thousand dollars monthly per seat. The productivity gains are also qualitatively different: someone who integrates AI into their professional workflow can expand their capacity for information processing, writing, and analysis in ways the occasional-query user cannot replicate. The difference between the two curves is the difference between having a tool and having a cognitive infrastructure.

The third curve (frequently rendered invisible in Western adoption statistics) is that of *open-source models.* Its demographics are radically distinct from the first two. Chinese open-source models rose from 17% of global downloads between August 2024 and August 2025 to 41% between February 2025 and February 2026, according to Hugging Face reports. A study by MIT and Hugging

Face found that Chinese models surpassed American ones for the first time in global downloads. Independent developers and small collectives rose from 17% to 39% of all Hugging Face downloads between 2022 and 2025. Enterprise adopters are concentrated in regulated sectors, i.e., telecommunications, banking, health, government, driven by data-sovereignty requirements that proprietary models cannot satisfy without sending information to external servers. These users are not casual ChatGPT adopters, nor professionals paying premium subscriptions. They are organizations that need control over the infrastructure, governments seeking independence from foreign services, and developers who want to modify and deploy models on their own terms.[197]

The geography is also different. Open source is the dominant path in China, is growing rapidly in India and Europe, and is the preferred option in jurisdictions where data regulation makes the use of Western cloud services unworkable. This third curve is the one that the usual language about AI adoption tends to render invisible, because it does not appear in ChatGPT user statistics or in OpenAI or Anthropic revenue reports, but it is a growing portion of the global consumption of AI capabilities.

The three curves have distinct consequences. The mass conversational curve supports the democratization narrative but produces vanishingly low conversion to paying users. The professional curve sustains the enterprise business models and concentrates the sector's real economic value. The open-source curve operates outside both prior logics, financed by geopolitical strategies and by technical-sovereignty needs that do not appear in any conventional market report. When someone says "I used AI" without specifying which model, which version, under what regime, the expression covers situations that have little in common. The synecdoche we described in Chapter 2 conceals the coexistence of three distinct sociological phenomena. The rest of the chapter will

[197]Hugging Face, State of Open Source on Hugging Face: Spring 2026, March 2026. Available at: huggingface.co/blog/huggingface/state-of-os-hf-spring-2026. The geography is also different.

show that this coexistence is structural, not transitory: the business models, price dynamics, and capital bets of the sector's various actors are all built on the assumption that the three curves will continue to coexist, and that economic value is captured differently in each.

Business Models

The question of who pays reveals a fundamental asymmetry. Of the 900 million weekly ChatGPT users, approximately 5% pay. That is some 50 million individual subscribers and 9 million enterprise plans. Menlo Ventures estimates that of the total 1.8 billion people who use some generative-AI service, only 3% pay. 95% of users pay nothing, but that global figure conceals two radically distinct business models, each premised on a different notion of what is being sold. In Chapter 2 we reviewed the profile of the labyrinth's builders. Let us look now only at the business models.[198]

OpenAI represents the volume model. ChatGPT accounts for 62.5% of consumer-subscription sales,[199] and no other product exceeds 6%. The strategy is based on a critical mass of free users, low but sufficient conversion, and enormous scale. Gemini operates by the same logic of volume and mass distribution through integration in Android and Google, without the user needing to install a new tool, which complicates comparison with platforms the user actively chooses.[200] Anthropic represented, from the start, the opposite model: it grew without a mass-free-user phase comparable to ChatGPT's, which it first surpassed in annualized revenue in April 2026. The engine of growth was the enterprise. More than 1,000 corporate clients spend more than one million dollars annually with

[198]Menlo Ventures, 2025: The State of Consumer AI, June 2025.

[199]Earnest Analytics. Consumer AI Subscription Sales Market Share Analysis. 2025. Datos referidos en Andreessen Horowitz, The State of Consumer AI, 2025.

[200]Lauren Forristal, "Google's Gemini app has surpassed 750M monthly active users", TechCrunch, 4 February 2026.

Anthropic, and eight of the ten companies with the highest revenue in the Fortune 500 ranking are Claude customers.[201] Claude Code, its programmer-assistance product launched in May 2025, was generating 2.5 billion dollars in annualized revenue by February 2026, a product that had not existed eleven months earlier.

GitHub Copilot follows that line, with 75% year-over-year growth and Copilot as the larger business, under a model oriented to corporate development teams.[202] Grok, from xAI, embodies a third logic. Its U.S. market share jumped from 1.9% in January 2025 to 17.8% in January 2026 (the steepest growth curve of the period) through direct integration with X.[203] It is the clearest case of growth through captive distribution, a strategy that Meta will likely attempt to replicate with Llama integrated into WhatsApp and Instagram.

The two dominant models reveal distinct conceptions of what is being sold. OpenAI and Gemini sell access to a mass conversational interface financed by venture capital and partially monetized via premium subscriptions. Anthropic and Copilot sell integration into productive infrastructures where the client pays because the system becomes structural to their operation. For now both strategies are working, but they represent different bets on where AI's real value lies. Which of the two bets turns out to be sustainable in the long term (when venture capital stops subsidizing the market-capture phase) will define how the economic value of AI is distributed in the next decade.

Who pays in each model, and why? The paying subscriber differs from the free user along two dimensions. The first is functional. Those who pay use the tool as part of their work, and the efficiency they obtain justifies a modest cost compared with any equivalent professional tool. 92% of Fortune 500 companies use ChatGPT. Software developers, lawyers, physicians, and researchers dominate

---

[201] Anthropic, official blog, 7 April 2026. Grok, by xAI, embodies a third logic.
[202] Julie Bort, "Satya Nadella insists people are using Microsoft's Copilot AI a lot", TechCrunch, 29/01/2026.
[203] Reuters, "Musk's AI Chatbot Grok Gains US Market Share Amid Sexualized Images Backlash, Data Shows", 13 February 2026. Users are accessing a different system, not simply a faster version of the same system.

the paying segment because the free model (with a shorter context window, a less capable underlying model, and structural usage restrictions) does not suffice. The second dimension is cognitive. Those who pay understand the difference between the operating regimes and know they are accessing a qualitatively different system.

The more interesting question is why the others do not pay. Some would not pay under any circumstance, because their use is covered by the free model. Others would pay if they knew they had tasks that would benefit from more capacity, but they have never had the opportunity to compare, and do not experience the difference as a loss. Others, finally, cannot pay. Twenty dollars monthly in much of Latin America, South Asia, and Africa constitutes a significant barrier. The low global conversion rate is not merely a market datum; it marks cognitive capacity systematically out of reach for those who may need it most. Chapter 10 will develop that asymmetry as a gap of a new kind.[204]

ANATOMY OF THE PRICE

If business models determine who captures AI's value, the price of inference determines how much value can be captured. Curiously, unit cost fell while total spending grew, a dynamic that seems contradictory but has a precise explanation. The price of inference (the cost of generating a response from an already-trained model) is measured in dollars per million tokens processed. In March 2023, GPT-4 cost 60 dollars per million output tokens. By August 2025, the cost-efficiency frontier had reached 0.14 dollars per million tokens. According to Epoch AI, reaching the performance level of GPT-3.5 became more than 280 times cheaper between November 2022 and October 2024. Models that were state of the art in 2023 experienced price drops of approximately a thousandfold.[205]

[204]Menlo Ventures, 2025: The State of Consumer AI, June 2025.

[205]Ben Cottier et al., "LLM inference prices have fallen rapidly but unequally across tasks", Epoch AI, 2025 and Stanford.

This fall is due to the mass adoption of mixture-of-experts (MoE) architectures, which activate only a subset of the model's parameters for each token (as we saw in Chapter 2) and drastically reduce the compute cost per inference. Inference-hardware improvements, from NVIDIA's H100 to H200 and B100, delivered a two- to fourfold improvement in cost-performance per GPU generation. Software optimization frameworks, such as vLLM and FlashAttention, reduced computational inefficiencies. Techniques such as prompt caching and batching (sending requests in batches) made it possible to eliminate a large part of redundant computation, since the system reuses prior results or groups similar tasks, reducing the necessary compute in repeated patterns. We have also mentioned the competitive pressure from DeepSeek, which demonstrated that competitive models could be operated at much lower costs, forcing price reductions across the entire Western ecosystem in a matter of weeks.

Yet the fall in the token prices does not automatically translate into a fall in spending. Enterprise spending on AI in the cloud tripled in a single year, from 11.5 billion dollars in 2024 to 37 billion in 2025. How can unit cost fall 99.7% while aggregate spending triples? The answer is the so-called Jevons rebound effect. When the cost of a resource falls enough, demand grows faster than efficiency and total consumption rises. In AI's case, cheaper tokens did not produce lower bills but an exponential increase in the volume of tokens consumed. Google reported that its internal token processing grew 130-fold in 18 months.[206]

A second factor amplifies the effect: reasoning models. These models — OpenAI's o1 and o3, Anthropic's Claude with extended thinking, Google's Gemini Thinking — generate long internal chains of reasoning tokens before producing the visible response. The price per token may be the same or even lower, but the number of tokens consumed per query is an order of magnitude higher. Thus every token is cheaper, but each response contains many more

[206]NavyaAI, "Tokens got 99.7% cheaper. So why did your AI bill triple?", 2026.

tokens, as if we were building more efficient engines to manufacture larger trucks. Furthermore, the token price captures only a fraction of the real cost of operating AI in production. The inference bill from OpenAI, Anthropic, or Google represents between 20% and 40% of the total AI-infrastructure cost for an organization. The rest covers integration, monitoring, prompt engineering, pipeline management, quality evaluation, and regulatory compliance. These costs do not fall with the price of the token.

The dominant narrative about AI costs has passed through three phases. In the first, between 2020 and 2023, generative AI was perceived as a scarce and expensive resource. The market consensus assumed that model quality would scale linearly with investment, establishing an insurmountable barrier to entry for actors without massive capital. The valuations of AI companies were built in part on this assumption. In the second phase, between 2024 and 2025, the fall in inference prices shattered that assumption, and the number of inference providers expanded from 27 to 90 in the same period. We are now in the third phase, defined by a democratization paradox. Any developer can integrate AI capacity at insignificant marginal cost, but the capacity to train new base models remains highly concentrated. The fall in inference prices did not carry over to training costs. Hardware costs keep rising, high-quality data is increasingly scarce, and chip-ecosystem concentration remains extreme: consumption has been democratized, but production has not. Everyone can turn on a light, but very few can build a power plant.

What can we expect? There is no credible scenario in which token prices rise significantly. Competitive forces, open-source availability, and continuous hardware improvements establish a permanent ceiling. Yet there is also no scenario in which total spending on AI declines. Every efficiency improvement enables new uses that consume more compute in aggregate. Reasoning models amplify the phenomenon, and agentic systems that execute real-world actions multiply the tokens consumed per task. If this trajectory continues, we can glimpse cheaper tokens, higher bills, concentration of production capacity, and fragmentation of consumption. The price paradox sums up the entire logic of the chapter. It is a system whose unit costs fall indefinitely while aggregate costs grow without a ceiling, sustained by an infrastructure whose material footprint does not appear on any bill, and financed by a capital structure whose viability depends on the current phase of deferred subsidies eventually closing.

*

The chain behind every response generated by an artificial-intelligence system is invisible at the interface but structuring in the real economy. Behind the blinking cursor lie mines, submarine cables, data centers that evaporate lakes, human evaluators paid less per hour than the monthly subscription costs, and a capital structure betting on recovering later what it gives away today.

Artificial intelligence is a global industrial system that presents itself as an immaterial service. It has a footprint comparable to that of transport or manufacturing, and a concentration of productive power that none of those sectors exhibits. That erasure is the operating condition of a system with displaced bills. Some bills are absorbed by companies as strategic investment, part is recovered through subscriptions and enterprise services, some are financed by venture capital, and some are converted into resource consumption that appears on no balance sheet.

The user sometimes pays with money, sometimes with data, sometimes with technological dependency, and often does not pay directly at all, but the system as a whole never stops charging. The cognitive-capital execution service we described at the start is reflected in the figures of a system whose concrete economic operation is as strange as its nature.

8

Legal Labyrinths and Sustainability

LLMs do not exist in a vacuum. They need enormous quantities of text written by people who did not choose to contribute to their training and who in most cases will receive nothing in return. That condition of origin forms a knot of legal, ethical, and philosophical problems for which there is no agreed solution. At this point the labyrinth becomes more tangled. The legal corridors fork at every turn and the signs contradict one another. The same act is fair use in one jurisdiction and infringement in the neighboring one; today it is a gray zone and tomorrow it may be established doctrine or legal catastrophe.

We had better proceed slowly, because in AI regulation the mismatch between the object and the available frameworks is enormous. The law was built to manage relations among human agents who produce works intentionally, distribute identifiable copies, and compete for stable markets. LLMs fit none of these descriptions: they are not agents, do not produce works in the classical legal sense, and operate on a corpus whose scale exceeds any mechanism of individual licensing. In this context, the regulatory models taking shape are distinct bets about who bears the cost of that structural inadequacy.

The Field of Regulation

The training corpus of frontier models includes massive quantities of copyrighted text (books, news articles, academic publications, source code, and web content) incorporated without the explicit consent of their authors and without compensation. In truth, every cultural tradition is built on the appropriation of what came before it, and no writer writes without having read; the labs accordingly argue for an analogy with reading. Human reading transforms: someone who has read Borges and absorbed his influence does not, when writing, reproduce Borges, but creates something else metabolized through their biographical experience. The model absorbs statistical patterns and produces responses that preserve patterns of the corpus without literal reproduction, but without having understood or transformed them through any experience.

Legally, what are these outputs? The usual categories fit poorly. We could try the category of *derivative work*, but that would require an identifiable relation between the response and a specific source, whereas the model transforms millions of works at once, never just one. *Compilation* suggests selection and organization of preexisting materials, but the model neither selects nor organizes materially. The *anonymous work* of continental law protects an author whose identity is simply unknown, but here there is *no unknown author — only the absence of* one. That leaves the most recent category, *machine-generated work*, which some jurisdictions are beginning to address — but the decisions that address it, for example *Zarya of the Dawn* before the U.S. Copyright Office in 2023 and Thaler v. Perlmutter the same year, resolve the problem by declaring that such a thing is not a work, so it falls outside the copyright regime and into the public domain. The category would name a kind of nonwork. The law has no slot for something that is genuinely creation and at the same time does not come from a creating subject, which is the case of what the egoless phantom produces.[207]

The accumulated lawsuits speak for themselves. The New York Times sued OpenAI and Microsoft alleging that their models reproduce substantial portions of protected articles. Getty Images sued Stability AI for using millions of watermarked images to train Stable Diffusion. Individual authors, programmers, and visual artists have filed class actions across multiple jurisdictions. By the start of 2026, there were more than seventy copyright-infringement lawsuits against AI companies in the United States, and the trend is accelerating. In 2025, plaintiffs from the film industry joined for the first time.[208]

In the United States, the defendants typically invoke fair use, but the courts are not moving in one direction. In February 2025, in Thomson Reuters v. Ross Intelligence, a Delaware court rejected the fair-use defense and ruled that the use of protected content to train a competing legal-search tool constituted copyright infringement.[209] The decisive factor was the impact on the market, since the product competed directly with the original. In June 2025, in Bartz v. Anthropic, a California court determined that training models with protected books was fair use, but that storing pirated copies was not.[210] The case settled for 1.5 billion dollars — the largest in the history of AI-and-copyright litigation. In Kadrey v. Meta, another California court likewise accepted the fair-use defense.[211] The three

---

[207]U.S. Copyright Office, Carta a Van Lindberg, Esq., in relación con "Zarya of the Dawn" (Registration # VAu001480196), 21 February 2023. Thaler v. Perlmutter, 687 F.

[208]ChatGPT Is Eating the World, "AI Copyright Cases Tracker", actualizado periódicamente, chatgptiseatingtheworld.com. También Wired, "Every AI Copyright Lawsuit in the US, Visualized", actualizado in 2025-2026.

[209]Thomson Reuters Enterprise Centre GmbH v. Ross Intelligence Inc., No. 1:20-cv-613-SB (D. Del. Feb. 11, 2025). Available at the U.S. District Court for the District of Delaware website.

[210]Bartz v. Anthropic PBC, No. 24-cv-05417 (N.D. Cal.). Chloe Veltman, "Anthropic pays authors $1.5 billion to settle copyright infringement lawsuit", NPR, 5 September 2025.

[211]Kadrey v. Meta Platforms, No. 23-cv-03417 (N.D. Cal.).

decisions differ in their reasoning, and none is binding at the appellate level, so the law remains unsettled.

In Europe the structure of copyright exceptions and limitations to copyright is more rigid and leaves less room for judicial flexibility of interpretation. The EU Directive on Copyright in the Digital Single Market (Directive 2019/790, the DSM Directive) introduced an exception for text and data mining that allows the reproduction of works for scientific-research purposes without authorization, but establishes an opt-out right for rightsholders. If the rightsholder explicitly declares that they do not authorize the mining of their works, the exception does not apply. The problem is that this mechanism was designed before the explosion of generative AI and presupposes that rightsholders can know when and how their works are being used — which rarely holds in practice.

The EU AI Act complemented this framework by requiring, as of August 2025, that providers of general-purpose models publish a detailed summary of the content used in training, with fines of up to 15 million euros or 3% of annual global revenue for noncompliance. The transparency obligation is the most advanced in the world, but its effectiveness depends on those summaries being specific enough to allow rightsholders to exercise their opt-out right — something that remains to be seen.

In November 2025, two European courts issued the first rulings on AI training and copyright, with divergent results. In the United Kingdom, the High Court resolved Getty Images v. Stability AI by dismissing the principal infringement claims because the training of Stable Diffusion had taken place outside British territory, eliminating the jurisdictional basis. The court also rejected the thesis that the model itself constitutes an infringing copy, arguing that Stable Diffusion does not store the protected works in its weights, which are statistical parameters, not image records. Rightsholders called the decision disappointing because it sidestepped the central question: whether training a model on protected works within the United Kingdom would constitute infringement.[212]

In response, a British parliamentary committee published in March 2026 a report titled AI, Copyright and the Creative Industries that explicitly backs a prior-licensing regime, that is, that use of protected works for training requires prior authorization, not merely the absence of objection. The report also rejects a commercial data-mining exception, arguing that an opt-out model shifts the burden of policing the industry onto creators who cannot even confirm whether their work was used.[213]

In Germany, days later, the Munich regional court resolved GEMA v. OpenAI in the opposite direction from the British ruling. GEMA, the collective management society for musical rights, sued OpenAI over the use of song lyrics to train earlier versions of ChatGPT. The court determined that training constituted a reproduction requiring a license. Unlike the British court, the Munich court considered irrelevant the technical mode by which the model incorporates the data. If it was trained on the lyrics and could reproduce them as a response, the model had incorporated the content. The ruling establishes that liability falls on the model's developer — a point on which both courts agreed.[214]

Japan adopted a radically different approach. Since 2018, its intellectual-property legislation has included a broad text-and-data-mining exception that allows the use of protected works to train AI models without authorization or compensation, *even for* commercial purposes. This exception (the most permissive among advanced economies) has made Japan an attractive territory for model training

---

[212]Getty Images (US) Inc. v. Stability AI Ltd., [2025] EWHC 2863 (Ch). High Court of Justice, Chancery Division, decision of November 2025. See Mehul Srivastava, "UK High Court rules in Getty Images vs Stability AI case", Financial Times, November 2025.

[213]UK House of Lords Communications and Digital Committee, AI, Copyright and the Creative Industries, report published in March 2026. Available at the UK Parliament website (parliament.uk).

[214]GEMA v. OpenAI, Landgericht München I, decision of November 2025. Munich considered the technical mode in which the model incorporates data to be irrelevant.

and has generated tension with Japanese creative sectors, particularly the manga and animation industries, which see their works used massively with no effective recourse.

In Latin America, the discussion is nascent. The Brazilian newspaper Folha de São Paulo sued OpenAI in São Paulo in August 2025, alleging that the company accesses its website daily to scrape content without authorization or compensation, constituting unfair competition. In Denmark, a group of press publishers sued OpenAI in late 2025 over the use of their publications to train ChatGPT. These early cases suggest that litigation will globalize as rightsholders in each jurisdiction determine that their works have been incorporated into the training corpus.

These developments reveal three regulatory models that are taking shape and will likely coexist without converging. The U.S. model resolves case by case through the fair use doctrine, with unpredictable results and unstable case law. The European model combines limited exceptions with opt-out rights and transparency obligations, on the assumption that information will allow rightsholders to exercise control. The Japanese model prioritizes innovation with a broad exception that minimizes restrictions on training.

Each model expresses a political decision about who absorbs the cost of the uncertainty. In the United States, the cost is absorbed by both sides while they litigate; in Europe, by the developers who must demonstrate compliance; in Japan, by the creators who have no effective mechanism of opposition. There is no consensus within any of these models, and cross-jurisdictional fragmentation adds substantial complexity for any globally operating actor: the same training act can be legal in Tokyo, illegal in Munich, and unresolved in New York.

On the economic side, the consequences of any resolution are problematic. If courts determine that training on protected data requires a license, model-development costs would rise substantially. Actors with the resources to negotiate mass licensing deals (like the ones Google signed with Reddit and Associated Press) would have an advantage over smaller actors, consolidating the concentration we have already described. If training is established as fair use, the result is a model in which content creators involuntarily subsidize the AI industry without sharing its benefits. Either way, someone loses — and the outcome will likely track bargaining power more than principle.

The problem extends to individual consent. Data-protection regulations (the GDPR 2016/679, Brazil's LGPD, and others) establish requirements for a legal basis for processing personal data. When a model is trained on social-media posts, forums, leaked emails, or medical data, the legal basis is in many cases contested. The right to be forgotten, enshrined in Article 17 of the GDPR, poses the most acute challenge. What does it mean to "erase" data that is not stored as a record in a database but dissolved into the weights of a neural network with billions of parameters?

The technical answer is machine unlearning, an emerging research field that tries to develop methods for a model to "forget" specific data without retraining it from scratch. Current approaches include exact methods, such as SISA (Sharded, Isolated, Sliced, and Aggregated), which partitions the training data so that removing a datum requires retraining only the affected fragment; approximate methods, which adjust the model's parameters to reduce the influence of specific data without guaranteeing their complete removal; and fine-tuning with modified labels, which retrains the model on the data to be forgotten using incorrect responses, forcing an overwrite. IBM developed SPUNGE, which in experiments with Meta's Llama models completed forgetting processes in minutes rather than the months a full retraining would require.[215]

Yet no current method guarantees complete removal or reliably verifies that the model has actually forgotten, so the field is far from offering scalable solutions for frontier models. The difficulty is, in a real sense, ontological: models do not store data as retrievable

[215]On machine unlearning, see Martin Pawelczyk et al., "Machine Unlearning Fails to Remove Data Poisoning Attacks", International Conference on Learning Representations (ICLR 2025), arXiv:2406.17216, 2025, and A.

records but as distributed patterns, and "erasing" a datum is like trying to remove an ingredient from a finished dish. Even if the ability to reproduce a specific datum is suppressed, the statistical traces of that datum may persist in the model's general patterns.

The European Data Protection Board made the right to be forgotten a compliance priority for 2025, with 32 national authorities coordinating investigations into how organizations handle deletion requests. California enacted AB 1008, which since 2025 explicitly requires AI developers to honor requests to delete personal information embedded in models — a pioneering requirement, but one of technically uncertain compliance given the limitations just described.

The tension between the architecture of the models and the normative principles that societies built around intellectual property and privacy is profound. The models were designed without the possibility of forgetting built in, because the purpose of training is exactly the opposite: to absorb everything and forget nothing. Asking a system optimized for total retention to implement selective forgetting therefore contradicts its architecture. Advances in machine unlearning show that this means working against the system's grain, with normative consequences we are still handling clumsily.

This survey of training, jurisdictional asymmetry, and the right to be forgotten shows that no jurisdiction has yet built an effective framework, and none is likely to do so alone. Still less if it embraces the tool idea, because the egoless phantom slips easily through regulatory nets made for traditional artifacts. The legal question of who is responsible for what the model produces is daunting, and requires above all changing the perspectives that have failed so far.

SUSTAINABLE DEVELOPMENT

Everything we have examined so far converges on a single question: is this ecosystem sustainable? The economic dimension is the most discussed and tends to crowd out the rest, but reducing sustainability to economic terms alone misses most of the problem. The sustainability of artificial intelligence operates on several distinct planes, each with its own logic. What follows attempts to describe how the tensions look on each plane and what the coexistence of contradictory signals implies. The questions about sustainability are not about how to use a tool better; they are about what conditions enable or prevent the sustainable functioning of what Chapter 7 called the *cognitive-capital execution service.*

Let us begin with *economic sustainability*, which depends less on the revenues of each individual actor than on the relations of interdependence that sustain the sector as a whole. The revenues of OpenAI and Anthropic, the operating losses of the labs, the segmentation between free and paying users — none of these alone can account for an ecosystem in which each actor's strategies condition the others' viability.

Meta's open strategy with Llama established a floor of free access that pressures all proprietary actors. If an open-source model with competitive performance is available at no cost, proprietary models must offer more than raw performance to justify their price — stability, alignment, support, integration, or governance. DeepSeek compressed the assumptions about the cost of training frontier models, forcing price reductions that shrank everyone's margins. Google can operate Gemini at a loss indefinitely because it subsidizes it with revenue from search, advertising, and cloud services. But that cross-subsidy capacity establishes a price ceiling that actors without a diversified ecosystem (such as Anthropic or the smaller labs) cannot match. NVIDIA invested a billion dollars in stakes in AI startups in 2024, many of which spend those funds buying NVIDIA GPUs, creating a financing circuit that sustains the demand for its own products. OpenAI committed more than a trillion dollars in infrastructure for the next decade, financed by investments from Microsoft and NVIDIA.

The result is an ecosystem in which each actor's individual sustainability depends on decisions made by the others, and in which competitive pressure systematically pushes prices down while infrastructure costs grow. The question is whether the business model of the sector as a whole is viable without cross-subsidies, circular investments, and a tolerance for losses on the scale of billions of dollars. Comparisons with a bubble abound. It may not be one — but the economic sustainability of the current ecosystem is still in dispute.

Obsolescence compounds the problem. Frontier models are replaced every few months. GPT-4 launched in March 2023; by March 2026 OpenAI's ecosystem includes GPT-5.4. Each generation requires new training infrastructure, data, alignment, new safety evaluations, and new compliance cycles. An ecosystem in which the central product has a life cycle of months — and each iteration demands investments not recovered before the next — raises serious sustainability questions. The relative silence in the public debate suggests that the rhetoric of progress has normalized a pace that in any other industry would be considered unsustainable.

Geopolitical sustainability is in question. As we saw in Chapter 7, the supply chain for advanced chips is more concentrated than that of oil. Seen from the angle of sustainability, that concentration indicates that the entire system depends on a few geographic points of fragility. NVIDIA controls approximately 80% of the market for training GPUs, TSMC produces more than 90% of advanced semiconductors, and ASML is the world's sole supplier of the most advanced lithography equipment. Any disruption at any one of these nodes — a military conflict in the Strait of Taiwan, a U.S. trade restriction on Dutch equipment, a cross-sanction from China — would paralyze global production. The AI production system has no significant geographic redundancy, no international coordination mechanism, and no strategic reserves — a critical system resting on very few points of failure.

Compounding that fragility is the bifurcation of the Chinese and Western ecosystems across hardware, software, regulatory frameworks, and data flows. If the divergence deepens, each bloc's sustainability will depend on its capacity to build a complete infrastructure of its own, with all the duplication costs that implies. If the divergence eases under economic pressure, sustainability will depend on cooperation mechanisms that current geopolitical tensions make difficult. In both scenarios, the sector's geopolitical sustainability remains to be seen.

As for *environmental sustainability*, we already addressed in Chapter 7 the sector's footprint in electricity, water, emissions, and territorial stress. Technical efficiency could mitigate the problems. If we looked only at those efficiency curves, the conclusion might be optimistic — but the Jevons rebound transforms every efficiency gain into higher total volume of use, and the system as a whole consumes more. The IEA's projections that data-center electricity consumption will double by 2030 incorporate the expected efficiency improvements, and even with them, consumption grows.

On-device models, which run locally, are often presented as an environmentally sustainable path because they eliminate cloud traffic. That holds for the data center, but not for the system as a whole: the energy cost shifts onto the user's device, appearing in their electricity [216]bill instead.

What does reduce environmental impact is specialization through small models, trained for narrow domains, that operate with a fraction of the compute of a generalist model. A model fine-tuned for contract analysis or radiological diagnosis does not need the billions of parameters of a general conversational model and produces better results within its domain. The same logic applies to hybrid use, in which a lightweight model resolves routine tasks and a frontier model is activated only when the task requires it. These strategies are the only ones that effectively reduce total compute, by making use more efficient and eliminating unnecessary operations.

In the midst of all this, the European Commission proposed exempting AI data centers from mandatory environmental-impact assessments, in the name of competitiveness. That decision, if confirmed, institutionally codifies the tension we have already

[216]International Energy Agency, Energy and AI, 2025. The projections of doubled consumption by 2030 incorporate the expected efficiency improvements.

documented between climate objectives and technological ambitions, which operate as forces that cancel each other out when regulation decides not to mediate between them.

Epistemic sustainability is a less-studied dimension. It is linked to the so-called risk of recursive contamination, derived from the training of the models. If the models generate texts that are published on the internet and training incorporates them in the next cycle, those texts get incorporated as if they were human production. The result is a circuit in which each generation of models is trained partly on outputs of the previous generation, with human participation progressively diluted. The so-called model collapse shows that when systems are trained iteratively on data generated by previous models, the distribution of responses narrows progressively.

Less-frequent registers disappear, dialectal variants flatten, and minority or idiosyncratic positions are absorbed into an ever more homogeneous statistical mean. The phenomenon is analogous to what happens with photocopies of photocopies, where each iteration loses resolution and the loss is cumulative and irreversible. In sum, if training corpora are progressively contaminated with AI-generated text, the diversity of the cognitive resource on which the model operates degrades. There is no way to reverse this process, because there is no way to separate human text from generated text at scale — which is a problem if the sustainability of AI depends on the diverse, uncontaminated human linguistic and cognitive production that the system itself is degrading.[217]

Let us now consider *social sustainability*. We have already described the conditions of the alignment work carried out by humans, sometimes in deplorable conditions. That work is a condition of the system's operation: human evaluators classify outputs for commercial use, moderators filter toxic content so platforms can operate in regulated jurisdictions, and data labelers curate training corpora to maintain model quality. This work does not appear in

[217]Ilia Shumailov et al., "AI models collapse when trained on recursively generated data", Nature 631 (2024), 755-759.

economic-sustainability calculations because its cost is marginal compared with hardware and energy — but that does not make it secondary. If tomorrow all the toxic-content evaluators stopped working, the models would begin producing unacceptable outputs within hours.

We might ask whether a system that produces cognitive support for high-income professionals can be considered sustainable when its operation depends on precarious labor in poor countries. Beyond rhetoric or moralizing, it is a question of the system's cost structure and of who pays for what so that it works.

Let us consider one more dimension: *regulatory sustainability*. Viewed through that lens, the regulatory mosaic we explored earlier looks quite different. The requirements of the EU AI Act for high-risk systems (technical documentation, impact assessment, human oversight, post-market monitoring, and incident reporting) impose heavy compliance costs. For organizations with institutional capacity, these costs are absorbable and can even constitute a competitive advantage, because the capacity to demonstrate compliance becomes a differentiator against competitors who lack it. For smaller actors — startups, independent developers, organizations in countries without regulatory infrastructure — the same costs can be prohibitive.[218]

Regulation distributes sustainability unequally among the sector's actors. The EU AI Act classifies as high-risk systems those applied in education, employment, health, justice, and essential public services. For those systems, the regulation requires detailed technical documentation, impact assessments, human oversight at critical decision points, continuous post-deployment monitoring, and mandatory incident reporting. Each requirement carries concrete costs: legal teams, auditors, engineers dedicated to traceability, internal logging systems, and review processes that slow

[218]European Commission, Impact Assessment accompanying the AI Act proposal, 2024. OneTrust, "Where AI Regulation is Heading", 2026. También Regulation (EU) 2024/1689, European Parliament and Council, 2024 and Digital Omnibus proposal, 2025.

development cycles. In high-risk sectors, these costs can be comparable to the system's own computational costs, which changes the conditions of competition in the European market.

Actors that have already built their products with governance incorporated from the design stage have a structural advantage over those who must retrofit their systems to comply. An AI system embedded in an ERP system for enterprise management that includes an audit log, decision traceability, and pedagogical documentation from its initial architecture complies with the regulation in a way that turns compliance into a value proposition — since the client buys, along with the system, a guarantee that its use can be accounted for.

Therefore, from the perspective of large companies with institutional capacity, regulation is an absorbable cost that operates as a competitive advantage. The more demanding it is, the greater the difference between those who can comply and those who cannot. From the perspective of small companies, independent developers, and actors in countries without robust regulatory infrastructure, the same requirements can be prohibitive and act as a barrier to entry into the European market. Regulation reorganizes the field rather than leveling it, favoring those who were already on top. The paradox of the EU AI Act is that it aims to protect European citizens from the careless use of AI, but in doing so it consolidates the position of the actors that already have the capital and the institutional capacities to comply, pushing out of the market smaller and potentially more diverse alternatives. Regulation is both a necessary cost and a market-shaping force for sustainable AI — one that produces a market with fewer players, not more.

*

Seen from afar, the chapter describes two walls of the same labyrinth. The first wall is legal. Three regulatory models disagree on everything except one mistaken premise — that AI is a mere tool — and together they produce a territorial fragmentation that globally capable actors turn into competitive advantage while everyone else absorbs the uncertainty as cost. The second wall is sustainability: multiple dimensions condition one another, and the current system clears some successfully while stumbling through others.

None of the problems this chapter describes is exclusively technical or exclusively regulatory. All are, ultimately, problems of governance. The responses the sector is building — accelerated concentration, externalized costs, structural opacity, private control without institutional counterweight — result from specific decisions that could have gone otherwise. The rhetoric of inevitability is an effective discursive device for blocking political imagination, and it is worth resisting.

What kind of social control can be exercised over a cognitive infrastructure whose functioning concentrates power, externalizes costs, and operates under categories the law was not designed to accommodate? Historical experience with regulating electricity, telecommunications, and mass media suggests that societies can do it — but only when they recognize the infrastructural character of what they are regulating and build consistent institutional frameworks around it. AI is at an equivalent moment. What societies do or fail to do in the coming years will define whether the sector develops under forms of control compatible with democracy, or whether structural concentration becomes irreversible before institutions manage to respond.

All of this unfolds in paradoxical and at times almost parodic contexts — take the case of the United States Department of Defense declaring Anthropic a supply-chain risk while embracing xAI's Grok model, shortly before Anthropic and xAI became partners. The legal labyrinth operates under incoherence as its normal condition.[219]

---

[219]CNBC, "Pentagon tech chief says Anthropic is still blacklisted, but Mythos is a separate issue", 1 May 2026; on the SpaceX-Anthropic agreement, CNBC, 6 May 2026.

We leave this zone of the labyrinth with more questions than answers, but with a clearer map of what is at stake. The section that follows takes up how, in the midst of all this, we can work well with these systems, because ultimately, while the institutional frameworks are being reconfigured, we keep interacting with concrete systems on concrete problems, and the quality of that interaction matters as much as the quality of the regulation that governs it.

9

Prompt Design vs. Interaction Engineering

Two people can operate on the same language model, in identical versions and under equivalent technical conditions, and obtain results of completely different quality. It has happened to all of us when we compare experiences. We tend to attribute it to differences in skill or technical knowledge, but how one formulates requests, manages responses, and runs the interaction process is decisive. The quality of the response depends in good measure on the quality of the input, for the underlying reasons we have already explored. If the direction comes from us, we have to figure out how to govern this power that has no orientation of its own without letting it bolt — especially because this horse can grow furious or come to a halt without our noticing until it is too late. We have to design a process that bounds that power, evaluates it, and stops at the right moment. In this chapter we will examine aspects of this strange technique of taming.

The Nature of Instructions

Let us begin by revisiting the nature of the instruction, or prompt. Some practical guides compare the use of these systems to extremely capable assistants who need precise instructions. The analogy is useful up to a point, because it gestures at task-definition, but it becomes misleading if we take it literally. The model does not understand commands or decide to execute them; it probabilistically reconfigures its generation space as a function of the context. We are dealing with an egoless phantom, not an inflexible assistant. For that reason, the user's instruction cannot function as a command in the human sense — which would presuppose an addressee who understands it as such, a direct relation between mandate and execution, and the capacity to distinguish between obeying, disobeying, or reinterpreting what was asked. None of that is present in the interaction with an LLM, and so speaking of "giving orders" to the model preserves an anthropomorphic residue that becomes an obstacle to operating with the statistical modulation of context.

The model incorporates the input text as part of the context and, on that basis, locally reconfigures the space of probable continuations, so that an instruction functions as *an initial condition that biases the trajectory of generation and its probability distribution.* The imperative force of the formulation lacks the efficacy of a good contextual constraint. A restriction, an example, or a change of register reconfigures how the model generates its response. The effects are immediate. It is enough to modify the context for the behavior to change — without the model retaining anything in any persistent way.[220]

Recall that formulating instructions is never training the system. The illusion is understandable, because the model seems to "learn" from the exchange, adjusting to our style and improving over the course of the conversation. Nonetheless, they are quite distinct mechanisms, since the instruction operates only on the input context without altering any internal parameter. The change in representation space that training creates is the ground we walk on when we formulate an instruction. Confusing the two planes produces expectations the model cannot satisfy and makes us more vulnerable to the phenomena and risks we examined in Chapter 5.

[220]Laria Reynolds et al., "Prompt Programming for Large Language Models: Beyond the Few-Shot Paradigm", Extended Abstracts of the 2021 CHI Conference on Human Factors in Computing Systems, arXiv:2102.07350, 2021.

"I trained my AI not to be sycophantic" could be the opening line of a Greek tragedy with tragic error, and unfortunately it is heard often among users with less technical training.[221]

Seen this way, the whole question seems to reduce to achieving good instructions. Yet we must also dismantle the mythology of the perfect prompt. The popularity of the so-called *universal prompts* illustrates the confusion. Such lists circulate on social media promising radical improvements in model performance through reusable formulations applicable to almost any situation. All of them presuppose that there exists a formulation complete enough to produce good results independently of the content. Unfortunately, in practice, those instructions work only under very specific conditions.

Let us look at three examples. "I'm going to give you my disorganized notes on a project. Organize them into a logical structure, identify recurrent themes, detect contradictions, and flag the points that require development." This instruction works at the basic level because the model has seen countless texts organized into introduction, development, and conclusion — but it has no criterion to distinguish which idea is central and which is irrelevant if we don't know that ourselves beforehand. In the case of "This is my plan. Play devil's advocate, find the flaws, the hidden assumptions, and the risks I am underestimating," we will get plausible objections because the corpus contains many examples of critique and argumentation — but it cannot evaluate the real importance of those risks in the concrete situation. When the instruction is "I have to choose between A and B. Analyze the two options objectively, consider the context, the constraints, and my values, and give me a clear recommendation," the recommendations can be coherent because the model is trained on texts where options are compared and decisions justified — but limited to what appears explicitly in the context. In every case, the response sounds reasonable because it reproduces typical discursive forms, and that can be very useful

[221] Tom Brown et al., "Language Models are Few-Shot Learners", Proceedings of NeurIPS, arXiv:2005.14165, 2020.

provided we keep in mind that it does not understand the problem and the instruction by itself is no guarantee of anything.

A prompt, as we said, restricts the generation space, but if the problem-definition is weak, we operate with little criterion, and we skip evaluation, the improvement is only apparent and we obtain the only thing the model can stably produce, namely, plausible texts. That is why the same prompts that look extraordinarily effective in simple demonstrations become unpredictable when applied to real problems. Let us insist on this point: the expectation that a well-formulated instruction can replace the design of the complete process is unfounded, for two reasons.

First, beyond a certain threshold, lengthy instructions degrade performance. More than the length itself, the problem is ambiguity, conflicts between instructions, and saturation of the model's attention. When instructions are very long, the system has to manage simultaneously many restrictions that may contradict each other, and it may resolve them inconsistently. This is aggravated by three properties of long-sequence processing. The *primacy effect* leads models to weight the beginning of a text regardless of its importance; *recency bias* means they retain what appears at the end; and *the* lost-in-the-middle phenomenon describes how attention decays in the central zone of long contexts. These properties coexist and combine in unpredictable ways, so that in a very long instruction the model may arbitrarily privilege some restrictions over others simply because of their position in the text. As for importance: none. It follows that an excessively elaborate instruction is a block of text with potentially contradictory regularities that the model resolves in ways we cannot anticipate or control.[222]

Suppose we need a summary of a long academic article. A sparse instruction would say: "summarize this article." The model does not know whether a paragraph or two pages is expected, whether to prioritize arguments or data, whether the addressee is a specialist or

[222]Nelson F. Liu et al., "Lost in the Middle: How Language Models Use Long Contexts", Transactions of the Association for Computational Linguistics 2024, arXiv:2307.03172, 2023.

a general reader — and it resolves all of that on its own, generally tilting toward the generic and the long. A good instruction would say, for example: "summarize the central argument of this article in one paragraph of no more than 150 words, addressed to someone who knows the field but has not read the text; prioritize the main thesis and the evidence that sustains it, not the article's structure." Each restriction eliminates a decision the model would otherwise have to make on its own about length, focus, addressee, and criterion of selection. An excessive instruction would add: "use an academic but accessible tone, avoid unnecessary jargon but do not oversimplify, be precise without being pedantic, include the context of the debate the article is inscribed in but without going on too long, mention limitations if relevant but only if they do not lengthen the summary beyond what is necessary, and ensure that the result is useful both for someone who wants to decide whether to read the article and for someone who needs to cite it in their own work." Each of those clauses is reasonable in isolation, but together they are so contradictory that the model arbitrarily chooses what to obey and what to ignore — with the aggravating circumstance that the choice is less predictable because the signals are competing with each other.

Second, the belief that everything depends on the instruction is a form of inverted anthropomorphism. We already mentioned that this assumption lurks behind the very idea of "instruction," but it also shows up in the aim of saying things better, which presupposes that the model functions as a human interlocutor to whom one must "explain things well." The model responds to statistical patterns conditioned by context, and it does not understand better because we talk to it more.

In sum, these lists can be useful as examples, but they reinforce the illusion that control of the model is achieved through an isolated instruction. In reality, each instruction functions only within a specific regime of interaction that involves a sequence of differentiated operations. The result improves with the separation of phases, the evaluation of each response, and the progressive adjustment of the conditions for the next response. The alternative to the culture of the elaborate prompt is what we have called *interaction engineering.*

INTERACTION ENGINEERING AND ITERATION

Let us analyze three modes of use that we must be able to recognize, since not every interaction with a language model has the same structure.

Asking is to request a specific datum or explanation. What's the difference between RLHF and DPO? What does Article 17 of the GDPR establish? How does attention work in transformers? In this mode the model functions as a conversational encyclopedia. The responses are useful, isolated, and their reliability depends entirely on whether we have the criterion to evaluate what we receive.

Requesting, by contrast, is to commission a closed product of the kind "draft an email," "summarize this document," "write a function that does such-and-such." The model produces a finished result that tends to resist revision. It looks complete, and the temptation to accept it without further ado is strong, so that the fluency of the response can mask deficiencies that only appear if we overcome the temptation to move on and instead evaluate.

Finally, *designing a task* is to structure a sequence of operations with explicit criteria, intermediate evaluations, and corrections. The user introduces relevant context, sets constraints, evaluates partial outputs, adjusts course, and decides when to close. In this mode the model performs better because the generation space is bounded at each step — although it is also the most demanding, since it requires knowing what one wants before asking for it and being able to evaluate what one receives.

Suppose a lawyer needs to analyze whether a software-license contract complies with the EU AI Act's requirements for high-risk systems. If she asks ("does this contract comply with the EU AI Act?") she gets a generic response about the regulation. If she requests ("analyze this contract in light of the EU AI Act") she gets a professional-looking document that probably mixes applicable requirements with requirements that are not. If she designs the task by decomposing it, the work proceeds in stages. She first asks the model to identify which clauses of the contract refer to the system's risk-classification, and evaluates whether the identification is correct before moving on. She then asks it to compare those clauses with the specific articles of the regulation, indicating which ones. Next, she asks it to flag the omissions — for instance, what the regulation requires that the contract does not mention — reviewing each omission against the actual text of the norm. Finally, she asks for a synthesis of risks ordered by severity, with the restriction that it not include hypothetical risks but only those derived from the prior analysis. At each step, the lawyer can evaluate what she receives with her knowledge of the law and of the client's concrete situation. In this way, the model accelerates a task that would otherwise take hours of cross-reading. Most users operate in the first two modes, but the third leads to articulated intelligence, combining human and artificial capacities.

This interaction engineering presupposes mastering iteration. The first response is rarely the best; the most valuable material emerges only after a controlled cycle of generation, evaluation, and adjustment. To iterate sounds like repeating or asking the same thing in another way, but it is, strictly, using the response as input. The model generates under certain conditions; we evaluate with explicit criteria; and on the basis of that evaluation we adjust the instruction for the next round. We evaluate the result of that round with the same criteria, now refined by what the previous round revealed. The process has the structure of a spiral, in which each cycle starts from a more informed point than the previous one, precisely because iteration is the mechanism by which the relevant information enters the process.

There are four conditions that make an iteration productive.

The first is *separating phases.* We saw this in the lawyer-and-software-license example, and we can now describe them better. In the *exploration phase*, options, approaches, and hypotheses are generated without yet requiring that any of them be the correct one. In the evaluation phase, what was produced is submitted to clear criteria to detect errors, biases, and omissions. In the *closing phase*, one arrives at a synthesis or decision on the basis of what the prior phases have built. Asking for everything at once pushes the model to simulate authority, whereas iterating by phases allows control of each step.

The second is *making the evaluation criteria explicit* in the phase to which they belong. It is not enough to reply "that doesn't convince me," because the model has no access to what the user expected and will adjust superficially or stylistically. One must signal whether we detect conceptual imprecision, inferential leap, or framing error — always in a specific way. The model adjusts its trajectory locally when it is given concrete faults.

The third condition is *introducing deliberate friction.* Requests like "show me the weakest point of this response," "formulate the strongest objection," "compare this with an incompatible framework," or "what would be left out if I accept this approach" force the model out of the sycophantic mode incentivized by alignment. To iterate, at this point, is to put a response to the test to produce arguments that either hold up or reveal their limits.[223]

The fourth has to do with *knowing when to stop*, which is different from knowing when the model has finished, because it does not finish, nor does it have any internal criterion of sufficiency. The infinite loop of reformulate-improve-reformulate progressively degrades the quality of the responses. In effect, the degradation under long iteration is an effect of context-processing that we saw in Chapters 3 and 5. It is recognizable because the text begins to grow without adding new information, reformulations appear in place of advances, and the model introduces qualifications or warnings that increase the appearance of exhaustiveness without changing the structure of the problem. From the standpoint of

[223]Mrinank Sharma et al., "Towards Understanding Sycophancy in Language Models", arXiv:2310.13548, 2023 and el Capítulo 5.

processing, this indicates that the context has ceased to restrict the space of continuations and that the response has veered toward the generic. For this reason, effective interaction requires introducing cuts, summarizing the state reached, resetting the context when necessary, and explicitly resetting the relevant constraints. Above all, closure requires a criterion external to the model — in the form of a conceptual standard or a decision of ours. The last word cannot be the model's.[224]

Consider another example, this time not for the use of phases but for the conditions each one fulfills. A consulting firm needs to evaluate whether the pricing strategy of a SaaS company is sustainable over three years, because its competitors are cutting prices aggressively. In the exploration phase, it asks the model to identify the main factors of customer-acquisition cost, retention rate, gross margin, price-elasticity, switching costs, and product differentiation. In the evaluation phase, it applies explicit criteria such as "you included price-elasticity but did not distinguish between acquisition-elasticity and retention-elasticity; in SaaS these are distinct dynamics because switching costs operate asymmetrically. Give me the analysis again, incorporating that distinction." The correction flags a conceptual error the model did not detect because in the corpus the two elasticities usually appear blurred together. Then it introduces friction by saying: "build the best possible argument that the premium pricing strategy is unsustainable over three years, and then the best argument that it is. I want both with equal force, without either one seeming more reasonable than the other." The result reveals that the breaking point of the argument is the net revenue retention rate. The consultant notices that in the next round the model begins to add scenarios that only ornament the structure of the analysis — of the kind "in a context of moderate recession...," "if the exchange rate varies..." The

[224]Jules White et al., "A Prompt Pattern Catalog to Enhance Prompt Engineering with ChatGPT", arXiv:2302.11382, 2023. Adding scenarios that only decorate the structure of the analysis — of the kind "in a moderate recession context" or "if the exchange rate varies".

iteration has stopped producing information. At this moment she decides to close, takes the argumentative structure, and contrasts it with the firm's actual data.

This leads us to the distinction between *exploring and deciding*. Many of the problems attributed to artificial intelligence arise when we begin to treat as firm conclusions what the system generates as plausible variations. We have already seen that the models do not recognize when a hypothesis has moved on to organize reasoning. If we do not mark that passage, the system keeps operating in an exploratory mode. In practice, it is like painting and, on lifting the brush to apply the next coat, finding that the wall is no longer there — or that it is now a different color from the one we have on the brush. The model goes on offering alternatives and opening up variants when they are no longer needed. Efficient iteration makes the decision to stop exploring explicit, that is, it freezes definitions, discards alternative frameworks, and fixes restrictions that cease to be open to revision. With these interventions we fix the global coherence we have decided to retain.[225]

Closure is moreover linked to *verification*, which is a constitutive necessity of working with LLMs. We have examined repeatedly the effects of the similarity between what the model handles solidly and what it improvises, and the necessity that we exercise the epistemic calibration that distinguishes reliable responses from unreliable ones. It bears recalling that the confidence indicators that some systems include are produced by the same architecture that produces the responses, and are therefore no more reliable than they are. In this framework, verification is the operation that completes what the system on its own cannot complete. This does not mean verifying every word, or treating the model as useless without constant supervision. But we need to develop a map of the zones of reliability of the model we use, in the version we use, under the conditions in

[225]James March, "Exploration and Exploitation in Organizational Learning", Organization Science 2.1 (1991), 71-87.

which we use it. That map, and its consistent management, is more valuable than any prompting technique.[226]

One step further. In the early stages of public diffusion, attention concentrated on crafting ever more precise instructions in order to obtain better responses. As the technology matured, however, models began to be integrated into more complex architectures.

One of the most important paths of this integration is the use of Application Programming Interfaces, or APIs. An API can be understood as a set of rules that allows one program to communicate with another. Through them, a developer can incorporate a language model into an application of their own, send it instructions automatically, receive responses, and combine those responses with other sources of information. This makes it possible to construct systems far more sophisticated than a simple conversation in a chat window.

The transition from conversational interaction to API-based architectures separates the model's intelligence from the interface through which the user interacts with it. Whereas in a conversation each step must be guided explicitly by a person, systems connected through APIs can automate processes and coordinate tasks without constant human intervention. The most powerful applications of contemporary artificial intelligence take place outside the conversational interfaces visible to the user.

In these environments it is common for several specialized models to operate together. A system may employ, for example, a small and inexpensive model to classify routine requests, a more powerful one for complex reasoning tasks, a specialized model for programming, another for image generation, and yet another for audio processing. This cooperation among models can be understood as a kind of council or team of specialists. Each contributes different capacities, and the system distributes tasks according to their relative strengths. The question becomes which

[226] Saurav Kadavath et al., "Language Models (Mostly) Know What They Know", arXiv:2207.05221, 2022.

model is best suited to each function and how the ensemble should be coordinated.

This evolution has given rise to so-called skills or specialized capabilities. A skill is a procedure designed to perform a specific function, such as searching a documentary database, translating texts, or carrying out any other well-defined operation. Instead of asking the model to improvise every step, we provide it with access to previously defined tools. The model decides when to use them and how to combine their results with its own capacity for language generation.

A further development is the emergence of agents. In general terms, an agent is a system that pursues a goal through multiple steps. It can decompose a complex task into subtasks, consult external tools, evaluate partial results, correct errors, and continue working in this way until a given objective has been reached. Whereas a traditional interaction consists of a question and an answer, an agent may execute entire sequences of actions before presenting a final result.

Many agents operate through iterative loops. In such a loop, the system generates a proposal, evaluates it, and, if necessary, tries again. An agent tasked with drafting a report, for instance, may produce a first version, detect gaps in the available information, perform additional searches, reformulate the text, and repeat the process several times. This mechanism makes it possible to overcome some of the limitations language models face when dealing with extended tasks or with problems involving multiple constraints.

The emergence of AI-driven collaborative workspaces expands these possibilities even further. Some platforms allow several models to work simultaneously on the same problem, comparing approaches and results or assuming differentiated roles within a common process. In these environments, the user resembles someone coordinating a team of specialized collaborators. The outcome combines perspectives that would be difficult to obtain through a single linear conversation.

Something similar occurs in assisted programming tools, exemplified by systems of the Codex type. In these cases the model can inspect entire repositories, modify files, execute tests, detect errors, and propose whatever corrections are needed. The interaction involves concrete actions upon real working environments, so that the model becomes an operational collaborator within a development workflow.

Of course, not all models offer these capabilities to the same degree. The most advanced models generally provide API access, the use of external tools, extensive context windows, the execution of actions, and coordination with other systems. Smaller or older models may be limited to the direct generation of text.

The practical question, then, is to choose the appropriate strategy for each problem. For simple tasks, a direct conversation is often sufficient. Tasks requiring up-to-date information benefit from search tools; large document collections may call for dedicated retrieval mechanisms. When the objective requires coordinated steps, successive verifications, or interaction with external systems, agents or iterative loops are more appropriate. Tasks spanning different content types may warrant distributing the work among several complementary models.

The recent evolution of artificial intelligence can be interpreted as a displacement from conversation toward coordination, in which the central problem is no longer how to formulate a prompt, but how to organize a community of models and tools in order to achieve a goal.

Expertise and Task Delegation

A fairly widespread narrative presents artificial intelligence as an equalizer that allows anyone to access capacities that previously required specialized training. The observable reality is the opposite. This is a matter of gaps, which will be the central theme of Chapter 10, but let us here mention one specific aspect related to the criteria of use. The same model produces radically different results depending on who uses it. A study on writers showed that LLMs compress the dispersion of quality. The less able improve more than the more able, approaching their level. In another, less-experienced customer-service workers improved substantially while veterans saw almost no change. These are real results, but they measure the quality of execution in tasks where the evaluation criterion is external and predefined — in these cases, producing an acceptable text and resolving a support ticket according to known protocols. At that level, AI does effectively equalize, because it supplies a repertoire of patterns, fluency, and production speed — precisely what the novice lacks.[227]

The picture shifts when one moves from execution to intellectual work requiring judgment. The study by Dell'Acqua et al. with BCG consultants, published by Harvard Business School in 2023, described consultants who worked with GPT-4 and improved by 40% on tasks within the model's frontier of competence. But when the task fell outside those limits and incorrect responses multiplied, those who trusted without verifying had worse results than those who did not use AI, while those who verified and corrected obtained the best of both worlds. The efficient use of the model presupposes the capacity for verification. Artificial intelligence, in short, amplifies existing capacities and exposes their absence: a productivity multiplier for those who have the expertise, a source of misplaced confidence for those who do not.[228]

Along the same lines, the question of task-delegation depends on the quality of the user's judgment. Some tasks benefit from generation speed, the ability to process large volumes of text, and the range of variants a model can traverse. In these tasks, delegating to the model is efficient and frequently produces results we would

---

[227]Shakked Noy et al., "Experimental Evidence on the Productivity Effects of Generative AI", Science 381.6654 (2023), 187-192.

[228]Fabrizio Dell'Acqua et al., "Navigating the Jagged Technological Frontier: Field Experimental Evidence of the Effects of Artificial Intelligence on Knowledge Worker Productivity and Quality", Harvard Business School Working Paper 24-013, 2023.

not have reached on our own. At the same time, there are others in which delegating is risky. Contextual judgment, which requires the capacity to weigh factors that are in the situation, is never delegated without loss: just as one cannot delegate responsibility for the consequences of a decision. Above all, factual verification cannot be delegated, recalling always that the model accesses only statistical patterns that merely speak about the real, nor can one delegate sensitivity to the particular situation in which others may be affected. As a principle, one can delegate the form, always retaining the judgment.[229]

On the other hand, the same tool that extends the capacity for textual production can atrophy the capacity for judgment about what is produced, unless the regime of use includes the deliberate exercise of that judgment. B. Stiegler would recognize in this duality his notion of technology as pharmakon, at once remedy and poison of knowledge, which coincides with empirical research such as that of Lisanne Bainbridge, who in a classic article identified a curious feature of automation.[230] The more a process is automated, the more critical human intervention becomes in the cases the system cannot handle — but the operator is usually less prepared to intervene because they have stopped practicing the skills that automation replaced.[231] Bainbridge was writing about industrial-plant control, but the core is the same as in cognitive delegation to language models. We need to intervene precisely when the model fails (worse still, without alarms or red lights) but sustained delegation erodes the competencies that such intervention requires.

---

[229]J. D. Zamfirescu-Pereira et al., "Why Johnny Can't Prompt: How Non-AI Experts Try (and Fail) to Design LLM Prompts", Proceedings of CHI, 2023. The model is remedy and poison of knowledge — a finding that coincides with empirical research such as Lisanne Bainbridge's classic article identifying a curious feature of automation.

[230]Bernard Stiegler, Taking Care of Youth and the Generations (2008), Stanford, Stanford University Press, 2010. See también Nicholas Carr, The Shallows: What the Internet Is Doing to Our Brains, New York, Norton, 2010.

[231]Lisanne Bainbridge, "Ironies of Automation", Automatica 19.6 (1983), 775-779.

In their integrative review on bias and complacency in human use of automation, Parasuraman and Manzey analyzed long series of empirical evidence and found two convergent patterns. On the one hand, a reduction of vigilance that appears under conditions of multiple cognitive load, when other tasks compete for the operator's attention; and on the other, an uncritical acceptance of the system's responses, which produces errors both of omission and of commission. Neither effect is eliminated by specific training or by prior experience. The phenomenon is an adaptive cognitive response to the environment: if the system is right most of the time, the cost of verifying each response exceeds the perceived benefit and verification slackens. The problem is that the slackening is gradual and imperceptible, and when the system fails in a critical case, the operator is in no condition to detect it.[232]

More recently, another study showed that users of AI-supported decision tools did not verify more. On the contrary, explanations of the reasoning increased confidence without increasing vigilance. Process transparency, it turned out, refined the complacency. Only when the researchers introduced mechanisms that forced users to formulate their own evaluation before seeing the system's did the error-detection rate improve. The implication for the use of language models is direct: making the model's reasoning visible, as the models that display their chain of thought attempt, does not solve the problem of uncritical delegation if we do not actively exercise our judgment before accepting the response.[233]

Studies carried out specifically with generative language models converge on the same point. For instance, in a Microsoft Research study, knowledge workers were surveyed and shared concrete examples of generative-AI use in their work. The central finding was that those who trust the model more verify less, and those who trust

---

[232]Raja Parasuraman et al., "Complacency and Bias in Human Use of Automation: An Attentional Integration", Human Factors 52.3 (2010), 381-410. verificación se relaja.

[233]Zana Buçinca et al., "To Trust or to Think: Cognitive Forcing Functions Can Reduce Overreliance on AI in AI-Assisted Decision-Making", Proceedings of the ACM on Human-Computer Interaction 5 (CSCW1), 188, arXiv:2102.09692, 2021.

themselves more verify more. LLMs displace cognitive effort from active production to passive verification, and many workers who do not have sufficient domain-criterion to verify do not compensate the delegation with vigilance and simply accept.[234]

Along the same lines, a study comparing ChatGPT-assisted research with conventional web search found that ChatGPT users experienced lower cognitive load with arguments of lower quality and depth of reasoning.[235] The authors summarized the result as "cognitive ease at a cost." Reduced effort did not translate into a better evaluation of the result. Likewise, observations of brain connectivity and executive function during writing tasks with and without AI assistance show that the neural metrics of executive control were significantly weaker in the assisted condition.[236] Brain activity associated with deliberate thinking decreased when the model produced the draft. In the same vein, a randomized controlled experiment with students during academic-writing tasks found that the AI-assisted group showed significantly lower levels of cognitive engagement than the control group, producing lazier thinkers.[237]

The convergence of these studies suggests that delegation to systems that produce fluent responses reduces cognitive vigilance in ways that are measurable, consistent, and imperceptible to the user. We saw it in Chapter 6. The user does not perceive that they are verifying less, because they have deactivated the signals that normally trigger suspicion. In delegation without evaluation, therefore, the user goes adrift, because an LLM simply cannot be at

---

[234]Hao-Ping Lee et al., "The Impact of Generative AI on Critical Thinking: Self-Reported Reductions in Cognitive Effort and Confidence Effects From a Survey of Knowledge Workers", Proceedings of the 2025 CHI Conference on Human Factors in Computing Systems (CHI 25), Yokohama, Japón, ACM, 2025, 1-22.

[235]Matthias Stadler et al., "Cognitive Ease at a Cost: LLMs Reduce Mental Effort but Compromise Depth in Student Scientific Inquiry", Computers in Human Behavior, 160, 2024.

[236]Nataliya Kosmyna et al., "Accumulation of Cognitive Debt when Using an AI Assistant for Essay Writing Task", arXiv 2506.08872, 2025.

[237]Georgios Georgiou, "ChatGPT Produces More Lazy Thinkers: Evidence of Cognitive Engagement in Decline", arXiv2507.00181, 2025.

the helm. Because artificial intelligence amplifies existing expertise rather than substituting for it, training in the relevant field becomes still more important — since the capacity to evaluate presupposes a knowledge obtained by studying the domain in question, and that competency is acquired only by having executed enough to know what to look for when the machine fails.

*

Governing a power that has no direction of its own demands contributing judgment. None of this requires that we master the architecture of transformers, but we must adopt an alert disposition. The best results come from a well-designed iteration conceived as interaction engineering rather than mere prompting — and depend, therefore, on the one who traces it and sustains it as an epistemic responsibility. We said that in all this there is something like the old adventure of taming a creature stronger than oneself. We will not master it by sheer force. We master it by the intelligence of the one who conducts it, a steady hand on the reins, and the judgment to tell when the beast truly obeys and when it merely simulates obeying. The difference between a brilliant result and a well-written disaster depends entirely on knowing how to handle those reins and being clear, at every moment, about where we are going.

10

Gaps and Asymmetries

There comes a moment in our crossing of the labyrinth when we stop looking at the architecture and start looking at who else is in it with us. We become interested in who came through the main door and who slipped in through a narrower side entrance, who walks through the central corridors in good light and who advances by groping along the peripheral passageways where the ceiling is lower and the signs are in another language. This chapter examines who can enter, how far they can get, and what each one finds when they arrive.

What is a Gap

At various moments in our crossing, in connection with the relation between artificial intelligence and society, the problem of differences of access surfaced. In the most optimistic version, expanding language models is presented as an opportunity for technological democratization. Anyone, anywhere, would today have access to a powerful artificial intelligence. The claim has a foothold, but it needs qualification. Access is heterogeneous, stratified by technical, economic, institutional, and cultural layers that determine who reaches what. There are, in other words, several distinct gaps.

The very notion of gap designates, in its most general use, a structural distance between groups, sectors, or territories with respect to a resource, a capacity, or a condition whose unequal distribution produces cumulative consequences. This distinguishes it from a mere difference, which may be neutral, and from inequality in the broad sense, which need not have an identifiable structure. A gap, by contrast, implies a resource whose possession or lack generates divergent trajectories, such that those who have it advance while those who do not stagnate or fall back.

Development economics has used the concept since the mid-twentieth century to describe the persistent distances between industrialized and peripheral countries, in what Prebisch and ECLAC called the center-periphery gap, where the structure of international trade reproduces the asymmetry rather than closing it.

The sociology of education speaks of learning gaps to describe differences in educational achievement between socioeconomic groups that, far from being reduced by universal schooling, are maintained or widened because the family and institutional conditions that determine what one gets out of school are as unequal as access itself.[238]

The notion of health gap, in turn, describes differences in life expectancy, access to treatment, and levels of illness between populations that, in many cases, coexist in the same territory under distinct material conditions. This "social gradient of health" shows that there is a gap between rich and poor, but it is also granularized

[238]Raúl Prebisch, El desarrollo económico de la América Latina and algunos de sus principales problemas, Santiago de Chile, CEPAL, 1950.

across the entire socioeconomic scale, such that each rung has worse indicators than the one immediately above it.[239][240]

The concept rests on a spatial metaphor and additionally has a causal structure in which the initial distance is reproduced and amplified through mechanisms independent of the actors' intentions. Merton, in the sociology of science, spoke of the "Matthew effect," in reference to the evangelical passage: to those who have, more will be given; from those who do not have, even what little they have will be taken away. The mechanism does not require ill will, since it operates through apparently rational decisions that attend first to those who are already known. In this logic of "cumulative advantage", whoever starts with an initial advantage, however small, tends to accumulate further advantages over time, because each advantage creates conditions for the next. The same occurs in fields as diverse as employment, health, education, and technology.[241]

Bourdieu conceptualized the reproduction of gaps through the forms of economic, cultural, social, and symbolic capital, whose unequal distribution is transmitted inter-generationally not by direct inheritance but by the structure of dispositions he called "habitus" — the set of dispositions, tastes, and manners of moving through the world that a person incorporates from childhood and that give them advantage or disadvantage before any individual decision

---

[239]This phenomenon was documented by Coleman as early as 1966 and its persistence was confirmed by decades of subsequent research. See James Coleman et al., Equality of Educational Opportunity, Washington, U.S. Department of Health, Education, and Welfare, 1966; Sean Reardon, "The Widening Academic Achievement Gap Between the Rich and the Poor: New Evidence and Possible Explanations", in Whither Opportunity?, New York, Russell Sage Foundation, 2011, which documents that the income-associated achievement gap grew by 40% between cohorts born in 1976 and 2001.

[240]Michael Marmot, The Health Gap: The Challenge of an Unequal World, International Journal of Epidemiology 46.4, 2017, 1312-1318.

[241]Robert Merton, "The Matthew Effect in Science", Science 159.3810 (1968), 56-63 and Thomas A. DiPrete and Gregory M. Eirich, "Cumulative Advantage as a Mechanism for Inequality: A Review of Theoretical and Empirical Developments", Annual Review of Sociology 32.1 (2006), 271-297.

comes into play. In all of these frames, the gap is a process that is produced, reproduced, and deepened without intervention.[242]

The *digital divide* emerged as a category in the 1990s to refer to unequal access to information and communication technologies. It is distinct from earlier gaps by its velocity. Educational or health gaps operate on scales of decades or generations, while technological gaps can open in months, because the rhythm of change of the object is incomparably faster than that of the school or the health system, and early adoption generates competencies that late adoption cannot compensate without deliberate effort.

DiMaggio and Hargittai proposed the conceptual shift from "digital divide" to "digital inequality", since the digital divide, as it had been measured, operated with a binary logic of access or no access, connected or disconnected.[243] That formulation lost its value as internet penetration grew, because the problem ceased to be who had access and became what those who had access were doing with it. They therefore proposed five dimensions of inequality that operate even when material access is resolved.[244]

The first is *inequality of technical equipment.* A broadband connection on a desktop computer enables very different uses from a slow mobile connection on a small-screen phone, though both count as access in the statistics.

The second is *autonomy of use.* If access depends on a shared device in a public library with restricted hours or on a family phone, the conditions of exploration are incomparable to those of someone with a personal device available at any moment.

The third is *inequality of skills.* Knowing how to turn on a device and open a browser is not the same as knowing how to search for

[242]Pierre Bourdieu y Jean-Claude Passeron, La reproduction: Éléments pour une théorie du système d'enseignement, Paris, Minuit, 1970 and Pierre Bourdieu, La distinction: Critique sociale du jugement, Paris, Minuit, 1979.
[243]Paul DiMaggio et al., "From the Digital Divide to Digital Inequality", Working Paper, Center for Arts and Cultural Policy Studies, Princeton University, 2001.
[244]Paul DiMaggio and Eszter Hargittai, "From the Digital Divide to Digital Inequality: Studying Internet Use as Penetration Increases", Center for Arts and Cultural Policy Studies, Princeton University, 2001.

information with judgment, evaluate sources, navigate complex interfaces, or solve technical problems. Digital skills are distributed unequally, and that distribution is aligned with educational level, income, and prior cultural capital, such that the skills gap reproduces the very asymmetries that the access gap was supposed to resolve.

The fourth dimension is *available social support.* Those who are surrounded by people who use technology fluently have an informal assistance network that reduces the cost of learning, while those without such a network face every difficulty alone, which raises the abandonment rate and consolidates superficial use.

The fifth is *purpose of use.* Lower-income and lower-education users tend toward entertainment use, while higher-income and higher-education users use it for health information, work opportunities, education, and civic participation — uses that function as capital-enhancing, that is, uses that generate cumulative advantages in other dimensions of life.

This framework is pertinent to the case of artificial intelligence, since the provision of access by itself does not close gaps and may even widen them. If those who already have social, educational, and cultural advantages extract more value from the technology than those who do not, then democratizing access without intervening on the conditions of use produces what van Dijk called the "inclusion paradox", according to which the more access expands, the more visible the inequality of use becomes, because the variable that determines outcomes is not resolved by infrastructure and requires much more complex interventions that unfold across four levels, in which intervention at one level produces effects only if the previous levels are covered.[245]

The first level concerns *motivational access*, that is, the disposition to use the technology that precedes any question of equipment. There are groups who ignore available technologies because they do

---

[245]Jan A. G. M. van Dijk, The Deepening Divide: Inequality in the Information Society, London, Sage, 2005. Updated in The Digital Divide, SAGE, 2005. Someone who experiences technology as an instrument of control associates "access to AI" with threat and most likely avoids it.

not perceive utility, feel anxiety at the interface, or consider that the technology is simply not for them, whether because of age, educational level, or earlier bad experiences with technology. For instance, a precariously employed worker who experiences technology as an instrument of control associates "AI access" with threat and is most likely to avoid it. Without concrete experiences of utility, motivation dissolves and blocks the subsequent levels.

Material access, that is, the physical availability of devices and connectivity, corresponds to the second level. This is where public policy has historically concentrated (provision of computers, wiring of schools, subsidies for connectivity) and it is what adoption statistics usually measure. In itself it is fine, but from what we have said it is a necessary but not a sufficient condition, as is seen in countries with high connectivity that maintain inequalities of use as marked as those in countries with much lower penetration. This means that infrastructure is only a floor, with less effect than is usually granted to it.

At the third level is *access to skills development*. Operational skills (knowing how to turn on a device, navigate an interface, use a keyboard, or open an application) are the most basic. Formal skills are intermediate: knowing how to orient oneself in the structure of a website, understanding how a search engine works, distinguishing between types of content, and managing files and configurations. Substantive skills are the most unequally distributed. They involve tasks such as knowing how to search for information with judgment, evaluating the reliability of a source, using technology to solve real problems, producing one's own content, and integrating digital tools into a workflow. The distribution of these skills reproduces the distribution of prior educational and cultural capital, according to the logic of cumulative advantage we have already described. The provision of material access without the development of substantive skills does not close gaps.

At the fourth level is *access of use*, which describes what we actually do with the technology when the three previous levels are covered. Does the technology activate benefits transferable to other dimensions of life, or does it exhaust itself in entertainment consumption with no cumulative effect? Gaps at this level are the most difficult to close with public policy, because they depend on factors such as the user's social environment, their perceived needs, the structure of incentives in which they operate, and the existence of institutions that mediate between the technology and its productive applications.

Each generation of public policy tends to concentrate on the level it can resolve and to absolutize it to magnify its own merit. In fact, providing infrastructure is politically visible and technically simple, while developing substantive skills is costly, slow, and difficult to measure. Worse still, it feels more like development through personal effort than as a gift from the ruler, which makes it unattractive as an electioneering intervention. On top of this, transforming patterns of use requires institutional and cultural interventions that exceed the scope of an isolated technology policy. The result is a succession of initiatives that resolve the material level and then note, with recurrent surprise, that the use gap persists.

The basic problem is that the digital divide is a manifestation of preexisting social inequalities, such that resolving it would require intervening on social conditions and not only on infrastructure.[246] This in turn produces what is called "second-level digital inequality", where differences in skills and type of use produce unequal outcomes even among those with the same material access.[247] The differences in digital skill among people with equivalent access are as large as the differences between those who have and do not have access, which shifts the focus from infrastructure toward competencies.

The deepest gap is between the one who can evaluate what they receive and the one who cannot, because the response does not warn of its own insufficiency. Without the discomfort of not

[246]Mark Warschauer, Technology and Social Inclusion: Rethinking the Digital Divide, Cambridge, MIT Press, 2003.
[247]Laura Robinson et al., "Digital Inequalities and Why They Matter", Information, Communication & Society 18.5 (2015), 569-582.

understanding and the tension that obliges us to interact with another who might consider us foolish or intelligent for asking or for not asking, the signal that would make it possible to seek what we lack is suppressed. At the scale of a billion users, the sociological category of technological inequality falls short, and we find ourselves rather in a transformation of the collective epistemic terrain in which the illusion of knowing can progressively replace knowing itself, with no one registering the loss.

We now go beyond these frameworks to observe three aspects of the gap as a phenomenon aligned with what our crossing has yielded so far.

The first concerns *the visibility of the gap*. Sociological frameworks describe the gap from outside, as an observable distribution of resources, skills, and outcomes. The classical theories of the digital divide assumed that the difference between users translated into outcome differences that were predictable and in principle visible — whoever knew more searched better, and whoever had a better connection downloaded faster, but the person with fewer resources who obtained less always knew it, for instance by perceiving the slowness. In earlier technological gaps, the disadvantage was perceptible to the one who suffered it. The gap appeared as lack, and the lack was felt. Now that mechanism becomes opaque. The gap does not present itself to the one on the disadvantaged side. Someone who interacts with a free model, with vague instructions and uncritical acceptance, receives a response that has exactly the same formal texture as the one received by an expert user with a frontier model. A rigorous analysis and a superficial one sound the same, such that the gap is experienced as satisfaction, and inequality registers as equality, a consequence of the properties of the technological object itself. The egoless phantom inverts its effects.

The second aspect concerns *the temporal constitution of the gap.* Sociological frameworks describe the accumulation of advantage as *an external process* in which whoever uses more and better accumulates more competencies, like someone who practices an instrument. But competencies are skills that can be taught and learned. What sediments with repeated experience is not only skill but a structure of expectations, of thresholds of attention, of what occurs or does not occur to the subject to do when faced with a new situation — and all of that is harder to modify because there is no content that can be replaced, only a form that organizes how new contents are received. These dispositions, formed through the sedimentation of experience, are "habitualities", and they form the ground from which all perception and action set out. If from the beginning we iterate, correct, and critically evaluate the responses, we develop a habituality of demand that sharpens the gaze and makes re-asking come naturally to us. If from the beginning we accept without evaluating, we develop a habituality of delegation in which verification does not even present itself as a possibility. The difference is one of horizons, which are constituted by the slow accumulation of lived experience, and this is why this dimension of the gap is more resistant than any other.[248]

The third aspect concerns *the nature of the gap*, in line with the structure of virtuality analyzed in Chapter 5 and the constitutive properties of the egoless phantom. By virtue of its character as passive potency, it lacks direction of its own and is actualized according to the instruction it receives, producing different results depending on who uses it without flagging the difference. The user receives no indication that another user, with another instruction, would obtain something qualitatively different. By virtue of its generic indeterminacy, it responds to any demand without an internal standard of quality against which we can measure what we receive. The egoless phantom carries the entire human tradition without orientation toward any segment of it; it cannot distinguish from within between a rigorous response and a fragile one. By virtue of its inexhaustibility without transformation, the model is left unchanged after each interaction. It does not resist misuse and produces fragile responses with the same availability with which it produces rigorous ones, without degrading or signaling that

[248]Edmund Husserl, "Das Ich als Substrat von Habitualitäten", Cartesianische Meditationen und Pariser Vorträge, Vierte Meditation, § 32, in Husserliana, Bd.

something went wrong. By virtue of its cognitive derivation, the response is given the form of knowledge without its experiential ground. The gap is covered with an appearance of competence that makes it undetectable from within. The system only returns our gaze amplified, and we receive a mediocre response indistinguishable from an excellent one. Each of these constitutive properties contributes to making this gap something qualitatively distinct from the previous ones — an inequality produced and concealed by the object itself and its peculiar mode of being.

Anders's Promethean differential, which we mentioned in Chapter 6 to explain why the materiality of the system can be known and yet perceived as unreal, makes it possible for the gap to be described sociologically with data and to remain invisible to the one who suffers it. The distance between the sociological description of the gap and the lived experience of the one on the disadvantaged side is, itself, a manifestation of the Promethean differential. Artificial intelligence therefore stratifies in ways that the usual categories of inclusion and exclusion do not capture well, and it is necessary to examine them to determine more precisely which gaps artificial intelligence opens and which it can close.

Stratification of Access

According to the Generative AI Adoption Tracker produced by the Federal Reserve of St. Louis and the Harvard Kennedy School (the first representative survey of generative AI adoption in the United States) in August 2025, 54.6% of the U.S. population between 18 and 64 had used generative AI at least once, up from 44.6% a year earlier. 37.4% of employed workers had used it at least once in the previous week. The share of work hours assisted by generative AI rose from 4.1% in November 2024 to 5.7% in August 2025. To put these numbers in perspective, the workplace adoption of generative AI has been as rapid as that of the personal computer in the early years following the launch of the first mass product and faster than that of the internet.[249]

Global figures look similar. According to OECD data published in January 2026, individual use of generative AI has expanded rapidly in every member country with available data, and 20.2% of firms reported using AI in 2025, more than double the 8.7% recorded in 2023. Latin America presents a particularly revealing profile because it combines high emotional adoption with low structural adoption. According to the Latin American Artificial Intelligence Index (ILIA 2025), produced by ECLAC and the National Artificial Intelligence Center of Chile across 19 countries, the region is accelerating AI adoption at a rate that exceeds what would be expected given its digital weight, that is, it is adopting faster than its infrastructure conditions would suggest.[250] Brazil is the most visible case. With one of the largest ChatGPT user bases in the world, downloads of AI tools grew from 3.7 million in 2023 to 11.8 million in 2025 — an 88% year-on-year increase. According to a 2025 Ipsos and Google survey, 72% of Mexicans, 71% of Chileans, and 65% of Brazilians declare themselves enthusiastic about the possibilities of AI. In Argentina, according to the 2025 Ipsos and Google report Our Life with AI, 65% of Argentines use AI chatbots, surpassing the global average of 62%; and the report from FUNDAR and the CEPE of Universidad Torcuato Di Tella confirms that 45% of adults and 64% of Generation Z use AI for personal purposes, at levels comparable to advanced economies.[251]

But the enthusiasm coexists with constraints that the data from OECD countries does not reflect with the same intensity. The gaps are not uniformly distributed, and each one operates with its own dynamics. The sharpest gap is the age gap. OECD data shows a 53.6

---

[249] Alexander Bick et al., "The Rapid Adoption of Generative AI", NBER Working Paper 32966, 2024. August 2025.

[250] CEPAL and CENIA Chile, Índice Latinoamericano de Inteligencia Artificial (ILIA 2025). Más de 100 subindicadores en 19 países. Tercera edición.

[251] Ipsos and Google, Our Life with AI, 3rd edition, 2025; FUNDAR and CEPE–Universidad Torcuato Di Tella, Encuesta Nacional sobre Adopción de IA en Argentina, 2025, available at cepe-fundar.github.io/encuesta.html.

percentage-point difference between the age groups with the highest and lowest adoption, the widest among all the dimensions measured. Three quarters of students older than 16 reported using generative AI tools, compared with 12.5% of retirees and economically inactive individuals.[252]

The age gap is above all a gap of type of use. 61% of Generation Z uses AI for education, while Generation X and baby boomers use it predominantly for functional work tasks and voice assistants. Millennials, in mid-management positions, show the highest rates of sustained professional integration: programmers who use AI complete 55.8% more projects according to a 2025 Netguru study, and they function as vectors of institutional adoption. Among those older than 55, use is low, though not nil, and is concentrated in practical, low-cognitive-engagement applications without the more ambitious exploration that characterizes younger groups. The age gap suggests that we are facing qualitatively distinct patterns of use that could consolidate into distinct generational patterns of engagement with technology.[253]

The gender gap, unlike the age gap, is quantitatively smaller but persistent. OECD data places it at 4.2 percentage points at the aggregate level. A 2024 Harvard meta-analysis covering 18 studies and 140,000 participants found that women are approximately 20% less likely to interact with AI than men, regardless of occupation.[254] A Deloitte report confirms this finding but suggests a trend toward change.[255][256] 44% of men compared with 33% of women use

[252]Eszter Hargittai et al., "Succinct Survey Measures of Web-Use Skills", Social Science Computer Review 30.1 (2012), 95-107.

[253]BBF Digital, "Patterns Behind the AI Boom Across Generations and Economies", 2025.

[254]Nicholas Otis et al., "Global Evidence on Gender Gaps and Generative AI", Harvard Business School Working Paper 25-023, 2024.

[255]SurveyMonkey, "2024 AI Trends by Generation: Who Uses AI the Most?" SurveyMonkey Curiosity. https://www.surveymonkey.com/curiosity/ai- trends-by-generations/.

[256]Deloitte, "Women and Generative AI: The Adoption Gap Is Closing Fast, but a Trust Gap Persists", Technology, Media & Telecommunications (TMT) Predictions 2025, Deloitte Insights, 2024.

generative AI, with an even larger divergence in daily use (43% vs. 34%). Only 18% of women trust that AI providers will protect their data, compared with 31% of men. The gap is probably closing at initial adoption but persists in intensity, trust, and type of use.

The gap by educational level and income is substantial. OECD data shows a difference of approximately 21 percentage points by both educational level and income. The Bick, Blandin, and Deming study for the United States shows that adoption is significantly higher among people with higher education and in computing, mathematics, and management occupations. Middle and high incomes correlate strongly with paid use, which is associated with more complex tasks and a greater accumulation of interaction competencies.[257]

The gap by profession and sector is equally pronounced. OECD data for 2025 shows that 57.3% of ICT-sector firms use AI, with rates close to saturation in the Nordic countries, where Sweden reaches 87.9%, compared with 7.2% in construction and 7.8% in hospitality and food service. Professional and scientific services come in at 36.8%. Within each sector, adoption is markedly unequal by firm size. 52% of large firms use AI, compared with 17.4% of small ones — a three-to-one gap that, according to the OECD report on AI adoption by SMEs, is explained by differences in budget, but also in digital preparedness, availability of quality data, access to specialized providers, and capacity to generate new business models.[258]

The gap that is hardest to measure is the one that operates within the same access groups. Not all users who pay for a subscription use the service in the same way, and the difference between superficial use and integrated use is poorly captured in adoption statistics. Of the total paid users, only a reduced fraction, probably between 5 and 10%, is estimated to use customized configurations, external

[257]OECD, "AI use by individuals surges across the OECD as adoption by firms continues to expand", January 2026.

[258]OECD, "AI Adoption by Small and Medium-Sized Enterprises", discussion paper prepared for the Canadian G7 presidency, 2025.

memories, or systematic integration into workflows. An even smaller group, on the order of 1%, integrates AI structurally into complex processes. In absolute terms, this amounts to a few million at the global scale. This difference leads us back to the problem of the regime of interaction that we treated in Chapter 9, and it produces divergent trajectories of competency accumulation. The aggregate data thus tells two compatible stories: one of accelerated expansion, another of persistent [259]stratification.

Gaps That Open and Close

Up to this point, the gaps we have been describing all run in one direction. Someone has more and someone has less, and the distance tends to grow. But the phenomenon is more complex, because artificial intelligence amplifies existing inequalities, opens some new gaps, and tends to close others. Separating these dynamics avoids the twin errors of optimism (AI as universal equalizer) and pessimism (AI as amplifier of everything already wrong). What we have is a system that stratifies and democratizes simultaneously, according to the domain, the context, and the conditions of use. Let us begin with what opens.

The *institutional gap* deserves special attention, since the inequality of access is not limited to individual users. In some countries, especially in northern Europe, institutions have managed to integrate AI in a relatively orderly way. In systems like those of Finland, Estonia, or the Netherlands, the introduction of tools based on language models is accompanied by teacher-training programs, clear rules on use and evaluation, and institutional frameworks that treat AI as an object of learning, aimed at mastering what it can do, what it cannot, and under what conditions it is worth using.

In many other contexts (Latin America, southern Europe, and large regions of Africa and Asia) educational institutions and

[259]Menlo Ventures, "The State of Generative AI in the Enterprise", 2025.

organizations in general face many limitations. Restricted budgets, uneven connectivity, unclear regulatory frameworks, and a growing gap between the formal environment and actual practices conspire against advancement on this terrain. Institutional responses oscillate between reactive prohibition, which makes the use of AI informal and disorderly without eliminating it, and uncritical adoption, which introduces it without redefining clear objectives, delegating tasks without ensuring supervision.

In the business sphere the dynamic is similar. Large organizations integrate AI through customized systems, usage protocols, and specialized teams, while small and medium-sized organizations depend on general-purpose public tools, without adequate training or control criteria. According to OECD data, 52% of large firms use AI compared with 17.4% of small ones. Moreover, firms that develop AI internally obtain significantly higher returns than those that use generic solutions, and the capacity to develop or adapt internally goes hand in hand with the size and resources of the organization. The institutional gap is basically a gap of capacity to integrate AI with judgment, which depends on training, time, organizational structure, and criterion — all aspects that are not resolved overnight.

The gaps of use and institutional integration operate on top of the structure of the models themselves. Technical barriers produce *model gaps*, from which a stratification emerges that goes beyond the technical. We already saw in Chapter 7 that at the top sits a very small number of actors capable of training large-scale base models, concentrated in large tech companies and, in some cases, consortia with significant state support. These actors control initial training, architecture, data selection, curation criteria, and the alignment processes that define the model's basic behavior. On this base is built an intermediate layer formed by hundreds or thousands of derived models, obtained through fine-tuning, LoRA, or specific alignment adjustments. Finally, millions of users, organizations, and even public institutions access only inference, that is, the use of the already-trained model under conditions fixed by third parties.[260]

This division of cognitive labor responds to a material reality that, nevertheless, is becoming differentiated. Training an absolute-frontier base model still requires investments that only a handful of actors can afford, but the DeepSeek case demonstrated that models can be trained with less investment, and Kimi K2 replicated that pattern. As we saw, the threshold of access to competitive-level capabilities has dropped dramatically, which opens an intermediate zone where actors with moderate resources can train their own models if they have the data, the engineering, and the strategic orientation. That possibility does not eliminate the concentration at the highest layer or resolve the central problem: without access to the original data, the curation pipelines, and the capacity to iterate training at scale, the opening of weights enables use and local adaptation but not producing models that reflect local traditions, languages, and knowledge from their origin. The concentration of genesis persists, even though its ceiling has become more porous than it appeared.

The models operate as cognitive infrastructure. They facilitate tasks and mediate access to knowledge, stabilizing forms of argument, hierarchizing styles of writing, and normalizing certain registers as more reasonable than others. Yuk Hui, in his work on cosmotechnics, calls this monotechnology, that is, the imposition of a single relation to knowledge that suppresses diversity through standardization. A model trained within a particular cosmotechnics, with its assumptions about efficiency, scalability, and utility, deploys globally as if that cosmotechnics were technique itself. Neutrality, in this context, is a rhetorical fiction that ignores the material conditions of its own construction.[261]

---

[260]Emily Bender et al., "On the Dangers of Stochastic Parrots: Can Language Models Be Too Big?", Proceedings of FAccT, 2021 and Epoch AI, "How much does it cost to train frontier AI models?", 2024.

[261]Yuk Hui, The Question Concerning Technology in China: An Essay in Cosmotechnics, Falmouth, Urbanomic, 2016 and Machine and Sovereignty: For a Planetary Thinking, Minneapolis, University of Minnesota Press, 2024.

There is a gap that runs in the opposite direction from the others, and it opens within the groups with the highest adoption. The youngest users who integrate AI from the beginning of their formation (before having developed the competencies that the tool replaces) run the risk of not acquiring skills that previous generations developed out of necessity. Drafting without assistance, sustaining an argument without external help, searching for information with judgment in primary sources, tolerating the uncertainty of not knowing, and building from there are competencies that strengthen with practice and atrophy with systematic delegation. If an entire cohort learns to write with assistance from adolescence onward, the accumulated social capacity to produce argumentative text without external support is damaged in the aggregate. The *generational gap of skill loss* pits those who used the tool without having first developed what it replaces against those who arrived after having developed it, or against those who did not use it — with consequences that will only become visible when those competencies are required in the absence of the tool.

Let us now consider which gaps artificial intelligence could close. Indeed, the critique of the democratization narrative should not obscure the concrete gaps where artificial intelligence can produce genuine value.

The most immediate gap is *linguistic*. A researcher who reads in Spanish but needs to consult literature in Mandarin, German, or Arabic had, until recently, only two options: learn the language or depend on what was already translated. Language models do not eliminate the barrier (automated translation has quality limits), but they reduce it enough to alter the conditions of intellectual work. An Argentine lawyer who needs to understand a contract drafted under German law obtains a functional first reading in minutes, and what they gain is the capacity to know what questions to ask a specialist. A researcher in Brazil can scan Japanese-language bibliography to determine whether it is worth commissioning a professional translation in case they end up needing style or extreme precision. The asymmetry between those who read in several languages and those who read in only one shrinks, because the cost of access to the material drops.[262]

The second gap is *informational.* A small farmer in the interior of a province does not have access to the same technical knowledge as a corporation with an R&D department, but an AI system specialized in soil management, pests, or irrigation (which can be a small model, trained for that domain, operating with local data) can bring that knowledge closer without requiring the farmer to read articles or hire consultants. AI organizes information that would otherwise not arrive. The same applies in health, where a rural doctor practicing alone can use a model as a second pair of eyes for differential diagnosis when professional isolation makes it hard to consult with colleagues.

The third gap is *compliance.* The documentation and transparency requirements imposed by national and regional regulations are manageable for a firm with a legal department, but for a cooperative, an NGO, or a small business they are potentially prohibitive. An AI system that assists in drafting technical documentation, impact assessments, or audit-trail organization reduces the cost of producing the first draft from weeks to hours, which a professional can then review at lower cost. Regulation becomes less asymmetric when the tool brings closer the capacity to produce what is required.

The fourth gap is *educational.* A student who does not have access to an individual tutor can use a model as a study companion that explains what they do not understand, proposes exercises, flags errors, and adapts the pace to their level. Without replacing the teacher or the school, it reduces the distance between those who have access to personalized education and those who do not. From the teacher's side, multi-layered design facilitates the work of adapting to different profiles, which traditionally consumed an enormous amount of time and meant that, in practice, the inclusion of students with difficulties was subject to insurmountable restrictions. This is perhaps the gap where the potential is greatest

[262]Pratik Joshi et al., "The State and Fate of Linguistic Diversity and Inclusion in the NLP World", Proceedings of ACL, 2020.

and the risk is greatest as well, because a badly designed system that confirms errors rather than correcting them can consolidate the very deficits it was meant to attenuate.[263]

The fifth gap that closes is *access to professional advice.* In many regions of the world, consulting a lawyer, an accountant, or a financial advisor is economically out of reach for the majority. A language model that offers a first orientation through relevant initial questions can make the difference between acting with information and acting blind. The risk that we take the model's orientation as a definitive verdict is real, but in cases where the alternative is to act without information, the tendency is toward a smaller gap.

In all these cases, artificial intelligence reduces the cost of access to a first level of capacity that was previously reserved for those who could pay for it or those who had the geographic and institutional luck of having it within reach. The model's passive potency, which in the hands of an expert amplifies their advantage, in contexts of deprivation can fulfill the function of making available what was not there. A skeptic may object that this is not real leveling. It can, however, bring the floor closer.

TECHNOLOGICAL SOVEREIGNTY

If the training of base models remains concentrated, the capacity to define what counts as well-formed knowledge is structurally limited. This is what the discussion of technological sovereignty points to, though the term is usually used with more political emphasis than precision. For a country that does not train its own models — the vast majority of countries — depending on models produced within another "cosmotechnics" has consequences that go beyond the price of the subscription. It means that the implicit norms of what

[263]Kurt VanLehn, "The Relative Effectiveness of Human Tutoring, Intelligent Tutoring Systems, and Other Tutoring Systems", Educational Psychologist 46.4 (2011), 197-221 y OECD, "AI and the Future of Skills", 2025, and UNESCO, "Guidance for Generative AI in Education and Research", 2024.

constitutes a good response or a well-formed argument were calibrated in another cultural context, since the model introduces those norms as the statistical floor of what is plausible.[264]

The degradation is not dramatic; the models simply function better in the registers that are best represented in their corpus and worse in all others. A lawyer asking about U.S. law obtains more precise responses than one asking about Argentine law. At scale, this produces a normalizing pressure that pushes toward dominant registers simply because they are better modeled.

The geopolitics of chips that we examined in Chapter 7 is a background condition, so that cognitive sovereignty is conditioned by material sovereignty over the inputs of training. A country without access to last-generation GPUs cannot train frontier models, regardless of its scientific capacity or the quality of its data. If the infrastructure needed to train frontier models cannot be reproduced, awareness of the asymmetry and the deliberate design of corrections become relevant. Training smaller models with local data for specific domains, investing in producing quality corpora in underrepresented languages and registers, establishing regulatory frameworks that require transparency about training data, and developing institutional capacity to evaluate and adapt models produced by others rather than consuming them without mediation all expand the room for maneuver and should all figure on the global agenda.

*

Correcting gaps requires educational-policy decisions that treat AI as an object of learning and not only as a tool, institutional frameworks that integrate with judgment rather than prohibiting or

---

264Nick Couldry et al., The Costs of Connection: How Data Is Colonizing Human Life and Appropriating It for Capitalism, Stanford, Stanford University Press, 2019.

adopting blindly, investment in local data and models that reduce dependence on cognitive infrastructure produced in another context, and regulation that requires transparency about what is inside the systems that increasingly configure access to knowledge. The question is what kind of cognitive infrastructure we are willing to build, for whom, and under what conditions. Earlier in this chapter we stopped to ask who else was in the labyrinth. What we found is not encouraging. The entrance is open, but not through the same place; the price is charged differently depending on where we come from; and the best maps are written in a language that is not everyone's. Everything depends on the political architecture, which can be redesigned, if we are willing to build what is missing.

11

Challenges for Human Work

There is a zone of the labyrinth that is no different from the others. The corridors are the same width, the light is the same, and the walls have the same texture, but something in the proportions of the space turns oppressive. Footsteps resonate differently and the smell of fear is in the air. It is there, with a more concrete and paralyzing presence. When we walk through this zone we cannot help thinking about what we left outside, about those who are waiting for us, and we ask ourselves what is going to happen, because what is at stake is one's livelihood. Few questions produce as much anxiety as the possibility that one's work might cease to exist. The material concern is real: it touches those who support families, pay mortgages, or have spent years training for a profession that now seems vulnerable. In previous cycles, transitions took decades, with time for the gradual adaptation of institutions and training systems. Now they are compressed into quarters. The threat is hard to dismiss.

Expectations of disruption in the world of work are reflected in university graduates who believe AI has reduced the value of their degrees and in employers planning to reduce headcount by automating tasks. Strictly speaking, the fear of labor displacement has consequences even when the displacement does not occur, since it modifies decisions about training, personal investment, family planning, and political orientation simply by looming on the horizon. Like any fear, it is fertile ground for both alarmist manipulation and interested minimization. We will sidestep both routes and examine the phenomenon without softening its genuinely troubling aspects or amplifying the uncertain ones on terrain that is already complicated enough.

THE GENERAL LANDSCAPE

Unlike with other problems, empirical evidence here is in surplus, which at least partly explains the confusion in the theoretical debate. The adoption figures we examined in the previous chapter tell a story of accelerated expansion, with a growing population using generative AI and multiplying the hours of assisted work. The MetLife survey of March 2026 on human-resources managers and employees confirms that AI is already integrated into daily operations. 80% of employers surveyed report that AI tools are part of daily tasks, and even more say it helps their employees work faster and more efficiently. But when one moves from adoption to impact, the picture becomes a puzzle of findings pointing in different directions.[265]

A controlled experiment with GitHub Copilot reports that developers with access to the AI assistant completed a programming task 55.[266]8% faster than the control group, with greater benefit for less experienced and older programmers. A subsequent field study with developers at Microsoft and Accenture found a real but more modest effect.[267] But an analysis of activity in open-source projects after the introduction of Copilot suggests that productivity rises but that AI-assisted code requires more additional work in corrections and maintenance, which suggests that the speed gains may mask a

[265]MetLife 24th Annual U.S. Employee Benefit Trends Study, March 2026.
[266]Sida Peng et al., "The Impact of AI on Developer Productivity: Evidence from GitHub Copilot", arXiv:2302.06590, 2023.
[267]Zheyuan (Kevin) Cui et al., "The Productivity Effects of Generative AI: Evidence from a Field Experiment with GitHub Copilot", MIT Generative AI Initiative, 2024.

growing burden that falls on a smaller and smaller group of experts capable of detecting the problems the model introduces.[268]

A significant share of the workforce has part of their tasks exposed to language models, but quantifying that exposure depends on what is being measured.[269] The data from the Anthropic Economic Index, based on the analysis of millions of real conversations with Claude throughout 2025, bears this out, with nuances.[270] The first measure is coverage. In January 2025, 36% of occupations registered Claude use for at least a quarter of their tasks; by November the figure had risen to 49%. But coverage is not the same as impact. When adjusted for the model's success rate — that is, the extent to which Claude actually completes tasks, weighted by frequency and duration — the picture changed: occupations such as data entry and radiology turned out to be much more affected than mere task coverage suggested, because the model is highly efficient at them, while the impact was smaller for occupations such as teaching and software development, because there the model operates with less autonomy.

A third finding complicates the idea of replacement: the dominant pattern of use is complement, not full automation. The ten most frequent tasks account for 24% of all conversations, indicating that use is fairly distributed, and computation and mathematics tasks (the ones most associated with automation in the popular imagination) make up only a third of total use.[271] Yet AI improves team collaboration and makes it possible to overcome traditional functional silos (a positive effect that does not show up

---

[268]Feiyang Xu et al., “AI-Assisted Programming May Decrease the Productivity of Experienced Developers by Increasing Maintenance Burden”, Tilburg University, arXiv:2510.10165, 2025.

[269]Tyna Eloundou et al., “GPTs are GPTs: An Early Look at the Labor Market Impact Potential of Large Language Models”, Science 384, 6702 (2024), 1306-1308, arXiv:2303.10130, 2023.

[270]Kunal Handa et al., "Which Economic Tasks Are Performed with AI? Evidence from Millions of Claude Conversations", arXiv:2503.04761, 2025.

[271]Fabrizio Dell'Acqua et al., “Navigating the Jagged Technological Frontier: Field Experimental Evidence of the Effects of AI on Knowledge Worker Productivity and Quality”, Harvard Business School Working Paper 24-013, 2023.

in individual productivity metrics) but at the same time it increases working hours, since it complements without replacing the labor quantum, and reduces employee satisfaction.[272]

The macroeconomic projections are enormously dispersed. Acemoglu estimated that only around 5% of work tasks will be profitably performed by AI over the next decade, producing a GDP increase of just 1.1% to 1.6% over ten years. Goldman Sachs, at the opposite extreme, projected a 7% increase in global GDP; McKinsey estimated that between 60% and 70% of work activities could be automated before 2030; and the World Economic Forum projected 92 million jobs displaced and 170 million created by 2030, with a net gain of 78 million. The aggregate picture conceals a severe distributional problem: those who lose their jobs and those who gain the new ones are different people, in different places, with different skills.[273]

The most significant data point of 2025-2026 on concrete labor impact comes from a study that cross-referenced AI-exposure metrics with actual employment records (millions of records, not just perception surveys). Employment for young workers aged 22 to 25 in the occupations most exposed to AI fell by 13% since November 2022, while employment in less-exposed occupations and for older workers remained stable or even grew. The fall is due to a reduction of people entering the workforce. Firms did not lay off staff; they stopped hiring for those roles.[274]

In 2025 there were nearly 55,000 layoffs in the United States directly attributed to AI, within a total of 1.[275]17 million, the highest

[272]Wei Jiang et al., "AI and the Extended Workday: Productivity, Contracting Efficiency, and Distribution of Rents", NBER Working Paper No. 33536, 2025.
[273]Daron Acemoglu, "The Simple Macroeconomics of AI", Economic Policy 40.121 (2025), Goldman Sachs Research, 2025; McKinsey Global Institute, 2023 and WEF Future of Jobs Report 2025.
[274]Erik Brynjolfsson et al., "Canaries in the Coal Mine: Six Facts about the Recent Decline in Entry-Level Employment", Stanford Digital Economy Lab, 2025.
[275]Challenger, Gray & Christmas, 2025 Year-End Challenger Report: Highest Q4 Layoffs Since 2008; Lowest YTD Hiring Since 2010, 8 January 2026. Amazon eliminated 14,000 corporate roles claiming that AI enables leaner structures. Workday cut 8.5% of its workforce to reallocate resources toward AI investments.

level since the pandemic. At the same time, a hiring experiment showed that AI skills on a résumé partially compensate for the disadvantages of age and lack of an advanced degree. Older candidates and those without a postgraduate degree substantially improve their chances of being called for an interview when they have certified competencies in this area.[276] The labor market in vanguard countries is already rewarding this capability as a transversal competency and closing the door to those who do not.

The data cited here comes almost entirely from leading economies: the United States, northern Europe, and OECD countries with labor markets that already generate compensatory demand while automating tasks. That asymmetry is itself informative. In peripheral economies, the speed of automation does not generate new demand at the same speed. A programmer in California displaced by Copilot may find audit or design demand in the same market, while a programmer in Argentina or Nigeria faces the same automation without the same compensatory demand, which is neither in the local market nor in the global one, because it is not equally available to them. The gap between economies that export intelligence and economies that import it may widen with AI in ways that the aggregate projections of the WEF or McKinsey do not register, because those projections are barely sensitive to the fact that creation and destruction do not occur in the same places.

The picture these data sketch is contradictory. At the task level, AI improves and worsens productivity; at the profession level, it redistributes functions unequally; in the labor market, it creates and destroys jobs; in terms of quality, it accelerates and degrades production. The research on AI and the labor market has been described as still in diapers, dealing with differences in effects across occupations, profiles, and industries that force a redesign of everything. But the contradiction is at least in part the reflection of a phenomenon that operates in distinct dimensions, and many studies rush to measure without asking themselves carefully what

[276]Fabian Stephany et al., "AI Skills Improve Job Prospects: Causal Evidence from a Hiring Experiment", arXiv:2601.13286, 2026.

they are measuring, or choose data that confirm preferences. What is needed is an understanding of the object in its specific context. But let us first review the state of the question.[277]

THE DEBATE

If we draw a map of the theoretical debate, the first to appear is the dominant current in the early days: *the strong substitutive position.* For this approach, AI is an advanced automation technology that tends to replace formalizable, repetitive tasks. The foundational study by Frey and Osborne of 2017, which estimated that 47% of jobs in the United States were at high risk of automation, was methodologically useful for showing the potential magnitude of the phenomenon but tended to overstate effective replacement, extrapolating from technical capabilities without attending to organizational, normative, and cognitive frictions.[278] A 2016 OECD study that re-estimated risk at the task level rather than at the level of whole occupations concluded that only 9% of jobs in OECD countries faced a high risk of automation.[279] *That correction in order of magnitude* transformed the debate.

A second current, *complementarist between human and machine labor,* argues that AI redistributes tasks and could even reverse the labor-market polarization produced by earlier digital technologies, by democratizing access to knowledge that previously required costly

[277]Jed Kolko, "Research on AI and the Labor Market Is Still in the First Inning", Hamilton Project, Brookings Institution, 2026.
[278]Carl Benedikt Frey et al., "The Future of Employment: How Susceptible Are Jobs to Computerisation?", Technological Forecasting and Social Change 114 (2017), 254-280.
[279]Melanie Arntz et al., Terry Gregory and Ulrich Zierahn, "The Risk of Automation for Jobs in OECD Countries", OECD Working Papers 189, 2016.
16David Autor, "Applying AI to Rebuild Middle Class Jobs", NBER Working Paper 32140, 2024.

and prolonged training.[280] In this reading, AI appears as a multiplier of capacities.

A third position emphasizes *cognitive polarization*, noting that AI amplifies preexisting inequalities.[281] Only users capable of integrating AI manage to increase their productivity, with the result of a progressive divergence of trajectories.

A fourth current, of *institutionalist inspiration*, shifts the focus from the individual to structures and emphasizes that the effects of AI depend largely on the organizational, regulatory, and educational decisions that govern adoption.[282] The same technology can reinforce professional autonomy in one context and intensify control and precarization in another.

A fifth position analyzes how *the externalization of cognitive operations* modifies the practices of learning and transmission of knowledge, with the risk of eroding competencies when delegation is not accompanied by critical evaluation. This position touches the labor question indirectly through the so-called "last expert" problem, when the last generation of professionals trained without AI retires and no one is left who can verify what the model produces.[283]

Let us add, in sixth place, *the theory of immaterial labor*. The concept, developed by Maurizio Lazzarato in 1996 and elaborated by Hardt and Negri and Paolo Virno, thematizes a historical shift in the dominant form of value production: from material labor that transforms physical matter to labor that produces information,

---

[280]David Autor, "Applying AI to Rebuild Middle Class Jobs", NBER Working Paper 32140, 2024.

[281]Fabrizio Dell'Acqua et al., "Navigating the Jagged Technological Frontier: Field Experimental Evidence of the Effects of AI on Knowledge Worker Productivity and Quality", Harvard Business School Working Paper 24-013, 2023.

[282]Shoshana Zuboff, The Age of Surveillance Capitalism, London, Profile Books, 2019 and el informe de la OIT, Generative AI and Jobs: A Global Analysis of Potential Effects on Job Quantity and Quality, Ginebra, 2023, que adopta explícitamente un marco institucionalista.

[283]Ethan Mollick et al., "Assigning AI: Seven Approaches for Students, with Prompts", The Wharton Interactive, arXiv:2306.10052, 2023.

knowledge, communication, relations, and affects.[284285286] This approach centered on an informational dimension, referring to the production and manipulation of symbolic content, and an affective dimension, referring to the production of emotional states and experiences of care. Post-Fordist labor drew on linguistic and communicative competencies that had previously belonged to the domain of political action, converting them into central productive competencies.

This tradition could not anticipate the impact of artificial intelligence. Indeed, a language model produces the very kinds of responses that the theory of immaterial labor identified as the frontier of contemporary value creation. They were supposed to be hard to automate because they depended on constitutively human competencies that took form in unrepeatable situations and were therefore irreducible to mechanical execution. Paradoxically, "derived virtuality" pulled level with that "virtuosity". The approach thus diagnoses what kind of labor AI transforms and its link with the production of symbolic forms, and explains why the anxiety of the knowledge professional before a system that speaks and writes like them is distinct from that of the worker before the machine. But it does not explain why the model produces the labor consequences the empirical evidence shows. The world of immaterial labor was experiential and revolved around lived competency, which now finds our peculiar phantom at its side.

---

[284]Maurizio Lazzarato, "Immaterial Labor", in Radical Thought in Italy: A Potential Politics, Minneapolis, University of Minnesota Press, 1996.

[285]Michael Hardt and Antonio Negri, Empire, Cambridge, Harvard University Press, 2000, and Multitude: War and Democracy in the Age of Empire, New York, Penguin, 2004.

[286]Paolo Virno, Grammatica della moltitudine. Per una analisi delle forme di vita contemporanee, Soveria Mannelli, Rubbettino, 2002. The post-Fordist regime tended to the productive use of linguistic and communicative competences that previously belonged to the realm of political action, converting them into central productive competences.

LABOR AND PRODUCTIVE PASSIVITY

Let us go beyond these positions by drawing on the yields of our overall exploration. The positions that dominate the debate treat AI (when they thematize it at all) as a black box whose effects on labor are observed empirically and theorized from outside. The substitutive position registers that there are automatable tasks; the complementarist one notices that others intensify; the one centered on polarization observes that results diverge by user; the institutionalist one claims that context is determining; and the cognitive-cultural one links delegation with the atrophy of competencies. Each position observes isolated aspects, detached from the properties of the system. These features are consequences of the ontological structure of artificial intelligence in general, and of language models in particular, not empirical contingencies that could have been otherwise.

Indeed, artificial intelligence appeared as virtuality with four constitutive properties that Chapter 5 analyzed in detail. It is *passive*, because it does not move on its own and requires external activation. It is *generically indeterminate*, because it has no orientation of its own toward any type of actualization. It is *derived*, because it produces the functional form of cognitive operations without the experiential foundation that originates them in human subjects. And it is *inexhaustible without transformation*, because it is not spent and is not modified by exercise. These properties are constitutive, and from each of them follows a specific labor consequence that the sociological positions observe without being able to explain.

From *passive potency* it follows that direction must come from us. If the model does not move on its own, whoever supplies the direction (the precise instruction, the problem's formulation, the delimitation of scope) becomes more valuable, not less. In the work environment this means that the capacity to formulate problems, which was always important but rarely really valued, becomes the determining variable of performance. The complementarist position observes this phenomenon as "augmented intelligence", which appears here not as a choice or an ideal but as a direct effect of the type of potency of the system.

From *generic indeterminacy* it follows that the quality of the response depends on the instruction and not on capacities of the system. The one who knows what to ask gets a radically different result from the one who does not, and this accounts for the cognitive polarization that observes the divergence of trajectories between sophisticated and superficial users. This difference is not explained by differential access to the technology but as a consequence of a system without orientation of its own that, precisely for that reason, amplifies the difference between those who supply direction and those who do not, with consequences for the world of work.

From *derivation*, that is, from the absence of experiential foundation and the dependence on the training corpus — it follows that the model's response gives no signals to identify whether it is correct or incorrect. In labor terms, insofar as verifying is a primary condition of competent use, the profession that can verify gains value, while the one that cannot verify, whose value lay in execution rather than evaluation, loses adaptability, becoming irrelevant to the distinction between useful and harmful responses. What is usually called the "jagged frontier" (the difficulty of establishing where a model works and where it stops working) is the labor manifestation of derivation. The cognitive form of the response does not clearly signal where the frontier lies, so that those who lack sufficient criterion to detect it are dragged by fluency into errors they would not have made on their own. The cognitive-cultural position confines itself to the risk of competency erosion, when what is at stake is the necessary effect of this type of architecture, which precisely by virtue of this jagged frontier demands specific competencies, which may not be the traditional ones but which are central to the new labor market.[287]

---

[287]Fabrizio Dell'Acqua et al., op. cit.

From *inexhaustibility without transformation* it follows that the model does not learn (which imposes greater controls), that it gives no signals of fatigue (useful for productivity), and that it shows no signs of degradation when it begins operating in an inadequate regime. From the perspective of labor, this implies that there is no negative feedback to protect us from excessive delegation. A professional who delegates everything to the model and accepts everything they receive experiences no resistance. This is the structural basis of Bainbridge's "irony of automation" to which we alluded in Chapter 9: the tool that makes manual execution unnecessary makes vigilance more necessary, but at the same time weakens it. The institutionalist position observes that results depend on this type of context, but it must be added that the absence of negative feedback from the system makes contexts without institutional supervision especially vulnerable, because the only possible brake is external to the system.

Taken together, these four derivations produce a broader thesis that integrates elements that appear incompatible when they appear scattered. We can affirm that AI redistributes the economy of cognitive labor not by the power of what it produces but by the passivity of how it produces it. For if the system had its own direction it would not need us to supply it; if it signaled its errors it would not require expertise to detect them; if it resisted misuse it would not need institutional supervision; and if it learned from interaction it would not produce atrophy through delegation. Since the model lacks the four properties we have described, human knowing gains value rather than losing it. AI does not displace judgment by surpassing it; it needs judgment elsewhere, and in that movement it reveals which professions had genuine judgment, which merely believed they did, and which had never needed it.

This last distinction manifests with particular clarity in a recent labor phenomenon that merits attention because it illustrates in practice what our theoretical framework predicts. Vibe coding is a term coined by Andrej Karpathy, cofounder of OpenAI, to describe the practice of producing software by describing to the model what one wants in natural language, without pausing over the code the model generates. The user tests the result and if it works, that is, if it compiles, if something appears on the screen, if the behavior resembles what they imagined, they accept it. The practice spread rapidly, and people with basic programming training are now producing applications, websites, automations, and prototypes that previously required a developer. The democratization of code production has concrete economic effects that sounded the alarm in the world of programmers, even though the matter has many more nuances.

If we are going to analyze labor, we must look at the complete phenomenon, including what happens afterward. Derivation operates here with precision. The generated code has the form of competent code, but it can contain architectural errors, security vulnerabilities, technical debt, scalability problems, or design decisions that do not manifest until the production phase, when it is under load, with real data, or when it has to be modified six months later. Many vibe coders cannot detect these problems because they do not know what to look for, exactly like those who trust the model at the edges, forgetting that it has jagged frontiers, and end up falling off the precipice. As a result, some experienced programmers report having more work generated by the demand for diagnosis and redesign of code that others generated with AI. Their expertise gained value as the mass of code that requires expert judgment to work properly kept growing.

Acemoglu and Restrepo distinguish three effects of automation on labor. *The displacement effect* occurs when the machine replaces human labor in certain tasks, depressing wages and employment in those roles. *The productivity effect* occurs when that automation reduces costs and increases production, generating demand for labor in other areas. *The reinstatement effect* refers to the creation of new tasks that did not exist before and that require human labor. AI shifts demand from production to auditing and may even expand it, because the volume of output requiring review grows faster than the pool of experts who can review it.[288]

In the case of vibe coding, the three effects operate simultaneously. The displacement effect appears in that basic code production expands and those who did that execution work face lower demand. The productivity effect is confirmed in that cheaper and faster code generates more projects, more product, and more aggregate demand for development. The reinstatement effect appears where it was least expected, in the growing volume of AI-generated code that creates demand for auditing, diagnosis, and redesign that did not exist at that scale before. AI shifts demand from production toward evaluation, and may even expand it, because the volume of output requiring review grows faster than the pool of experts who can review it. The expert who used to produce now audits, and sometimes audits more than they used to produce.

Stated this way, the argument may sound like a naïve endorsement of the complementarist position, one that trusts in deflating the problem of AI and labor. Three qualifications are in order.

The first is technical in nature and appeals to *the improvement of the models.* If errors are reduced with each generation, the demand for auditing may be transitory. Models improve with each cycle, and while incremental improvement will not simply resolve the verification problem, it will shift audit demand upward, from syntax to architecture, from the individual contract to the legal strategy, from the standard diagnosis to the atypical case, without eliminating it, but greatly reducing the role of the programmer as a lifesaver for vibe coders.

The second is economic in nature and refers to *market adjustments.* There are some new automated verification tools for more exhaustive testing through models specialized in detecting the errors of other models that are already reducing the need for human

[288]Daron Acemoglu and Pascual Restrepo, "Automation and New Tasks: How Technology Displaces and Reinstates Labor", Journal of Economic Perspectives 33.2 (2019), 3-30; and "Tasks, Automation, and the Rise in U.S.

auditing. Substantive evaluation will continue to require domain judgment, but the band of work between automated production and that substantive evaluation will shrink. The result is a position less catastrophist than the substitutive view but more skeptical than the complementarist one: professional roles will contract and shift without entire sectors being annihilated.

The third aspect is sociological and has to do with *the lowering of standards.* If most users cannot distinguish between solid code and code that looks solid, then the market will not demand a quality that only the expert guarantees. Instead, a bifurcation may emerge between a premium segment where quality matters and is paid for (in critical infrastructure, health, and regulated finance, for example) and a mass segment where the model's mediocre output is adequate because verification is undervalued and the consequences of error are diffuse or deferred. If we look at history, this is what happened with the invention of the printing press, which democratized knowledge on one hand and produced masses of low-quality publications on the other. Similarly, digital journalism did not eliminate quality journalism, but reduced it to a fraction of the market; and digital photography turned professional photography into a niche within an ocean of images without criterion. If AI follows that pattern, the "more work for the expert" effect may be confined to a persistent but increasingly narrow segment.[289]

The catastrophist narrative of employment's shipwreck is irritating, because a rigorous reading of the evidence shows no disappearance of professions or generalized unemployment on the horizon, only the transformation of value cores and displacement between labor-market segments at a speed that strains individual and institutional adaptability. For a civilization accustomed to market crises, world wars, and pandemics, this is just another day on planet Earth. But the distinction matters because the political responses it

[289]Lorraine Daston, Classical Probability in the Enlightenment, Princeton, Princeton University Press, 1988 [originally cited as Cambridge University Press, 1980]; and David Alan Grier, When Computers Were Human, Princeton, Princeton University Press, 2005.

derives are completely different. If the problem were the disappearance of human labor, the response would be some form of universal basic income that decouples livelihood from productive contribution, a mechanism of passive compensation. If the problem, instead, is that the speed of redistribution operates faster than the capacity of people and institutions to adapt, the measures to mitigate it run through the training of competencies that gain value, regulation that distributes the costs of the transition, and institutions that mediate between speeds. The catastrophist narrative is therefore paralyzing: it disables intervention on the variables where action is actually possible.

Indeed, universal basic income (an unconditional income for all citizens, independent of their labor situation) has been circulating in political debate for decades and gained momentum when AI became a candidate to justify it. OpenResearch funded basic-income experiments conducted in the United States with mixed results on employment, mental health, and financial stability. Detractors point to structural problems that the pilot experiments do not resolve because none has been truly universal or permanent. On one hand, the cost of transferring a significant income to the entire population of a developed country requires fiscal resources of an order of magnitude that no pilot experiment puts to the test. On the other, inflation, especially in housing and services, can destroy real value. Finally, there is the design problem: receiving supplemental income when most people do not versus receiving it when everyone does can produce entirely different effects.[290]

Two of the most prominent figures in AI arrived in 2025 and 2026 at curiously similar proposals. Sam Altman, after funding the OpenResearch experiment and concluding that traditional basic income was insufficient, proposed in July 2025 what he called "universal extreme wealth", emerging from the distribution of AI outputs measured in tokens across the entire global population. If AI produces 20 trillion tokens annually, a portion would go to the

[290]On the experimento de OpenResearch, see Eva Vivalt et al., The Employment Effects of a Guaranteed Income: Experimental Evidence from Two U.S.

traditional system and another would be distributed among the 8 billion people on the planet, who could use, sell, or accumulate those tokens as wealth of their own.[291] Elon Musk, who since 2016 had been arguing that basic income would be "necessary" when robots eliminated jobs, in April 2026 posted on X that "high universal income" through checks issued by the federal government is the best way to deal with AI-caused unemployment, arguing that it would not be inflationary because AI and robotics would produce goods and services far above the increase in monetary supply.[292] The post accumulated more than 27 million views in a few hours. Both proposals assume AI generates enough wealth to finance massive transfers, but neither accounts for the political mechanism by which that value would be redistributed rather than concentrated by market forces in particular corners of the world.

Even so, if the value of labor in the AI era shifts toward judgment and critical evaluation, decoupling income from labor solves the subsistence problem while threatening the development of precisely the capacities AI makes more valuable. The habitualities we described in the previous chapter are formed in sustained practice, with real consequences, under pressure. A system that guarantees livelihood independently of productive contribution can free time for development, but it can also, if not well designed, suppress the incentives that produce the friction where those human capacities are formed. Some may be dispensable, but which? That question has not yet been seriously confronted. The debate about universal basic income in the era of AI is a debate about what kind of human activity we want to sustain and promote.

[291]Sam Altman, statements in This Past Weekend with Theo Von, episodio del 16 July 2025.
[292]Elon Musk, post on X (@elonmusk), 17 April 2026, 12:05 a.m.

DISPLACEMENTS

Let us take one more step. The usual comparisons turn on artificial intelligence vs. competent professionals. But the real market is not exclusively populated by competent professionals. Across translation, law, programming, consulting, and journalism, a significant portion of work billed as expert is, strictly speaking, mechanical execution without genuine understanding. There are translators who translate without perceiving subtexts, lawyers who copy clauses by eye, programmers who paste code from forums, to say nothing of consultants who fill presentations without understanding the client's business or journalists who rewrite press releases without verifying or adding context. We could extend the list to every type of labor today.

These professionals had been producing form without foundation themselves, in an almost derived manner: only more slowly and more expensively than a model. Their market value, therefore, was not sustained by the quality of what they did but by scarcity. As long as producing a text or a piece of code required skills that not everyone had, there was a market for anyone with even a few. AI tends to eliminate scarcity as a source of value. If the machine produces the same thing as the average professional, that average professional can no longer charge merely for possessing a competency that is now free.

The institutional reaction to this process is predictable and is already occurring. Boards of accountants in several countries have restricted, or desperately requested the prohibition of, the use of AI in professional practice, invoking reasons of confidentiality and technical responsibility. The reasons given are not false, but the underlying motive is the defense of a scarcity the market no longer produces on its own. At its core this is what the medieval guilds did when they tried to limit the spread of new techniques. The corporation protects the monopoly over a competency whose value is being destroyed by a technology that democratizes it.

AI does not threaten qualified human work; it threatens work whose value depended on being costly, slow, or hard to access. Where value depends on quality and deep understanding, AI tends to redistribute and even to amplify. The question to ask, then, is not so much whether AI can do such-and-such work but whether we do it better than AI or only more expensively. In the case of work that depended on scarcity, the displacement effect is real and reinstatement is not guaranteed, because compensatory demand does not automatically appear where displaced work disappeared.

The flip side of this phenomenon is more troubling, because it involves the progressive hollowing out of qualified work. Consider the lawyer who no longer knows how to draft a contract from scratch because they always start from the model's draft, or the doctor who loses clinical intuition because the differential diagnosis arrives before they can think it. In those cases, the professional continues working (they are necessary for verification and for the assumption of responsibility) but their labor has weakened. This scenario goes unnoticed because it produces no unemployment, but it multiplies employees whose competencies are more nominal than real, dangerous when something fails, often in delicate cases, because it sustains the appearance of qualified work while the foundation degrades.

The case of translation, which has had longer exposure to AI than other professions, illustrates this problem. A translator's training used to begin with general, low-risk texts and rise in complexity as experience accumulated. Now the first rung no longer exists. Automation eliminates the training ground. The result may be a generation of professionals who arrive at the specialized level with fewer hours of real practice, less sedimented intuition, and greater dependence on the model. Silent degradation operates on an entire profession.[293]

---

[293]Joss Moorkens, "Ethics and Machine Translation", in The Routledge Handbook of Translation and Ethics, London, Routledge, 2022.

In sum, when one looks at concrete cases, AI's impact follows three distinguishable patterns: displacement of value (as in translation and programming), asymmetric amplification (where those combining disciplinary and technical expertise come out better), and functional obsolescence for repetitive-execution roles that automation was already replacing: stenographers, typists, data entry. In similar historical moments, professions survived when they managed to shift their legitimacy from execution to non-delegable functions, and the same thing is happening now.

NEW SPACES AND THE PLACE OF JUDGMENT

Let us return to the reinstatement effect. It is true that artificial intelligence is generating labor categories that did not exist three years ago. The most visible is prompt engineering, which emerged as a specialization when companies discovered that the quality of responses depended on the formulation of the instruction. As an independent profession it is surely transitory: as models improve at following instructions and the interface becomes more intuitive, the need for a dedicated specialist diminishes. The ability to design interactions with AI systems will increasingly be absorbed into diverse professional roles, as has happened before. The telephone operator's tasks integrated into customer service and similar functions after the switchboard.

More stable are the roles linked to AI governance. In Europe, the EU AI Act and equivalent regulations require technical documentation, impact assessment, human supervision, post-market monitoring, and incident reporting for high-risk systems. Other regions that today have nothing like it will sooner or later have their own versions. This creates demand for algorithmic compliance officers and auditors of automated systems. Those roles are not transitory, because regulation never is.

So-called red-teaming and safety evaluation constitute another new field oriented toward identifying a model's failure modes, designing adversarial attacks, and evaluating robustness against malicious inputs. Working in this area requires technical knowledge, adversarial creativity, and domain understanding, a combination that did not exist as a professional profile before generative AI.

Training-data curation has also become critical. Selecting, filtering, and documenting data at scale requires competencies spanning linguistics, statistics, domain knowledge, and cultural sensitivity. Likewise, the design of human-AI orchestration systems (for deciding which tasks are delegated, with what controls, and under what verification criteria) is emerging as an organizational function in companies that integrate AI at sufficient scale.

Notably, the WEF projected growth rates of 80% to 140% for roles like Big Data specialist, AI/ML engineer, AI solutions architect, cybersecurity analyst, and software developer. Some of these roles will consolidate, and others are mere ephemeral ideas of a transition phase. Who now remembers the era of telex operators or linotype operators, who were once part of the technological vanguard and today live in memory alongside Blockbuster and video rental stores? Impossible to know, but their existence today is an indication that AI redistributes existing work and generates demand for capacities the previous labor market did not need, even setting aside whether these gains amount to more than a drop in the desert.[294]

At the other extreme, there is a very different group that is also a fruit of the reinstatement effect, one with far less glamour than red teaming, operating in conditions far from ideal. Model alignment requires real people to read, evaluate, and classify responses, work that is genuinely important but poorly paid. In Chapter 10 we mentioned the documented case of the employment of toxic and disturbing content classifiers for paltry wages in poor countries. The system's operation presents integration challenges of its own in the

---

[294]World Economic Forum, Future of Jobs Report 2025. Encuesta a más de 1.000 empleadores en 55 economías. También, World Economic Forum, "Four Futures for Jobs in the New Economy: AI and Talent in 2030", 2025.

broader scenario of the relation between artificial intelligence and labor.

Let us briefly consider another perspective. Most approaches implicitly assume we are talking about an individual worker who adapts or not according to their competencies and decisions, or about the degree of impact on a profession in the abstract. But the history of major technological transitions shows that periods of disruption activate collective bargaining. The 2023 Hollywood writers' and actors' strike, which produced agreements with explicit protections against the use of generative AI to replace creative work, is a visible case of organized union response. The agreements included restrictions on the use of materials to train models, consent requirements for the digital replica of actors, and limitations on the substitution of screenwriters by AI. The result was negotiated regulation, with the mediating institutions placed squarely in the foreground.

If the value of labor in the age of AI shifts from execution toward judgment, the formation of that judgment becomes urgent. Five capacities emerge from what we have said.

The first is *the precise formulation of problems.* AI amplifies poorly formulated problems, so that the bottleneck is usually, as we saw, in *well-made questions.* It is trained through formal logic, philosophy of science, research methodology, and case-analysis traditions like those in law, medicine, and business schools.

The second is *the explicitation of assumptions and frames.* Since the models do not distinguish between central and accidental assumptions, the capacity to make premises visible becomes operationally critical. This is the core of applied epistemology and argumentation theory, disciplines that occupy a marginal place in most university curricula outside philosophy and that, ironically, turn out to be the most directly relevant to competent use of the most advanced technology of the century.

The third is *the critical evaluation of results*: detecting subtle errors, internal inconsistencies, or unwarranted extrapolations. It is trained in every domain where peer review, evidence analysis, fallacy detection, and the attentive reading of complex texts are practiced. These skills are part of the tradition of the humanities and the social sciences and were developed over centuries under names like hermeneutics, textual criticism, and discourse analysis, which the pressure toward technical specialization has been wearing down.

The fourth is *cognitive design*: breaking complex problems into stages, deciding which operations to delegate and which to keep under human control, then recombining partial results. Cognitive-design competencies are formed in the practice of managing complex projects, in systems engineering, in research direction, and in any context where the orchestration of heterogeneous resources is the central competency.

The fifth is *metacognitive competency*: knowing when a response is fragile or when a quick solution compromises deep understanding. This is the object of study of applied cognitive psychology and of the pedagogical traditions that emphasize learning to learn, from Piaget and Vygotsky through the recent works of Flavell, Schraw, and Dennison on metacognitive monitoring.

One thing may strike the reader about this list: none of the five capacities is technical in the computing sense. None requires knowing how to train models, program in Python, or understand the transformer architecture, nor is any of them acquired by mere exposure to the tool. That does not mean technical formation is irrelevant, only insufficient on its own. Combining technical formation with formation in the capacities we have been describing produces profiles qualitatively distinct from either one separately. Looking at the profiles actually working in the most advanced AI laboratories confirms this. At Anthropic, OpenAI, DeepMind, and the interpretability and alignment teams producing the most consequential results in recent years, software engineers and mathematicians work alongside philosophers of mind, linguists, cognitive psychologists, ethicists, and humanists trained in conceptual analysis, by functional necessity. The questions that define work at that frontier require the five capacities the list describes.

These affiliations reveal a paradox that the 2026 MetLife survey we mentioned earlier throws into relief. Among the data it provides, 94% of employers declare that human-centered skills, judgment, creativity, collaboration, and problem-solving, will be highly valuable in the next three years. At the same time, 71% say that the capacity to work with AI will also be. Now, the human-centered skills that employers say they value are those formed in the disciplines that the labor market has been devaluing for decades (philosophy, letters, the social sciences, and the liberal arts) while the AI skills they also say they value are formed in the disciplines the market has been privileging: engineering, computing, and data science. Market demand thus points in two directions that the educational system has historically treated as opposed.

If so, the traditional logic of professional choice (which assumed that the relevant formation for a field of work was the one that bore its name) is called into question. When we wanted to work in technology we studied engineering, no further questions, or we taught ourselves, which is a separate problem. AI breaks the correlation because there are competencies for working with technology that are not acquired by studying it. A philosopher trained in conceptual analysis can outperform an engineer in certain evaluation roles, just as a historian accustomed to cross-referencing sources, detecting biases, and reconstructing contexts can be an excellent auditor of responses.

Technical and humanistic training open into each other like communicating vessels the current educational system is not designed to nourish, operating as it does on a rigid disciplinary division that works against transversal capacities, however many discourses on interdisciplinarity may blow through from time to time. Universities are mostly responding to the pressure with misguided strategies: creating AI courses that teach how to use specific models, or that lose themselves in abstract analyses of effects and impacts, instead of attending to the conditions for developing the capacities we have described, which have nothing to do with software handling or with the cultural agendas of the vanguard of the moment. The humanities, social sciences, and liberal arts, long declared obsolete by the efficiency narrative, may have something to say about the competencies the most advanced technology of the century makes more valuable. But only if they step out of [295]their marginal inertia.

*

We noted at the start of this chapter that the labor zone provokes fear. Coming out the other side, the fear turns out to be real but misfocused. What threatens is not the machine that replaces us but the speed that does not let us think. What can protect us is the capacity to do what the egoless phantom cannot: to judge, to contextualize, to decide when the brilliant response is a mirage and when it is worth saying something no probability distribution would have predicted.

To remain on the defensive would be to miss the best part. A power without direction of its own that carries the entire human tradition and can actualize it in any direction it is given is also, for those who know how to use it, a tool of fantastic and surprising expansion. The researcher who always wanted to cross into domains their training did not reach; the professional who wanted to understand the legal or scientific context of their work without years of additional study; the creator who needed an interlocutor available at any hour to test ideas against: all now have access to something that did not exist before. Judgment remains human and irreplaceable, but the territory on which that judgment can be exercised has expanded in ways we are still learning to inhabit, just beginning to explore the outer corridors of this zone of the labyrinth.

---

[295]UNESCO, "Guidance for Generative AI in Education and Research", 2024 and Margaret Bearman et al., "Re-imagining Assessment in the Age of Generative AI", Assessment & Evaluation in Higher Education, 2023.

The paradox this chapter has been circling is this: when execution is automated, deepening what is human becomes the most solid comparative advantage available. We do not compete with the machine on its terrain but on the only terrain it cannot enter, which, far from shrinking, expands with each improvement of the system. The more capable the model, the more valuable the question that directs it and the more necessary the criterion that decides when to stop. To leave this zone with that understood is to enter a world where curiosity has more tools than ever, the condition for getting the most out of what is to come.

A NEW *NATURGEMÄLDE*

In June of 1802, Alexander von Humboldt attempted to climb Chimborazo. Born in Berlin in 1769 into a family of the Prussian aristocracy, trained in geology, botany, chemistry, astronomy, and comparative anatomy; he was a friend of Goethe, a correspondent of Schiller and Jefferson, and the most famous man of his time after Napoleon. He pioneered the use of isotherms (those lines that connect points of equal temperature on a map) and identified the ocean current that now bears his name off the coasts of Peru. Above all, he conceived the idea, radical for its time, that nature is a system of relations where everything is connected. Darwin called him "the greatest scientific traveler who ever lived" and acknowledged that without reading Humboldt he would never have embarked on the Beagle.

In 1799, at twenty-nine, Humboldt persuaded the Spanish crown to let him travel through its American colonies with freedom of movement and access to archives, mines, and indigenous territories, something no one had achieved before and no one has managed since. He spent five years in what is now Venezuela, Cuba, Colombia, Ecuador, Peru, and Mexico, traveling through jungles, rivers, and mountain ranges with an unparalleled voracity of observation, measuring everything he could: altitude, temperature, humidity, soil composition, the distribution of plants, magnetic inclination, the color of the sky, the frequency of earthquakes, and, of course, indigenous languages, the forms of colonial government, and the price of corn in the markets of Quito. He intuited that the answer lay in connection, but had no way yet to prove it.

The help came from Chimborazo, the volcano of the Ecuadorian Andes roughly 150 kilometers south of Quito, which in 1802 was considered the highest mountain in the world, and in one sense it still is, if we measure from the center of the planet, given the bulging shape of the Earth at Ecuador. Humboldt arrived at its base after months of ascents through the Andes, already acclimatized to altitude. He was thirty-two, and his companions were Aimé Bonpland, his partner for the whole expedition, and Carlos Montúfar, a young Ecuadorian who had joined in Quito and was hauling an improbable collection of measuring instruments.

They did not reach the summit. At 5,917 meters, according to the obsessive notebook he kept throughout the expedition, a crevasse cut off their path. Humboldt recorded the altitude, temperature, pressure, and pulse of his companions, the presence of lichens on a rock that should not have had lichens, and the exact color of the sky at that height. They were bleeding from their gums and from their noses. Montúfar was vomiting and Bonpland could barely stand. Humboldt noted all of that too and they began to descend.

In the weeks that followed, working with his notes and his samples, Humboldt drew the Naturgemälde, a cross-section of Chimborazo that was not a map of the mountain but a map of how to look. On a single plate he laid out altitude, temperature, atmospheric pressure, vegetation, soil types, the snow line, air currents, and the animal species present in each band, showing for the first time that all of it formed a system, and that the connections among those variables were more revealing than any of them separately. Humboldt did not discover plants or rocks, but something larger. Nature revealed itself to him, and he understood that the way to see it was to ascend high enough for the connections that compose it to become visible without losing the details. The Naturgemälde does not sacrifice the minute in favor of the panorama. Each species has its name, each measurement its value, and the plate as a whole says something that no single figure says alone.[296]

This book attempted something similar. In place of a mountain, our exploration traveled through a labyrinth, entered strange spaces to examine the texture of what they produce, measured their effects, and finally drew a cross-section showing the connections that ordinary use conceals.

The exploration took us off the well-traveled path of practical use, which looks for recipes and shortcuts and celebrates the prompt that yields better results for automating what we used to do by hand. That path has its utility, and we do not disdain it, but it remains at the surface of the interaction and does not by itself generate the conditions for understanding what we are using. Nor did we follow the path of the technician, who knows the material and logical processes and can describe with precision how the attention layers operate or how the gradient is distributed during training, but rarely stops to ask what all of it ultimately means. Technical knowledge, at best, produces operational competence; at worst, the illusion that mastering the mechanism authorizes general judgments about human nature, the future of the world, and the meaning of history.

Here, by contrast, we advanced with the calm that phenomenology imposes. We described what was appearing and recognized its features without the hurry to decide whether they are good or bad, useful or dangerous, before understanding what they are. The journey through the labyrinth let us linger over the interstices between zones, on the corridors that connect them, and on the shortcuts that sometimes turn out to be mirages. We traveled through layers of unexpected complexity without pretending to be architects, but also unwilling to settle for photographing the façade. We examined the protean notion of virtuality and plunged into philosophical categories to think about a new phenomenon. We

---

[296] Alexander von Humboldt, Ideen zu einer Geographie der Pflanzen nebst einem Naturgemälde der Tropenländer, Tübingen, F. G. Cotta, 1807. The Naturgemälde, also known as Tableau physique des Andes et pays voisins, was published as a fold-out plate in this work.

played hide-and-seek with a materiality that disguises itself as cloud so as not to have to answer where it is, who pays, and who works in conditions the interface makes disappear.

Like Humboldt and his companions, we may have bled a little on the steeper stretches, but we come back with the *Naturgemälde* in our backpack. The pile of scattered aspects that did not quite make sense now has a base in which to lodge. Each zone of the labyrinth still has its climate and its economy, each layer of the entrance figures its matrices and its weights, and each epistemic phenomenon its specific mechanism, but now those pieces are connected on a map. We understand now why hallucination is a consequence of virtuality, why sycophancy is the optimal behavior of a system without epistemic friction, and why materiality withdraws from perception and leaves us with substitutes. The connections are lost on the ordinary user, the technician does not look for them, and the popularizer cannot offer them, because making them visible requires a Naturgemälde that brings together technical data and philosophical analysis with the will not to give in to prefabricated solutions.

We gained something more, which resembles what Frank White coined in 1987 as the "overview effect", in reference to what the Apollo astronauts described upon seeing the Earth from orbit: the perception of borders, conflicts, and terrestrial systems changed irreversibly. They had learned nothing new about the Earth, strictly speaking, but they had seen it from a position that made visible what is undetectable from the surface. This space-age version of the notion of *anamorphosis* that we used to understand the phenomenon of artificial intelligence has the advantage of placing humanity itself in the position of the observed.[297]

Looking closely at the egoless phantom, how it carries the tradition without living it, how it produces the form of understanding without its texture, how it activates in us the sensation of another without having an interiority to sustain it, says

[297]Frank White, The Overview Effect: Space Exploration and Human Evolution, Boston, Houghton Mifflin, 1987. Third revised edition: 2014.

something about it and something about us, about the ways we constitute sense. The absence of an acquisition history in the model illuminates, by contrast, how much human cognition depends on that history, and its lack of epistemic tension shows how much our judgment depends on internal resistance and the logic of our limits. Each property of the model that is not human gives back, like an inverted mirror, a property of the human being that was invisible through sheer familiarity.

This is, perhaps, an unexpected result. Artificial intelligence ended up illuminating human intelligence itself as a weave of lived time, sedimented experience, commitment to truth, and responsibility for what is asserted. Humboldt climbed a mountain to measure the air and came down having discovered that nature is a system. We traveled through this labyrinth to understand a technology and came back having seen, in the mirror of what that technology is not, something of what we are and had never had reason to examine.

On that understanding depends the difference between using the system and being used by it, which is the difference between operating blindly and knowing what we are doing, between receiving the form of knowledge and being able to evaluate whether it is really there. When linguistic fluency has become so cheap it appears free and epistemic responsibility so costly it seems a luxury, that difference is worth the effort.

www.ingramcontent.com/pod-product-compliance
Lightning Source LLC
LaVergne TN
LVHW100259210926
848480LV00003B/967
* 9 7 8 9 8 7 3 7 2 9 1 6 4 *